siberian dream

•

IRINA PANTAEVA

BARD

AN AVON BOOK

AVON BOOKS, INC.
1350 Avenue of the Americas
New York, New York 10019

Library of Congress Cataloging in Publication Data:

Pantaeva, Irina.
    Siberian dream / Irina Pantaeva.
        p.   cm.
    I. Title.
PS3566.A587S5 1998   98-23799
813'.54—dc21   CIP

First Bard Printing: October 1998

BARD TRADEMARK REG. U.S. PAT. OFF. AND IN OTHER COUNTRIES, MARCA REGISTRADA, HECHO
EN U.S.A.

FIRST EDITION

Printed in the U.S.A.

QPM   10   9   8   7   6   5   4   3   2   1

To Ruslan

ACKNOWLEDGMENTS

I am very grateful and would like to thank the following for their assistance, guidance, support and editing: Quinton Skinner, Elyse Cheney, Jennifer Hershey, Larissa Dagdanova, Elena Prokopieva, Vladlen & Tatiana Pantaev and Roland Levin.

EXPERIENCE IS ALL:
ALL KNOWING, ALL LEARNING, ALL SEEKING
EACH SHAPE AND COLOR IT COMMANDS
WITH BURNING STEPS THROUGH FOREIGN LANDS
COMPREHENSION ARRIVES AT BEING.

M. Voloshin

BETWEEN TWO WORLDS LIFE HOVERS LIKE A STAR,
'TWIXT NIGHT AND MORN, UPON HORIZON'S VERGE

Lord Byron

i am looking out at the audience from behind the parted curtains of the stage.

I see the fanlike sweep of the seats, the star-flake lights recessed into the walls. Faces that have smiled at me from movie screens all my life fill the hall. Could it really be that I am seeing them live, in the swirling current of the present? The women in the audience wear glamorous, glittering dresses, the men are dressed in tuxedoes. Jewelry sparkles in the light, creating multicolored explosions—visions from fairy tales or exquisite, impossible dreams.

I take a step forward as the curtain parts and the light hits my eyes. I hear music and the silent voices of my ancestors. In a moment beyond history I transform into someone else.

What are you doing, little girl? an old man asks me. Isn't it too late for you to still be awake?

The lights are hot. I stand motionless, ready to walk across the stage when it is my turn. I hear the audience applaud. There is a smell of electricity in the air, a tang like a charged wire.

Isn't it too late for you to still be awake? the old man asks me. Perhaps I should go fetch your mother.

She knows I'm here, I reply politely. It's not too late for me. I am three years old.

I peer through the slightly parted curtain. The young prince on stage roars his murderous anger, his soul aflame with the desire to avenge his father's death. His eyes bulge with fury and his voice echoes in the tiny Siberian theater. No one can see me, but I can observe everyone.

All right, I believe you, you can stay, the old man says to me with a smile. His name is Vasily, and he has constructed sets and controlled the lights at the theater for more than twenty years.

Once again I have convinced my parents to take me to the theater, where my father is an important man. He conducts an orchestra.

Outside the snow is piled high against the theater walls. The endless Siberian skies are dark and cloudless; the stars shine down with infinite incandescence. When it is silent I can hear the wind whisper from the great lake.

The audience watches with rapt attention as the prince drops to his knees in anguish. The musicians begin a slow, melancholy melody.

I live between the sky and the earth. In the wind are the whispers of my ancestors. In the town square Lenin's head scowls down into the cold awaiting the country's bright future. The great lake is buried under ice.

I part the curtains a little more and allow the stage lights to shine in my eyes. I hope that I will never awaken.

I move across the stage in my beautiful, elaborate dress— inspired by Jane Austen's *Sense and Sensibility*, flowing and high-waisted in the Empire style of the eighteenth century. My hair is in curls, a small crown rests atop my head. I am wearing clothing based on this year's Academy Award nominees. It is up to me to present them to the millions of people around the world who watch the sixty-ninth Oscars.

I turn and look out from the stage. Irina Panteava, I hear the announcer say.

My spirit is peeking out into the future and past, seeing a little girl growing older on the stage of life. A voice moves through time and space, and as it enters me I hear: *We dwell between the sky and the earth, awaiting our fate.*

i am a Buryat from the land of Lake Baikal in Russia. I was born in the lands which were once roamed by Ghenghis Khan; my ancestors rode across the plains with the voices of the wind and the land strong in their ears. I spent my childhood as a citizen of the Soviet Union, pledging my obedience to Lenin's teachings. My people were nomads for millennia, and in time their blood compelled me across the world.

The air was chill and clean the morning I was to begin kindergarten. I had risen early in my family's apartment and dressed close to the heat of the stove, lacing my hand-crafted shoes and buttoning the homemade jacket that my mother had sewn. I was three years old.

The sky was still dark when my parents led me out to the street. They clapped their hands together in the cold and our breath turned to vapor in front of our faces. They grasped my hands to either side of me and led me up the slight hill in the direction of the school. On either side of the street were Stalinist concrete apartment buildings, their regimented square windows bright with the morning lights of other Soviet citizens.

The three of us walked quickly. When I complained about our speed, my father told me that I would be late if we didn't hurry. It was my first day; I didn't want to be tardy. I quick-ened my pace to match theirs. This was a bad time of the month for me to make waves; my parents' salaries from the theater where they worked had nearly run out, and a week remained before their next payment. They were artists, and they earned less than factory workers or clerks in the regional planning offices.

We will have to borrow a little money, my father said as we waited for a truck to slowly move through a mud-speckled intersection. My mother glanced at him and nodded. I'll take care of it between rehearsals, he added, squeezing my hand a little harder.

The city of Ulan Ude had awoken during our walk together; a bus wound toward the city center, where a gigantic steel head of Lenin glowered at the people. Workers hiked the streets toward their factories and shops, their faces bent down to avoid the wind. Elderly women walked in their slow steady way into the morning, all with the same scarves on their heads to ward off the chill, hands grasping the rope baskets which they would fill with whatever wares were to be found that day.

My parents led me through a band of withered birch trees and the school came into sight. It seemed to expand with the dimensions of a castle, though it was more drab and grimly imposing than any palace I had ever envisioned. I was so small and it was so large.

Inside the front door was a long quiet hall. An old woman was mopping at the far end, her head bent down.

For a moment we were all silent. I looked at the gray walls, the old-fashioned wooden doors with their glass transoms. A feeling had been with me since I stepped outside that morning. It had accompanied me on this journey. Now it filled my head like a buzzing in my ears, insisting that I pay attention.

Your first day of school, Father said meditatively. He looked down at me as though he had just noticed I was no longer a baby.

It's just kindergarten, Mother said to him. It will be very nice.

What will happen today? I wondered, excitement growing inside me.

Be good and do as you're told, Father said; he let go of my hand. We'll come for you later, Irina.

But by then I barely heard him. Inside me I felt heat, a burst of energy that compelled me to give it definition. Glancing down at my feet and hands, I understood that I was expanding. My soul had grown—I didn't know just when, perhaps during the night—and though my tiny body remained the same, I had transformed into a giant. So this was how you traversed worlds. You just took a single step.

Go on in, Irina, my mother said. Don't just stand there dreaming.

She and my father exchanged knowing smiles as I emerged from this fantasy. Inside the classroom nearly all the wooden desks were occupied by students. I was the last to arrive, and I saw all their eyes—Russian and Buryat—turn to examine me. I set my face into a tough mask and looked back at them. They couldn't intimidate a giant.

This was the moment when my life began. I sat down at an open desk and ran my fingers across its surface. It was the soil of the world, and I could cross it with a single gesture. With my legs I could touch the bottom of the deepest sea. The globe itself was a plaything, a ball that I could bounce and toss into the air. A hunger for experience had filled me like the gas that propels a balloon into the sky.

My existence has traced a path from that cold autumn morning all the way to Europe, and then to America, from a Soviet childhood to a New York high-rise. In my mind it is an unbroken, continuous line. I was a little girl who never felt small. No matter how many years I live, I have never felt old or young. I come from the other side of the planet, but in my soul, I have seen the world shrink to the size of a pebble.

When the school day ended I waited more than an hour for my brothers to pick me up as they had promised. All of the other children filtered into the surrounding streets, accompanied by their mothers and fathers and siblings. I thought that waiting alone by the school's stacked concrete porch was appropriate for me; now that I was a giant, I would have to be strong.

My brothers never arrived. I was only three, but I understood the concept of hatred. I understood that this was what they felt for me. They were my mother's sons from her first marriage, a time in her life of which we never spoke. They were older, wiser, I thought. So why did they never take me into their hearts like a true sister?

I had begun to shiver from the chill of late afternoon when I saw my mother turn the corner, hurrying, looking for me. When she took my hand she was shaking her head, wondering aloud what was wrong with her boys.

Together we walked home to our building, where the Soviets had granted my parents a two-bedroom apartment. I had been born in a little room my mother and father had shared above a theater; it was a house that had been provided for actors. Just a year before they had been granted their new apartment. I remembered walking into it, how the distance from one end of the living room to the other seemed like miles.

My mother opened the door for me. I can't come inside, she said. I have to go back for rehearsal.

Can I come tonight for the performance? I asked. I was getting older, and I had learned to fight for what I wanted. I was ready to begin whining and crying if she said no.

Mother seemed to sense my resolve. All right, she said. Because this has been a special day for you, have your uncle bring you after dinner.

She left me in the foyer. I heard her footsteps echo on the concrete stairs as she descended to the street. The pulse of her steps was soon replaced by the familiar din of voices.

Hey out there! I heard my uncle shout. Come on in, little girl.

Is that Irina? my grandmother asked from the kitchen. I had heard that she was coming to visit from the country, and my heart beat with excitement to know she had arrived. I stepped inside and heard her knocking pots, humming to herself.

I took off my coat and hung it in the corner. My uncle resumed a story he had been telling about a relative of ours.

Will you please be quiet? said a voice from across the room. My aunt Tamara appeared in the doorway to the second bedroom. She was pretty, slim, and high-strung. She was twenty-one and had come to live with us since she got pregnant. As soon as she walked into a room I felt myself tense, wary that she might have one of her violent epileptic seizures. I was terrified of being alone with her because I wondered if I could save her if one of her attacks went out of control.

Oh God, listen to her, my older brother said. Hey, we're quiet enough. Why don't you go back in there and rest?

I can't, with your laughing and drinking, Tamara said. She sat on the edge of the sofa. Irina, how was your first day of kindergarten?

I liked it very much, I said. I made friends with a big fish who lives in a glass bowl at the school. I thought all the fish live in Lake Baikal. But this one doesn't.

Tamara smiled and ran her hand through my hair. I didn't speak Russian yet, only Buryat, and I considered the fish my friend because I wasn't able to talk to anyone in kindergarten.

Are there nice things at school? Uncle asked me.

So many, I replied, my voice high with the thrilling memory. Toys. Dolls with dresses. Little cars. Wooden chairs and tables where we ate three times. A little bed that folded out so we could sleep. And a big playground. I never saw so many things before. I want to go back. I want to go there again.

Tamara laughed. You'll go back tomorrow, she said. I think you can wait until then.

My grandmother came into the room from the kitchen with a small dish containing *penka*—a skin from boiled milk that she froze in the frigid air of the countryside until it turned hard like candy. She covered it with sugar, sour cream, and jam, then gave it to me.

I sat down at the table and ate, humming a melody to myself.

Irina likes new things, she likes to travel, my grandmother said to the room in a soft voice. She will travel far someday.

I looked at the faces of the adults, trying to divine the mysteries that lay behind their eyes.

Have you seen this, Tamara? my uncle asked. He rose from the sofa and took down a piece of newsprint that had been tacked on the wall above the work table in the dining area.

Tamara looked closely at the carefully cut clipping. This is Irina, she announced, in the park.

Go ahead, read the quote, Uncle said.

It says, My name is Irina. I don't like it when it is noisy and chaotic around me, because I am a very serious person.

I looked down at my milk. Little had I known, when a photographer from the local party newspaper had approached my father and me on the street, that this would happen. I thrilled to the attention, even though I wasn't sure how to behave.

That's very sweet, Tamara said, replacing the clipping. Peace and quiet. It's a shame she'll never have any around here.

My life maintained its rhythm. After dinner Uncle dropped me off at the theater where my parents worked. It was nearly dark outside, and I could feel the first frigid winds of winter insinuating their way across the plains. It was late for a Russian child to be out, but Buryats believed in allowing their children greater freedoms. Also, the apartment would be deserted that night except for my brothers. I would be better cared for by the cast and crew at the theater than by my half-siblings.

The lobby was half-lit, the ticket booth still closed. I walked through the small auditorium toward backstage, where I found my mother conferring with an actress over a costume. There wasn't enough fabric to finish the actress's regal gown, she said as they tried to pin it together in order to hide the bare spots.

The Buryat Drama Theater was the center of my dream life. I had spent my childhood exploring in my heart the differences between dreams and reality—and finding that the separation was almost meaningless. The theater had space for an audience of perhaps two hundred. The orchestra pit was the size of our apartment balcony. The backstage was a trio of cramped, stuffy rooms which the actors filled with smoke and the smell of tea.

To me it was a kingdom in the clouds. I failed to understand why anyone in Ulan Ude spent time anywhere else. Outside there was soot-stained concrete, mud, and ice. Inside there were kings and queens, intrigues, noble acts, and unspeakable cowardice. Other than the bitter moments when the cast and crew discussed their paychecks, the Soviet Union didn't exist inside the theater doors. I smelled the dusty odor of old costumes arranged on racks against the back wall; my fingers outlined the stitches where the old stage curtain had been repaired. When no one was looking I would rummage through huge wooden crates full of old props: weapons, false jewelry, wigs, eyeglasses, cups from which the actors pretended to drink and dishes from which they pretended to eat.

Irina! an old man in rags and a stained white beard called out to me. Come here, we saved you a piece of cake.

With him by the samovar were two men dressed in tunics and tights, holding staffs with sharp points. Though I didn't understand Shakespeare yet, I recognized the trappings of his dramas.

I also understood the power of sweets, which were hard to find in the city. The theater often obtained them because of an actor's connections to a small bakery. I took a slice of frosted cake from the old man and sat next to him at the table.

I hear that you're going to kindergarten now, he said. His name was Alexei, and I had known him all my life. One month I would see him dressed as a prince, the next a beggar. He was perhaps fifty years old.

Are you playing that evil man again? I asked.

Alexei put his chin in his hands and considered for a moment. Buryat children were free to speak to adults on an equal basis; it went without saying that my thoughts were worth responding to with respect.

I don't know if you would call him evil, Alexei said thoughtfully. He has many troubles in his mind.

But you kill your brother! I declared, finishing the cake. How could you do that?

Alexei slipped into character. Perhaps you should consider your words, young lady, or the royal ax might find you next.

I squealed and slapped Alexei's hand. The courtiers waiting for the samovar to warm up laughed with us. What fabulous people, I thought as I waited for my father to finish meeting with his orchestra. They were spirited, intelligent, creative. They moved and spoke like no one else in Ulan Ude, as though they knew a secret they might one day share with me. My parents were unorthodox in their own way; they weren't Party members, and they had never registered their marriage with the government.

Later in life I would understand that their costumes granted them a sort of immunity from the eyes of the government. The plays were set in faraway lands, yet the characters spoke in allegory about the problems and truths of life in the contemporary Soviet Union. I learned that today's truth can be hidden behind the guise of years past, and that in this way an artist can speak to the audience without using words that might otherwise bring her trouble.

I couldn't comprehend why everyone in the theater always talked about how little money they had. Or why from time to time a cultural officer would arrive for a couple of days. Each play had to be premiered for a government censor. The man in the drab coat would sit in the front row, frowning and taking notes as though what the actors were doing was all wrong.

My mother and father had met through the theater in which they still worked. Sometimes when we were having dinner together or walking home from a performance, I asked them how their love began.

I found her on the moon, Father said, pointing up at the sky.

I picked him in a potato patch, Mother corrected. Can't you see how lumpy his head is?

Mother had grown up in the small village where her parents still lived, one child among many brothers and sisters. She was very beautiful and intelligent, and she decided to make her own way in the world by becoming a tailor. Her will was strong, and soon she was making her own living sewing clothes.

She met and married a man who was much older than her; he took Mother from her village to live in his. She sewed day and night to make money for her new family, which soon included two sons, but her life turned sour. Her husband criticized her constantly. He drank, and when he was drunk he beat her for things he only imagined she had done. There was no law in her world to protect her, so one day she took her sons in her arms and left.

She couldn't return to her village because she was now divorced and would be scorned as a fallen woman. So she took her sons to the city—Ulan Ude—and tried to survive. She had no money and no friends, only her ability to sew clothing. A kind family took her in, and soon she found work in the theater. She was self-sufficient, whole, and free from the fists of her husband. A year later my father arrived at the theater from his music training at the conservatory.

How did your romance begin? I would ask in the heat of summer, our balcony door open to the cool breezes. When did you know you loved her? I would ask again, during deadliest winter when we dined on pickled cabbage and carrots.

Our love began a thousand years ago, Mother said, fanning herself with a newspaper. I knew I loved her when she laid a golden egg, Father replied, tracing a line with his finger on the iced-over window.

My mother, Tatiana, had never before known love. She had never enjoyed a connection with anyone to whom she could speak freely and explore life. She had accepted her pain as though it was all that she deserved.

My father, Vladlen, was like an angel to her. He was open, kind, emotional. He was an artist full of unique thoughts. He was full of love and was bursting to express it. She had never known much about music—tape recorders and stereos were rare in Siberia then, owned only by well-placed Party members. My father exposed her to the aching beauty of composition and melody by playing the piano for her in the shadows of the theater after performances.

The productions at the theater often were classics of Russia and the West: Shakespeare, Ibsen, Chekov. My father led the orchestra and, when an extra player was needed, would assume a role in the play and take the stage. I watched everything from behind his shoulder in the cramped orchestra section in front of the audience.

I remained quiet, part of the bargain I made for staying out so late and keeping the company of adults. Alexei looked up at the spotlight shining down and lamented the fate which I felt he deserved. The orchestra played a melancholy song which I had first heard my father humming in our apartment kitchen. Then it was all over.

The lights came up after the audience's applause had died away and the cast retreated backstage. The silence was punctuated by voices commenting on what they had seen, and the shuffle of autumn coats and wraps being tightened against the wind outside. The musical players put their instruments inside their worn and frayed cases.

My father stacked his sheet music and ordered it carefully in a folder as tears burned paths down my cheeks. When he turned to raise me from my seat, his expression dropped with surprise.

Irina, why are you crying? he asked, taking my hand.

I shook my head as he walked me backstage. It can't be over, I said. How can the fantasy end just like that? How can people just walk away?

My mother stood at the end of the hall, giving orders for storing costumes and props for the night. When she saw me she stopped what she was doing and joined us.

Have you stayed up too late? she asked, wiping my face with a handkerchief.

Irina is sad because the play is over, my father said.

Mother cocked her head at me. But we will stage the same play tomorrow night, and the night after that, she said. It's over just for a little while.

But how can it end? I asked. It was so beautiful, so sad. How can we act as though it never happened?

My father picked me up in his arms and bounced me a couple of times. I felt my tears subside a bit.

It's all right to cry, he said. Now that you explain it to me, I think I understand precisely what you mean. It's enough to make me cry, too.

Mother rolled her eyes at us. Maybe we should skip the play tomorrow night, she said. Or the whole family will become hysterical.

My parents explained to me that children are born as full people. A mother and father's primary task is to step aside and wait for their children's personalities to emerge like flowers after the winter. I was still a baby, in kindergarten, living beneath the notice of the Soviets. But residing within myself was a permanent spirit whose outline I felt as solidly as a cement block or a marble monument.

In our apartment there were about ten relatives, including my parents and half-brothers, a constantly shifting cast that also included the neighbors on either side of our thin walls. My grandparents arrived from their village then left again, my grandfather silent and mysterious, my grandmother with a will that hit you like a wave.

My parents started to speak in low voices to each other about the neighbor down the hall. Her name was Baba Pana. She was an old woman we shared food with, and who the men would help whenever she needed something heavy lifted or help with her aged stove. Baba Pana had been sick since last winter, and my mother and I had gone to her apartment several times to help with the wash. The old woman's spare furniture encircled the room in a gloom, and I had started to feel frightened and uncomfortable every time we went there.

Baba Pana had grown sicker, and now another winter was only weeks away. My parents had made no secret of the fact that we were low enough on money and food without trying to assist the old woman again. Of course we would try—it was unthinkable that we wouldn't—but Baba Pana had grown so ill that she had shrunken into an old chair near her dusty window. She barely moved, and when she spoke her voice was crackly and dry like old newspapers rustling in the wind. Fortunately, so we thought at first, her daughter Nina had come from another town to care for her.

It's Nina who's the problem, my mother whispered to Father. Tamara was sleeping in the living room; my brothers and uncle were out at their jobs.

I joined them at the table. Pana was so sick now that she required care all the time. She couldn't feed herself, wash herself, or go to the bathroom without being helped by someone. Nina had been living in Pana's apartment for almost a week, and I knew she wasn't to be trusted.

I don't like her, I announced. She's very rough in the way she moves, and her eyes are very mean.

I wonder how well she is caring for Baba Pana? my mother said. She left the question hanging among the three of us.

Father looked up from his tea. He was tireless around our household, always cleaning and straightening the place to help my mother. She was more likely to help the neighbors and other families, so he listened to her pronouncement with great seriousness.

Before she was sick, Baba Pana was always over here, and we were always over there, Father recalled aloud. We've done a lot for her this year, but in the past she was always there for us. She's a good woman. This Nina, though, I know nothing about. Are you saying that she's trying to hurt Baba Pana?

My mother glanced at me. An old sick person is hard to care for, she said. I think she might be doing . . . little things.

That night I saw Baba Pana in my dream, an old woman whose mind had deserted her and whose body was nearly useless. She looked out the window, crying softly to herself as she remembered moments and dead friends who would soon disappear with her. I also pictured Nina, thick-waisted, her eyes bleary, her voice sharp when it cut the air. Both times I had seen her she had pulled sips from a vodka bottle all the time my mother spoke to her.

At the end of the week I came home from kindergarten with a paper doll our teacher had taught us how to make. I had dressed it in strips of paper that matched my own coat and cloth dress. My uncle had accompanied me home and dropped me off at the apartment, where Tamara was supposed to watch me until my parents came home. But when I stood outside our place, I looked down the hall and saw Baba Pana's door partly opened. A ray of light sneaked out of the apartment and painted a finger on the uncarpeted floor.

I went to the door and pushed it open without considering what I was doing. I went into the apartment, where my nostrils immediately burned with a familiar scent of age and impending death. Baba Pana lay on the couch in the corner, staring up at the ceiling, her lips moving with words I couldn't hear.

I looked around for Nina and heard noise coming from the bathroom. Before I could run out she walked into the living room smoking a cigarette. She let out a little sound when she noticed me.

You live down the hall, don't you? The Pantaevas?

Both times I had seen her she had been drunk, but that day her eyes were clear and her voice steady. It made me even more frightened of her; her body seemed even larger, and I could feel her capacity for anger and violence.

Why don't you talk, little girl? she asked. What's the matter, are you scared of me?

I remembered the things my mother had told my father. Baba Pana wasn't being fed enough, she wasn't clean enough, she wasn't getting medicine. It seemed to her that Nina wanted to let her mother slip away. Then the problem would be solved.

My parents had both shook their heads sadly. What could they do?

You are not right. You are a bad woman, I said to Nina. She was about the same age as my own mother, yet much bigger and stronger. I took a step toward her. How can you do these things to your mother? How can you want her to die? Didn't she take care of you when you were a little girl? Don't you want your own children to take good care of you when you are old?

There was a long silence. My ears began to ring with fear. I had spoken to her very loudly in a voice that I had never heard come from me before.

Nina's mouth hung open with shock. She took a drag from her cigarette and looked once at me, then at her mother. I knew what she would say. Who did I think I was? I was just a little girl, not even part of this family. It was none of my business. I should have kept my mouth shut.

I read all these thoughts in her eyes, but then her expression changed. Suddenly she looked directly into my eyes for the first time, as though she had just noticed that I was a real person and not an apparition. I was even more frightened. She was so rough, I was sure she knew how to fight. She was a drinker, she was crazy, I knew what kind of person she was. My legs shook, and I would have run away if I had been able.

I'm sorry, she said to me. I saw her huge shoulders start to quake. I didn't mean to do it. I don't want to do this. She is my mother.

Nina covered her face with her hands. I couldn't understand just what had happened. I had never spoken like that before, certainly never to an adult. But I no longer felt scared. I hadn't been full of fear when I spoke to Nina, I realized. Fear would have stopped me.

The next time Nina and I saw each other in the hall, we both averted our eyes. After a moment such as we had shared, it was as though normal contact would never again be possible.

I began to sense that the lives of those around me were defined by a sort of combat; whether they chose to fight for, and what they chose to fight, determined who they were. My father fought against the crowding in our home and the constant chatter of voices so that he might have time in which to compose. Mother fought to manage our money, to make our clothes, to make sure there was enough to eat. Her fight was against everything around us, from the food shops to the government offices, though she remained steely and I had to watch her closely to understand the extent of her struggle.

It became clear to me that I would have to fight as well, though I couldn't have said precisely who or what my life's sparring partner would be. I had grown tired of fighting with my brothers; their affections were the spoils of a battle I would never win.

My mother kept an old trunk full of fabrics, buttons, trim, thread, and needles. When I was alone in their bedroom I went through it like an archaeologist, the different textures and colors aspects of my mother's personality. The world was there, too; in shimmering blues I conjured Lake Baikal, in rough brown cloth the ancestral spirit of trees.

For weeks I selected and secreted away bits of fabric in order to make a ballgown. I planned to transform into a princess soon, and I needed to be dressed appropriately when the moment arrived. From my mother's hidden treasure I had found silky silver and sea-floor greens. All that remained was to assemble them into an outfit worthy of royalty.

Mother often worked at home on her antiquated, noisy sewing machine. It was a heavy metal device with a rotating bobbin and imposing lengths of steel and brass. I had watched her manipulate it with a professional's hand, and I could use it to make simple stitches. As long as I pledged to be careful, it was mine to experiment with.

It was Sunday, no school until tomorrow. Outside the shadows grew longer by the day. Mother was in the kitchen using our big pot to stew beets for borscht. The center room and the sewing machine were mine alone. But the machine sat in the corner, shoved out of the way for the weekend. The big wooden dining table, the only one in the house capable of bearing its weight, was ten feet away and its surface three feet off the ground.

I heard my mother humming one of my father's compositions softly to herself in the kitchen. He was away in the countryside with his orchestra, earning a little extra money playing at a collective farm.

I listened to her voice, looked up at the table, then at the solidity of the sewing machine. A call to her for help died in my throat. I would do this myself.

The machine was so heavy that my first push caused it to merely teeter on its side. I pushed again, my body nearly parallel to the floor, until the long muscles in my thighs and calves started to burn. With a groan, the machine moved a couple of feet across the floor.

Pots banged in the kitchen. Mother was still singing. I knew she was a little angry that day, because the beets father had waited in line three hours for were too dried out and stringy for her taste.

This time I tried to drag the machine; my back pulsed with effort, but I made it move another foot. The machine and I were locked in a sort of dance, a struggle which I insisted that I would win.

You will move, I said to it in a whisper.

I pulled again and now it was next to the table. But how could I raise it up to the table's surface? I became enraged again and tried to lift it all at once. No good. I barely lifted it off the floor. I pried one side of it from the ground and put my knee under it, bracing it while I pulled up at the other side.

You're not so big, I said to it. You think I'm just a girl, just a little person. Well, I'm going to show you. I can do anything I want.

I yanked again and now the whole thing was off the floor. I didn't know how much the damned thing weighed, maybe half as much as I did. But now I was winning. It was going where I wanted. What flashed through my mind then were my brothers, and the look on my parents' faces when they had to borrow money yet again, and the tone of my family's voices whenever they talked about the government or the very idea that life might ever change.

I fought with the sewing machine because it was there for me to fight with. Alone in the long shadows of afternoon I played out this scene that would repeat itself again and again in different forms.

I looked up and saw my mother watching me from the door-

way. At first she didn't offer to help. I think she knew precisely
what was going on.

I finished the gown on Tuesday afternoon amid the bustle
of my brothers and aunt and uncle eating dinner and arguing
about the whether winter would come sooner or later that year.
The dress hung from my small body, I thought, like a waterfall
floating gently down to earth under the warm caress of the
sun. I waited for my parents to return home from that night's
performance until it grew dark and the apartment was quiet.
I lay down and fell asleep near the front door, where their
entrance would surely wake me.

I woke to their voices talking softly. In my father's quiet
laugh I could hear his fatigue. He started straightening a pile
of papers and books in the living room as soon as he had taken
his coat off. I opened my eyes and saw my mother's face.

Well, look at you, she said. You've finished. It's very nice.

Don't look! I said to her. You can't look yet.

Father took off his glasses and began to wipe them. Before I
could admonish him, he said, Okay, Okay, I'm not looking. Let
me clean these, or I won't be able to see when it's permitted
again.

I sat them down on the sofa; they exhaled at the same time,
their tired bodies sinking down. Mother glanced at the clock
on the wall.

Wait here, I said. The theater is about to open. The play
begins.

I lunged behind the balcony curtain and caught my breath.
I had run through the play in my mind several times, feeling
that its nuances were all known to me. When I heard nothing
but silence on the other side I emerged.

Presenting Princess Irina, I said in a stage whisper. Prepare
yourself for a performance by the greatest actress in the Soviet Union.

I stepped out and bowed to them, pulling out the fabric of
my dress so they could see every facet of its beauty. My father
oohed with appreciation.

I began to sing a song. *I am a nice little girl. I haven't started
school yet, but please buy me sandals. Because I am getting
married.*

Sing another one, Father said.

I took a deep breath. *Love has just passed me by, and I am sad. The tomatoes are rotten now. And my coat is hiding from me in the corner.*

I started a dramatic scene that I had memorized. I have traveled far to reach this kingdom, I said, already feeling my grasp of the lines escape me. But I know that it is here where I will meet my prince. He will take me back to my kingdom and regain the throne for myself and my royal family.

I glanced at the audience. Their hands were folded in their laps, their mouths curled into serene smiles. They were enjoying themselves.

I spoke on, mixing up anything I could remember from the last six months of productions at their theater. I spoke of chivalry and honor, love and duty, until I could think of no more. Humming a melody Father composed, I performed a dance that in my mind communicated the grace and beauty I saw on their stage.

When it was over I bowed again and hid behind the curtain. They clapped on, insisting I come out again and receive my due. Father flipped on the lamp, signaling that the play was over. When I came out, they treated me with the hushed excitement of an actress after a particularly good performance. I grasped my mother's dress and my father's jacket, kneading the fabric, wishing to savor every element of this perfect blend of dream and reality.

I performed for them many times when I was a little girl, and they were always a receptive and appreciative audience. They laughed and clapped, insisted I sing another song, and addressed me as Princess Irina. I suppose they understood very well that in Russia we would never live as princesses and princes. They enjoyed the fantasy as much as I did.

My childhood was spent in the theater, where I was the princess and the orchestra section was a moat around the castle of the stage. The audience were the kingdom's subjects, devoted to the reign of fantasy. My childhood sounded like my father's music. It felt like the fabrics in my mother's sewing chest. It smelled like the flowering blossoms in my grandparents' village, where my parents took me on holidays.

Childhood ended for every Soviet young person at the same time—when they were seven years old. I was no different. This was the age when official schooling began. It marked the point at which we became full members of Soviet society. From that moment the State no longer would leave us to our blissful games.

The week before my first day of school I awoke in my grandparents' village. I had a breakfast of fresh berries and milk from the cow, then I wandered the fields after helping Grandfather feed the horses. The sky was so clear and wide that I could have reached up and made ripples in its surface as though it were a pond.

My parents would take me back to the city early that evening. In the afternoon my grandparents summoned me to their room in their tiny home. Inside the curtains gently swayed in the cool breeze. My grandparents sat on their bed, their shoulders hunched, their eyes searching my face. They had never taken me aside before with such a feeling of seriousness.

We want to share something with you, Grandmother said.

I nodded my head. Grandfather looked at me with his usual quiet kindness. Only now I sensed something else in him, a spirit of caution.

You've grown so fast, she continued. She took my hand and pulled me closer to them.

I started to pull away, reflexively behaving as though this was a game in which I would make them chase after me. But she held onto my hand tighter, making it impossible for me to get away.

The first day of September is coming soon, she said. This will be a very important day in your life. Be a good girl in school. Study the teachings of Lenin. We are all working hard, every day of our lives, to attain pure communism. Then we will always live nicely. We will never have to borrow money.

Her hand held mine tightly. And remember the proverb, she said, *Don't take the rubbish from the house to the street.*

I knew what she meant. Things that were said at home were private, not to be repeated to people who weren't in our family. I wasn't sure why this was so but I knew it was very serious.

You're a good girl, she added, looking into my eyes. You'll

become an Octobrist, a Pioneer, a Comsomol. You'll make us all proud.

These ideas were so powerful and true that they burned in my heart. I was a patriot.

She made me repeat what she said to make sure I understood. In kindergarten they had talked about Soviet society, the October Revolution, the Communist Party, happy ideals that would be elaborated upon when we were old enough to comprehend their beauty and gravity.

I knew the face of Lenin, with his steely eyes and tight mouth. He seemed like a stern but loving grandfather who always exhorted his children to do better and better. And the older children had told me about the great things that lay ahead—becoming an Octobrist, then a Party member when I came of age and demonstrated political rectitude. I looked forward to every stage of my life as it had been designed and lain out before me by the wise fathers of the Communist Party.

My grandparents told me to go outside and play. There was only an hour left before I would return to the city. I walked alone on a crest rising above a grassy field that extended luxuriantly to the lake. Potatoes and grass—winter food for the animals—grew in carefully tended patches where the breeze lifted the smell of rich soil to my nose. Next to a tall tree was the barn, where I said goodbye to the two cows, the horses, lambs, pigs, and chickens. I told them I would be back for the holidays, looking into their trusting eyes and searching for words that they could understand.

I was bigger now. My arms could lift more, my legs could run faster. I could carry feed for the animals and milk from the cows to the house. I was becoming smarter, learning from watching and listening.

Don't take the rubbish from the house to the street. One of my parents' few requirements of me was truthfulness. When something was wrong or hurtful, I was encouraged to say so. Perhaps my grandparents didn't entirely understand. They had lived their lives in the country, never attending school in the city.

The night my mother and I rode the bus into the twilight, sitting together next to a cracked window that allowed in a whistling wind. When we had talked for some time I repeated in a lighthearted voice what her parents had told me.

Instead she listened closely. She looked out the window at the fields passing by.

I'm glad they spoke to you, she finally said. I want you to remember what they said and make sure you follow it. Communism is our hope for the future. It's the way things are, and it's the way things are going to be. For a long time.

My homeland was called the Buryat Autonomous Socialist Republic, or Buryatia. Under the Soviets it was a remote part of the USSR; now it is a sector of Siberian Russia. Look at a map of Russia, with your finger covering Moscow. Drift east across the green farmlands, over the dark rocky face of the Ural Mountains into Asia and Siberia. By now you have traveled across five time zones.

There is Ulan Ude, the city of 300,000 that was my home. Ulan Ude translates into "Red Gate" in Russian. The word *red* in Russian folklore predates the Soviet Union as a synonym for *beautiful*. In the thirteenth century Genghis Khan journeyed with his army from the lands east of Baikal and conquered the steppes of Russia to the Caspian Sea. The history of Buryat Mongols, always intertwined with the forest lands near the great lake, was passed down for centuries in folk tales like the epic of Geser Khan.

The Buryats are the northernmost of the Mongol peoples. We are Eskimos, Inuits. We are the largest indigenous group in Siberia, with a population of more than 400,000. Our history is nomadic, but when Russians came to our lands in the seventeenth century we were settled into towns and cities, often against our choice. The Soviet Union continued this policy, trying to eradicate the Buryat folklore, language, and history.

The majority of people in Ulan Ude are ethnic Russians. I was the only Buryat in my school class. I learned to be tough, to make jokes, to be ready with a reply when I received an insult.

Your eyes are like saucers, a boy said to me.

But look at you, I replied. Your ears make your head look like a pouring pitcher.

His friends pointed at him and screamed. Outwitted by a girl!

In the Soviet Union there were no ethnic divisions, no prejudice—this was one of the first lessons that was taught to us in school. I wouldn't argue that it wasn't the truth, but I also knew better than to contradict my teacher when she spoke of Ghenghis Khan as a bloodthirsty conqueror. He might have been a hero to my people, but I was living in the Russians' country.

From the first day of school everything was different. I was assigned a desk of scarred wood with a hard straight back. We all wore uniforms now. The boys were dressed in dark suits and white shirts, the girls in blue or brown dresses under white aprons. I had turned back and forth in the mirror at home that morning, finally deciding that I liked these clothes. But already I understood that I would have to wear the same outfit every day. Like the army, my father had said under his breath.

The teacher held up her hand for silence. She looked around the room at us as though she were assessing our collective character.

You are not children anymore, she said. You are part of the Soviet Union, citizens of the Dictatorship of the Proletariat. Each of you is a part of the shining future and the only hope for humanity. We will learn about the teachings and philosophy of the Communist Party and about the great achievements of the state.

I heard a titter of high-pitched laughter on the other side of the room. One of the boys, a cut-up I knew from kindergarten, was pulling faces for his friends. The teacher walked slowly toward him.

Perhaps you do not understand what I mean when I say you are no longer children, she added in a monotone. You are old enough to know the difference between obedience and rebellion. There are two paths. Down one path lies the worker's paradise and a good life for every person in this country.

She stopped in front of the boy's desk. His name was Sasha, and he struggled to keep from laughing.

Do you know what lies down the other path? she asked him. He shook his head and she leaned close to him. Betrayal of the Soviet Union, she hissed. Betrayal of the people. Our country in flames, all of us enslaved by the capitalists because you wanted to make stupid faces and not pay attention.

Sasha's eyes widened and he squirmed in his chair. I watched his bewildered expression beneath his hair, which was cropped close to his scalp. We contemplated what we had been told. We were no longer children. Our every act and thought had an almost supernatural power to affect the fate of our people and our country.

It was flattering. It was intoxicating to be treated with such gravity, to have the future of humanity placed at our feet. I swung my legs back and forth under my desk, listening.

We began to learn about the world outside Ulan Ude. In the Soviet Union were fifteen republics, all working together happily for the common good. Ethnic differences were irrelevant, individual personalities didn't matter. We were not given a chance to learn to speak or write the Buryat language of my people; this was so, we were told, because Russian was the language of the Party and the language we would need as adults.

I craved to become strong enough to meet the demands of socialism. I believed in the system with all my being. Every Soviet citizen had been blessed with the opportunity to contribute to the greatest collective project in the history of our species: the perpetuation and perfection of a state based on absolute equality and economic justice.

In the West there were poor people and rich people, and no one in between. In my lesson book was a drawing of a fat man in a tuxedo with a thick mustache and a monocle. He held onto huge bags of money with a greedy, almost drunken expression. The sides of the bags were ripped and coins and bills were falling out all over the place, but the fat man didn't seem to notice or care. Outside his window, on a filthy street covered with trash and rats, a family of skeletons starved in agony.

In the USSR everyone had food to eat. Everyone had the same rights and privileges, and the same opportunities under the law. The State would always take care of us, providing medicine and education for free. The reason America and Western Europe didn't live like this was because the wealthy were greedy and used their armies to keep the power and money from the workers. Someday, we hoped, the workers there would also rise up and assume control of the state. The world would move closer to total justice.

I listened to every word with all my attention. The idea of other countries fascinated me, even while I accepted the basic truth that their systems of government were bad and unfair. I knew it was practically impossible that I would ever travel outside the Soviet Union. My teachers knew so much, but none of them had ever traveled anywhere. To Moscow, perhaps, or to Vladivostok, but the world outside the USSR was farther even than the moon in the sky.

Some people had left the country—famous dancers and actors. But of course no one knew any of them personally; they were thousands of miles away in Moscow. There was no one in our school, no one we could speak to, who could give a firsthand picture of life outside our country.

There was a girl in our class whose father was a sailor in the navy. He travels to other countries, she declared.

Oh, really? our teacher asked. She looked a little uncomfortable, but she told the girl to continue.

He brings me little toys, but sometimes he's not allowed to, she said in a proud voice. He's not always allowed to leave the boat in other countries because it's so dangerous. When he is allowed to leave, two other men have to come with him. That's to make sure none of them talks to anyone they're not supposed to. If one of them does, then the other two can tell the captain what happened.

My teacher complimented the girl on her complex grasp of the hazards of contact with other cultures. She failed to explain why a simple conversation might be so destructive to our society.

When I came home at night I thought I saw a wariness in my parents' eyes when they asked me about my day. They must have wondered how I was adapting. They must have been curious what sort of person I would become after the influence of Soviet indoctrination.

I had begun a task that was essential for every citizen: splitting my mind and spirit into compartments. I did what was asked of me at school, and believed what I was expected to believe. But I also remembered my grandparents' warnings, and I didn't repeat the jokes I heard at the theater about communist bureaucrats and I kept my mouth shut whenever the teacher accused one of the students of being traitorous.

In late October the snow piled up on the streets, turning the apartment buildings into white layer cakes. When I walked to school now it was under bundled layers beneath the new coat my mother had sewed to warm my quickly growing body. The worst of winter was weeks away, but my flesh stung then grew numb in the wind.

That morning the teacher informed us, with an air of seriousness she reserved for the gravest proclamations, we now would be granted the opportunity to become Young Octobrists. Even the name was glorious, with its connotations of the Revolution. Membership in the Octobrists was the first step in our becoming honored communist citizens. It would set us apart and above other children.

That was true, in a limited fashion. But the Octobrists would set us apart only from those rare children who lived in the remotest countryside and never attended school. Everyone in my class would become an Octobrist, for not to do so would be an open revolt against the Soviet Union. This was a test of our loyalty. Because it was the first, it was designed to be very easy.

At home that night we ate steamed cabbage and carrots. The fresh food was running out and soon we would survive on pickled vegetables and preserves.

I turned to my father and said, Today they gave me the opportunity to become an Octobrist. I think I should join. The teachers say it will be so much fun—they will give me a beautiful pin with a red star on it if I promise to be a nice girl.

My father put his fork on his plate and looked at me. Of course you should, he said.

Yes, it will be a good thing, Mother said.

I laughed with joy. I never imagined school would be such a delight.

I wished to be good enough to become an Octobrist. The school would take a photograph of me, they would send a nice note to my parents' theater. Perhaps my becoming an Octobrist would help them somehow with their government reviews.

It's an honor to become an Octobrist, my father said. It means you are growing. It's an achievement.

We'll throw a party for you, my mother said. I'll get some cakes and we'll invite the neighbors.

My father's eyes shone. I'm very proud of you, he said.

She's becoming a big girl, Mother said to him.

I continued eating my dinner. Inside me swelled a pool of warmth and happiness. My parents had confirmed everything I felt. I wanted to be a patriot; my enthusiasm for communism felt like the greatest freedom I had ever known.

I had learned about the best facets of communism, the qualities that would remain with me throughout my life. I gained belief in something greater than myself, pride of achievement for the common good, a sense of morality and selflessness, the discipline to achieve my personal goals, and the maturity to see my destiny as something that would only come to pass by combining the previous four elements. It felt as though life was a constant upward march toward a spectacular future.

In class a spirit of excitement started to move through us. When I was at home I was able to analyze the Octobrists and keep the concept at arm's length; at school, though, my public self took over. It was clear that joining was for the best. My parents wished it, the other children strove for it.

This is a great moment for all of you, the teacher told us. In her features was displayed more genuine emotion than she had ever showed us before. You are taking the first step toward a great future. I congratulate and welcome each of you as comrades.

I was given a red pin shaped like the five-pointed Soviet star. Inside the star was a portrait of Lenin as a cute seven-year-old little boy. His expression was serious and focused. I turned the pin in the light to see closer his sullen, determined face. That day we sang patriotic songs whose genesis dated back to the 1917 revolution. Our teacher gave us chocolates and explained that we were all now part of something greater than ourselves. We were changed for the better.

We learned the Octobrist marching song, which we sang as we stepped in tight lines to lunch, or in and out of the classroom:

One, two, three, four
Three, four, one, two
Who is marching in a steady row?
It is our Octobrist Platoon.
Friendly and cheerful—we're always in the vanguard,
The star of Lenin shining on our chests.
Young Leninists—that's who we are!

We learned our new oath: *Vsyegda gotov! Always ready!* We learned that Young Communists were sent to the trenches during the war, that they had been prepared for any sacrifice. And we were taught that the Germans had killed communists with nearly as much fervor as they had tried to annihilate the Jews. We were to live our lives in a state of readiness; life would not be easy for a communist, but it would be a splendid life.

By the end of October the winds grew harsher and more serious in their intent. The leaves had abandoned all the trees in the city, and the accumulated snow turned gray with street dirt and smoke from the factories. From the apartment I listened to the equipment trying to keep the streets passable after every fresh snowfall. During the storms I could barely see to the end of our street. We began to feel even more isolated and closed in.

At school we now had to learn simple political lessons in addition to math and science. In the beginning it was simple, boiled-down Leninism for children: capitalism led to inequality; that was bad. The workers should own their means of production, which was communism; that was good. These were the last days of Brezhnev's reign, with its sense of peacefulness and stability. I walked home in the afternoon wearing my Octobrist pin on my coat, tracing my steps between snow drifts that soon would be as tall as me. The city had begun to feel like the mythic kingdom I had always pretended it was.

My friends from the neighborhood gathered in front of a building with a deep yard where the snow had been shoveled by the cleaning crews. There we played war games—the Russians against the Fascists. Our newsprint Octobrist readers cost our families money—mere pennies, but we understood the symbolism of our contributions, as we had begun to comprehend the symbolism of our every act—so we sheltered all our workbooks in a portico to keep them dry while we waged war.

I huddled behind a mountain of snow and screamed when a neighbor boy dumped a pile of ice on my head. Though I was playing, there was a tinge of justification in my fear; the Great War lingered in all our minds, more than thirty years after it ended. Why else would we re-create the battles of our grandparents?

I made a snowball out of crystalline ice and hurled it at my attacker. My mother had once told me that she remembered her father returning home from the war, bandaged and frail as he stepped from the train. His leg had been injured and then gotten infected, and he had barely survived. Like so many other things, he never spoke of it. I threw another ice-ball, pretending that I was protecting my wounded grandfather.

A couple of girls broke off ice spears hanging from a steel gutter and began fencing. I joined them, jabbing and parrying with my own sword until it was too small to use. In my mind were other battles fought by my distant ancestors in mythic stories. The girls I fought were Russians; I was Buryat. But there was no history of conflict taught to us to reenact. We were all Soviets. Focusing on ethnic heritage was decadent and anti-communist.

I was finally so wet and cold that I had to go inside. Ice caked my eyebrows and snow made its way into the cuffs of my coat and down my back. I walked with a shuffling step, careful not to slip. Though our teeth were chattering, we stood outside a few minutes longer in the cold. In all our apartments a quiet night waited for us. Soon it would be too cold for such play to take place at all. Our silence was like the vigil for a life that would soon come to a halt.

Inside I put my book by the oven to dry away moisture that had seeped into it. Our teacher noticed those students with sloppy materials and made pointed mention of them every morning. I walked past my uncle sleeping on the living room sofa to the kitchen, where my aunt and a neighbor were drinking tea, smoking, and talking in quiet voices.

The slowness had begun, that grinding sensation of time. I took a glass of warmed milk to the window, where I stripped off one of my several layers of sweaters. I bundled my wet feet in a blanket and blew milk vapor onto the windowpane. Its surface looked like stained glass, filigrees of ice creating a distorted mosaic. My breath warmed a small spot, and I could see outside to the battleground where we had defeated the Germans for the third time that week. In the morning the spot on the glass would be frozen over again, thicker than before. The light shining into the room cast blues and yellows like a cathedral.

The winter would last as long as seven months. In Moscow, I was told, the cold weather was bad, but not as bad as ours. In Kazhakstan and Uzbekistan it was nowhere near as severe. When the cold grew unbearable my father would joke about moving to the Crimea. But I never hated the freeze; it was imprinted on me by countless generations.

In 1908 there was a vast explosion in a remote part of the Siberian tundra. In my childhood people spoke of it with such vivid imagery that it almost seemed as though they had witnessed it. I pictured a great flat field roiling with flames, trees splintering like twigs, dirt hurtling miles into the air.

The blast was heard throughout Siberia. Dust from the explosion spread around the world and made warm days cold by blocking the sun. The shock wave was felt almost a thousand miles away. The explosion had been as great as that from a nuclear bomb. Many scientists felt that the event had been created by a meteor impacting the earth. Yet no large fragments of rock were ever found to support this opinion.

In Siberia the night sky is an ocean of blackness spotted by thousands of brilliant stars. The full moon looks down, its craters dotting the great circle of yellow light. My father wrote a song about the full moon after being inspired by its brilliance.

One night my mother woke me from a deep sleep. Dawn was still hours away.

Look out the window, she said, her voice tight with fear. There's something going on in the sky.

I got out of bed, my eyes blurred. I had never heard my mother sound frightened before. Outside the window a red fire played in the blackness above. I was a young girl, full of dreams, but I knew that this wasn't supposed to happen. Bright redness flickered against my eyes. I wondered if I were dreaming.

My mother held onto the windowsill next to me. She stared out, almost uncomprehending.

Go back to sleep, she said. Forget about this.

She left the room. I sat on my bed and rocked gently back and forth. The light from outside played in the shadows of my room. I felt a blurring in my mind as though there was a new logic to life that I could barely comprehend.

I heard a buzzing noise, sharp and pointed. Loud, strong. It seemed to bore directly into my head. It rocked through my body like a shock wave.

Something was in the room with me. There were two of them. One was long and thin, with no neck. His head sat atop his shoulders. He had eyes and a nose. I thought I recognized him.

I didn't know the other. His body was strange, almost round like a ball. He was shorter. His eyes looked into mine. The three of us stood in silence. I realized that they were speaking to me without making a sound.

I wasn't frightened of them; somewhere inside myself I understood that I was ready to meet them. Maybe they had known to come to me from their planet because I often thought of other worlds, because dreams and reality were for me one and the same.

My brain felt like a tape recorder. They were making a recording in my mind.

Don't be scared, the tall one said.

I heard a noise like a piano playing itself. The sounds were clear and pleasant, like Beethoven. I heard the strains of an orchestra joining in.

Can you hear what we're telling you? they asked.

Where is your world? I said aloud.

Do you understand what we've said? they asked.

As soon as they made an impression on the tape of my mind, the information seemed to disappear. I grasped for its meaning.

I don't know, I said.

In the morning I couldn't remember what they had tried to tell me. I couldn't remember how or when they had left me. They had returned to whatever place was their home. I had never asked them who they were; for a reason I couldn't comprehend, such a question hadn't been necessary. I searched my memory for the message they had imparted; though I couldn't recall what they had said to me, I hoped that one day it would return.

When the winter holiday arrived it was time to help my grandparents in their village. It was more difficult to reach them in the snows, but I campaigned weeks in advance to be allowed to go. My mother said it was always good for me to see village life. It taught me that there had been people before there were cities.

I climbed onto the bus alone and maneuvered my way to a window seat. There were always plenty of other passengers. Buryat families stayed close even when they weren't living in the same physical space. Riding into the countryside twice or three times a week wasn't a trial for people who had once ridden horses five thousand miles.

The journey itself required a lot of faith in the driver. Not only did he have to keep the bus on the road, he had to find the road in the drifting snow. Inside the bus was filled was smoke, body heat, the smell of vodka and hot tea, and conversation. I lost myself in the landscape outside. Evergreen trees lined the edges of the horizon like sentinels. I felt the smallness of the bus in the vast whiteness of Siberia. I thought the journey would never end, that I would always be in this pristine white space. I thought about the futility of life against the infinity of the elements, then about the heroic stand of people's search for meaning in the face of a world that was so much greater than the individual.

Heat and motion lulled me into a dream state. Through my half-closed eyes I saw the white fields passing by as though they would go on forever. I knew that nature had to be essentially benevolent to allow us to survive in such a place. I would remember things I had heard from my grandparents, spoken to other adults. The Soviets were foolish to think they could conquer nature, I had heard, and someday everyone would suffer from their tampering. It took bravery to hold our place against nature, but it was insanity to try to defeat the heavens and the earth.

The bus dropped me off at the village and receded into the distance. Dotting the hills were brown and black patches standing out from the absolute whiteness, and from the splotches came plumes of smoke and vapor. These were the small village houses, all handbuilt, already sunken into the snow. Inside each burned a single Russian stove, the center of domestic life and the difference between living and freezing to death.

Grandfather met me and walked with me down the lane. Evergreens ringed the horizon like ramparts against the limitless power of the cold. He was dressed in furs, his wrinkled face squinting into the wind. As usual he said nearly nothing during our walk. He gestured toward familiar landmarks, the homes of people I knew, the trails into the forest we walked together during the summer. I watched his face, interpreting his smiles and ironic glances with as much detail as if he had carried on a monologue the entire way.

One afternoon when he was very young, Grandfather rode through the forest between his village and the next; the sun shone on the dewy trees and cool breezes whispered through the grass. He stopped to let his horse drink at a stream, then walked through the high grass to stretch his legs. When he came to a clearing he saw a group of young women picking berries and mushrooms near the road.

His eye caught on a very attractive, strong girl, and he stopped to watch her work. When he returned to his horse and rode back to his village, he knew that his destiny had changed. That night he rode to the girl's village, found her, and put a burlap hood over her head. He placed her on his horse and rode back through the night with her to his village. When they arrived at his home he removed the hood and looked into her eyes.

You will be my wife, he said to the girl.

My grandmother said nothing; she simply smiled, too young and shy to raise her eyes to his. He was tall, handsome, dignified. She would become his wife.

Grandfather had returned from Sverdlovsk in 1944 scarred from the war; he spent a year in the hospital recovering from his wounds. The family had thought he was dead for months before he returned home, his face bandaged and his strong walk reduced to a limp. My grandmother had stood by the door looking into the eyes of a man she thought was a stranger, asking who he was and who he had come to see.

The door to their house opened as we approached and Grandmother hurried us inside. The table was set for lunch. I took off my coat and sweaters and found my little Lenin pin affixed to my dress. People from the village joined us, eager to see me and hear news from the city.

The night was almost impossibly cold. Northern winds set in and froze everything tight to the grasp of the earth; everyone in the village knew better than to go outside until the sun rose low again the next morning.

A Russian stove burned in the middle of the little house my grandfather had built many years ago. It was the heart of the home, the place for cooking, baking, for providing heat. I walked up to it to warm my hands, hearing the wind moan outside the door.

Atop the stove was a place for warming and drying shoes, gloves, hats. It was my favorite place. I climbed above the stove, careful not to burn myself, and lay down inside a blanket. Within moments I was daydreaming, then I was asleep.

I woke up very early in the morning; outside it was still dark. The stars and moon shone down and reflected on the snow. I heard my grandmother say my name, and I looked down from my perch above the stove. She held out a piece of fresh bread for me, the first of the morning.

I got down from the stove, the blanket still wrapped around my shoulders. I poured a glass of milk that was still fresh and warm from the cow. I added sour cream and sugar to it from the containers on the table. My grandmother passed me on the way to the stove and squeezed my shoulder gently. I closed my eyes and sipped the milk, almost dreaming again.

The world outside didn't exist. I was safe, I was warm. Though I would have to work that day—feeding the cows and chickens, giving water to the horses—I knew that none of the trials of life in the city could reach me.

I looked up. Grandfather was watching me from his chair next to the stove, smiling gently as though I had spoken my every thought aloud.

He began to sing a song in his deep voice; a moment later,

my grandmother joined him, improvising on themes centuries old.

The wind, so strong and cold last night,
The icicles hang from the roof.
The moon floats in the sky and looks down upon us.
Telling us that the spring, when it comes, will be warm and
*   plentiful.*

I closed my eyes and listened. Everyone in the village communicated at times in song, the lyrics reflecting village news or how a person had filled the day. It was the music of life, joyous and wise. Once a man from the city had come with a tape recorder to make a record of the villagers' songs; he had sat much like me, swaying gently with the melody, amazed by the beauty of what he heard.

When we were nine years old we were introduced to the next step in the process of becoming a good Soviet citizen: joining the Young Pioneers. Little by little during the past two years our teachers had developed less patience for any transgression of discipline or expression of individuality. Ivan, a boy who lived on my street, had been called into the director's office several times because his uniform was sloppy. I had seen Ivan and his father walking home together one afternoon; Ivan's father had been tight-lipped, his eyes ringed with fatigue. Ivan soon had one of the cleanest and neatest uniforms of all the boys.

We all knew that our actions reflected on our parents, though we couldn't have explained precisely why that was so. Any activity that deviated from study and obedience was a slap in the face of the worker's revolution, we were told. A girl in my class who was caught kissing an older boy was exhibiting counterrevolutionary decadence. For my part, I talked too much in class. A note sent home to my mother said that I was in danger of becoming a disruptive influence.

I worked hard and received good marks. But I couldn't see anything wrong with speaking the truth aloud in class at times. Our humanities lessons were like sermons that we were supposed to digest without question or analysis. We were taught math and science with an attitude of hope—after all, the USSR put the first satellite in space, and we had many women in science and medicine, unlike the West. Then political lessons began, and we were no longer people but vessels for an undeviating line of truth.

Becoming a Young Pioneer wasn't automatic—you didn't just hold out your hand and receive your membership as had been the case with the Octobrists. At first only the most zealous students would become Pioneers, a few at a time, and receive the red triangular Young Pioneer scarf. We all knew who would be taken first: classmates like Luda, whose father was a regional Party Secretary, and Andrei, whose voice always rose the loudest when it was time to recite Lenin. They were the students who could recite Party ideology from memory when they were called upon. I had to flip through my books, trying to remember what Lenin had said about farming or academic discipline.

The Pioneers were another test, more difficult than the Octobrists, but easier, I was told, than joining the Comsomol and eventually the Party. Differences began to emerge between the students. Some of us were more effective propagandists, others hung back and seemed uninspired by Party ideology. Our teachers watched carefully, making notes that would stay in our files forever. I was inducted into the Pioneers in the middle of my class, saving me from the ignominy of being the last to receive my scarf.

I had seen others' triangular scarves, even touched them. Our teacher had held one up for us with the dainty grip of a believer holding a sacred relic. She laid it out on her desk, pointing away from us, and explained its profound symbolism: one front tip represented the Young Pioneers; the other represented the Comsomol; the back corner embodied the Party. It was red to evoke the blood spilled during the Revolution and the Civil War that followed. The act of tying the scarf linked together all three branches of Soviet youth and adults into a sacred bond.

My day of induction was April 22—Lenin's birthday. A lot of children in my class were taken into the Pioneers that day, but we were each convinced that our individual loyalty and dedication had earned us this honor. The teacher opened a small box containing several small triangular red scarves, then announced that we would collectively journey to the city square.

Ulan Ude's city square was ringed by boulevards full of gray, ugly apartment buildings and government offices. There were trees and shrubs, and people would take baskets of food there in the summer for picnics. It was a place where a person could not forget for an instant that they were a citizen of the Soviet Union, because it was dominated by a massive metal statue of Lenin's head. This was nothing unusual—every city in the USSR had its Lenin statue and museums dedicated to Revolutionary history. But this statue burned itself into the memory of everyone who saw it. It was a towering, monumental head— no neck, no body—with Lenin's face glowering over his citizens. When I saw *The Wizard of Oz* a few years later, I pointed up at the screen and yelled out in recognition at the wizard. This head of Lenin was perfectly Soviet: imposing, gravely serious, ultimately ridiculous.

We reached the square. My class marched in strict military-style formation across the concrete. Ahead of me was a boy called Shura, and I stared at his straight auburn hair as we walked, trying to keep my steps even and true. To rebel at such a moment by talking out of turn or stepping out of line was unthinkable. Out of the corner of my eye I saw old men and women sitting together on steel benches, watching us in our uniforms and stiff style of moving. When we reached the statue, we all stood in the very shadow of Lenin's head; the frowning adult father of the State looked down on the boy's face pinned to my dress. I fought against the urge to shift from one foot to the other.

Some older children had accompanied us. I knew some of them, older siblings of classmates from my street. A few had been in the Pioneers for several years, while others had already joined the Comsomol. Those of us being inducted stepped forward and stood with our chins up in the air, the weak autumn sun blocked by the giant steel head as we pledged our deep belief in the communist system. I swore my everlasting loyalty to the Party and the State. I would commit every day of my life, until my last breath, to making communist theory and ideology into reality.

I accepted my scarf and tied it around my neck the way I had been taught. The teacher smiled at us with genuine affection. The older students looked down their noses at us, as if to say: You've made it this far, let's see how well you do now. As I accepted their congratulations, I felt that I had joined a very special and exclusive club.

I was gloriously happy. I felt blessed to live in a country with such a humane and fair system of government; I looked ahead to a future in which I would accomplish more and more. Afterwards there was a party for the new Pioneers, with white cakes cut into the shapes of beautiful swans.

Back in the classroom that day we received another ideological lesson. True communism is just over the horizon, our teacher said. Her eyes gleamed as she spoke. This was her only passion. When we achieve communism, she added, the trains and buses will be free. Food will be free. There will be free plays and carnivals in the park. Everything in life will be available for no cost if we are willing to work together to make it happen.

How far away is communism? a student asked. How long do we have to wait?

Sometimes it felt to me as though a script was being read in class of which I hadn't been given a copy. Very soon, if you remain faithful, our teacher said with satisfaction.

I struggled to keep up with the concepts she taught. Some contradictions were already evident to me. Communism would give us equality and freedom, but why did my parents have to borrow to live? The answer was always the same: We are not there yet. Perfection will come only with hard work and sacrifice. I listen and absorbed. I believed, because conformity and belief were the highest values I was taught. I tried to learn to ask the right questions, and I tried to be a good propagandist. But I was never entirely successful. The fear of failure was already beginning to bloom within me.

That day was also a state holiday throughout the Soviet Union. For the entire day the buses and trains charged no fares. After school my friends and I got on the bus together and rode through the streets just for the pleasure of it.

Free bus rides! we called out. It's communism! We've made it!

Some of the adults looked back at us and smiled; others didn't.

Every autumn in the city the weather would take a turn, and everyone would intuitively understand that the temperate days were nearly gone. The storm clouds released slivers of ice and drizzle, and the gray streets seemed perpetually gray and muddy. Soon the fresh food supplies into Siberia would dwindle to nearly nothing. Arrangements had to be made for surviving the winter.

An announcement was made that the main food store was receiving a large shipment of cabbage and carrots. It would be the last fresh vegetable shipment of any size until spring. A line began to form outside the store a few days before the shipment was due. My father walked to the store alone, dressed in several warm sweaters and a coat, and took a place in line for our family. He stayed through the night until my brother came to relieve him.

Lines were nothing new to us. They were an elemental fact of life in the Soviet Union. Lines formed for food, clothing, and supplies. They might contain a dozen people, or they might extend all the way around a city block. It all depended on what was to be sold and how much of it was available. We lived with shortages on a daily basis, always wondering when food and clothes would be available to us and for how long. People in every Soviet city walked around carrying their *avoiska,* a collapsible burlap rope bag that could carry twenty pounds of goods on a moment's notice. When a store started to put of a fresh supply of oranges, or toothpaste, or underwear, the word would spread through the streets and the line would grow.

One store carried vegetables, another meats. People got into lines without knowing what was at the end. They would have their place saved and go to the front, returning to tell everyone what they were waiting for. Perhaps Bulgarian tomatoes were available that day. Anything from outside Russia was commonly accepted to be better. If food was apportioned according to how many people arrived in line, entire families, even two-week old babies, would wait together.

At the front of the line the food sellers were dressed in white aprons which became dirty and smeared. They had strict orders for how much to charge for their product and how much each customer was allowed to purchase. Everyone knew that there were special stores for highly placed Party members and people with connections, where there were no lines and better things were available. But no one I knew had ever been to such a secret market. Of course if they had, they would never have spoken of it.

Now that I was a Pioneer and I was a few years older, I had to help my family wait in line. My father arrived home early in the morning after his shift in line. He told us that, according to rumor, when the shipment arrived each family would be allowed to buy thirty-two pounds of carrots and cabbage. That was slightly better than the year before. My mother agreed to take a shift in line that afternoon; I said I would join her. The line would be full and would continue to grow throughout the day. It was accepted and tolerated that a person had to leave their job when something important became available.

I joined my mother after school. The line extended out from the vegetable store around the corner and would soon snake back around the next block. I walked it from back to front, looking out for my mother's green wool hat.

I found her near the middle of the line, the place where my father had waited through the cold night. She was talking to a fair-skinned, blue-veined old woman bundled up in a cloth coat that had begun to leak stuffing from the sleeves.

Oh yes, of course it was much worse during the war, the old woman was telling my mother. The farms around here were all shipping west for the soldiers and the cities. People were starving.

I know, my mother responded respectfully. My mother and father have told me about that time.

Behind us in line two men were arguing. You know why we don't get pineapple anymore? one of them said. It's because we're spending all our money on Cuba.

Give it a chance, a second man implored. We're making strides. We have to keep a presence in the Caribbean, or America will have its way with the entire region.

I can't remember the last time I tasted a pineapple, the first man said plaintively.

And on it went. The people were used to making adversity tolerable, and they transformed the lines into living social meeting grounds. I heard joking, laughing, bitching, people running into friends, making new ones. A married couple in our building had even met in a line. I sat down on the ground to rest and let my gaze wander to all those standing ahead of us. On their feet I saw sneakers falling apart, old army boots, dress shoes worn by the office workers, heavy oil-proof shoes for the workers. I saw children's shoes and women's heels. We were all there together, all the same. No one was better than anyone else, I remembered from school. Now it was coming true in front of me. We had united in our quest to survive the winter.

We were allowed to buy twenty-eight pounds of carrots and cabbage per family that winter, the same as the year before— the rumor-traders in line had been wrong. We learned about the allocation soon after the lines opened, a few hours after the trucks arrived from the fields. A wave of disappointment went through the line, but who was there to complain to?

The next day I worked with my mother clearing out the living room. The men were on their way back from the vegetable store, each carrying two or three sacks. When they came through the door their faces were serious. There would be no joking or play until our job was finished.

My father dumped the vegetables out on the floor a bag at a time. I pushed the carrots to one side and the cabbage to the other and my brothers joined in. Sergei even helped me move a chair into our entryway, speaking to me in a kind tone of voice. There was no time for bickering or pettiness, even from my brothers. When we began to work, a chill wind pushed against our window from outside, like a beast hungering to get in and eat us.

All the vegetables laid out on the floor took up the entire living room. The cabbage was pale and had already begun to smell. The carrots still carried dirt from the fields.

Irina, I would like you to begin with the carrots, my father said. We'll start the cabbage. If we work hard we can all be done by tomorrow.

I felt a flush of warmth; for the first time I had a job of my own. I had to wash, cut, and shred the carrots. I had a bucket of warm water and a paring knife. My father and brothers began to joylessly hack away at the cabbage, isolating the edible parts from the bitter tasteless leaves. For the first hour or two the work was fun. My small pile of shredded carrots began to grow. Then my fingers grew raw from the knife handle and my nose stung from the acrid smell of raw vegetables.

My work turned increasingly mechanical; after I took a break for dinner I checked my pile of shredded carrots against those that were still whole. It looked like a little anthill next to a mountain. We worked until it was late, not talking much, all of us working and working until one by one we went to sleep.

I woke up in my bed without remembering how I got there. Immediately I smelled the overpowering, rude odor of cabbage. I lifted my hands out from under my blankets. They were stained yellow-orange all the way up to my elbows. My fingers and palms were covered with small cuts where I had been careless and blisters where the knife had rubbed away my skin.

It was Saturday, so I didn't have to go to school. I walked out to the living room and found my mother hacking away at cabbage. I wondered if she had been there all night. My brother Sergei drank slowly from a cup of tea, staring into space. At his feet was a pile of cabbage debris.

The sun shone through the balcony window with an orange tint that made me feel as though the entire world was now made of carrots. But now I looked around more carefully and saw that my family had finished much of the seemingly impossible pile of cabbage. I examined my own section of the floor and was surprised to see how many carrots I had finished before bed.

We have to get started again, my mother said. These vegetables are going to dry out by tonight. We'll be sorry in January if the cabbage is bitter.

In the afternoon my father arrived home from rehearsal. He worked faster now, chopping cabbage at the big wooden table he had made years before. I continued to hack at the carrots, trying not to think about the sun shining outside on what might be one of the final warm days of autumn. Across the city, I knew, other children were performing the same task as me.

As I labored I thought about the lessons I had been taught at school. We were a tough people. Napoleon had found that out, then Hitler. We were willing to work hard and grit our teeth in order to survive.

We worked even faster. Every half hour or so Mother would remind us that the vegetables were beginning to dry out and lose their juice. The very idea was enough to frighten me, because my grandparents had told me about *cinga,* a form of malnutrition that affected people who didn't get enough nutrients in the winter. It made people's teeth fall out, and it exposed bleeding sores in their mouths. People had died from it in their time, and it still haunted the dark places of our memories.

My mother added salt and sugar to the shredded vegetables. I sliced, shredded, stacked, and moved on to the next. My brothers dragged the hand-made wooden barrels inside from the balcony. I sliced and shredded, juice running between my fingers. The vegetables smelled like a person's sweating body, a thick cloying odor that stuck to my clothes.

Mother loaded the processed food into our three barrels. This would be more than enough food for us. It would leave us with enough to share and trade. I sliced and shredded, ignoring the pain in my hands and back. My uncle arrived from the countryside and helped my mother seal up the barrels. I fell asleep very soon after I realized that there were no more carrots or cabbage to shred.

When I woke up it was dark outside; the apartment was lit only by the small lamp next to the table. My mother and father sat there together. His sleeves were rolled up and his shirt was soaked with sweat. Her dress was wrinkled, though she had put on a colorful scarf. They drank tea together and spoke in low voices until they saw that I was awake.

It's never easy, is it? my father asked me.

I don't know, it wasn't so bad, I bluffed.

They laughed softly. Look at those hands, my mother said. Make sure you wash them to get the stains out.

We would leave the barrels on the balcony through the winter; the elements outside created a natural refrigerator. These pickled vegetables would be the mainstay of our diet from November until April. This salad, along with some green onions and chives we grew in windowboxes, would make up all the vegetables we would eat until tomatoes and cucumbers came to market in the warm weather.

That was no fun, but we'll be glad in a couple of months to have something green to eat, my father said.

We'll thank ourselves then, Mother agreed.

They let me stay up late that night. It was like a holiday. The next morning, as though the elements wished to signal our good timing, there were several inches of fresh snow on the ground.

part
t w o

$\mathcal{N}$ow that I was a Pioneer I hoped desperately to succeed. But almost as soon as I took my oath I began to harbor doubts which I felt I shouldn't share with anyone. Being a Pioneer meant living by a long set of instructions on how to be, what to think, how to talk. This would train us to be good Communist Party members, if we were strict and vigilant enough. But what if I couldn't meet those standards? Sometimes I felt distracted. Questions died on my lips at the very moment my teacher moved onto the next political idea. What if I wasn't able to listen and obey the way my teachers and the state demanded?

I felt patriotic; I still believed in the communist system. I wished for that belief to transform itself within me into the strongest of hope, but still I couldn't see the bright future I had always desired. In a few years I would be considered for the Comsomol, and if I didn't make the grade I would never be considered for the Party as an adult. And without Comsomol membership, a girl from the provinces would find it very difficult to be admitted to a university. I would never get a good job. I would never be able to live well in Soviet society.

When I came home from school I was quiet around my family. I couldn't sleep at night. Dark thoughts seemed to press my body down into my bed. I was part of the system. I was only eleven years old, but I knew what lay ahead for me: taking orders, obeying, always striving for approval. I tried to imagine myself as a woman in a severe suit with my Party membership pin. I saw my adult self with her hair pulled back, frozen in time, as she spoke to someone at her job. I closed my eyes, trying to see where she worked. The image was murky, like a picture at the bottom of a pool. Perhaps it was a government office somewhere. She had obeyed, she had conformed, she was part of the system. She was my future, yet no matter how much I concentrated I couldn't clearly see her. I wondered if she would ever exist.

When I went to the theater I felt part of myself pull back as I never had before. My parents weren't Party members, some of the actors were. But when they talked about their lives they always mentioned their hardships and the ways in which the state discriminated against them.

I would bring my school lessons to the theater. My father stopped between acts and looked over my shoulder.

Lenin, I see, he muttered in a neutral voice. Very good.

I stared into his eyes and tried to divine what was in his heart. He had played by the Soviet rules only enough to survive; my mother had done the same. But life was always changing. The State was tolerant sometimes, but throughout our history it had lashed out against those who didn't satisfy its desires. I had just begun to walk the balance beam that was always under the feet of a Soviet citizen. He had been doing it for decades.

Do well in school, he said, it will help your future. Then he joined his orchestra and led them through a song of longing and loss.

In class our teacher announced that we were falling behind in our ideological studies. No matter how hard we worked it always felt as though we weren't doing enough for her. She was a stocky woman, with big hips and wide shoulders. She looked like a woman in the fields from a Soviet painting.

Some of you are distracted, she said. She looked around the room, and I thought her gaze stopped on me for an instant too long. I took school very seriously and still received very good marks. In math my homework was among the best in class. My Russian was very good. But I felt that I wore my inner doubts on my face like a scar everyone could see. I was growing taller. My Buryat features were different from everyone else's. At moments I thought my fate was to always be different and somehow lesser.

This morning's lesson is designed for Young Pioneers, she said. It is a political discussion on heroes of the Revolution. Listen closely. You will learn about those who were martyred so that you can enjoy freedom and a good life. From these stories you will learn to be a strong and true communist. You will learn how to live and what to do in trying times.

I glanced around the room. All the other students, like me, wore clean uniforms. Our feet were planted firmly on the floor, our hands folded on our desks. We stared straight ahead and listened to the story of Pavlik Morosov.

Pavlik lived in a village a little more than a decade after the Revolution. During this time Stalin sent his armed militia to the country farms in order to gather food for the cities, where people were starving. When they reached Pavlik's family's farm they searched everywhere. No grain was to be found there. They were very disappointed, but they left.

I tried to concentrate very hard on what I heard. Perhaps I was becoming a lazy revolutionary, I thought. Maybe I lacked dedication. I would absorb what I was taught. I would be a good girl.

But Pavlik was a true Pioneer. And here is the lesson of this story. Pavlik went to the authorities and told them that his father had hidden the harvest. He told them where to find the food. The militia returned to the farm to confiscate it. Pavlik's father, mother, sisters, and brothers were sent to Siberia for the crime of withholding food from the People.

When Pavlik's grandfather heard about what had happened, he became enraged and murdered Pavlik with an ax. The authorities then executed the grandfather for this crime. Since then, Pavlik has been remembered as a hero of the people for his sacrifice, and an example for all children.

The teacher closed her book with a snap of satisfaction. She allowed us a moment of silence before she spoke.

You see, Pavlik was willing to do anything for the Party, she explained in a steely voice. Because the Party serves the needs of the People. The good of the Party is the good of the People. This is more important than individuals or families. A true Soviet revolutionary understands this.

I interpreted what she had said. Pavlik was good because he betrayed his family and had them all sent to the gulag. Pavlik's father was a criminal because he hid away food for his own family. I should be prepared to do the same. I should betray my mother and father who had raised me and loved me. If it served the needs of the Party, I should be willing to see them sent away without a moment of regret.

It wasn't such a terrible thing to me that Pavlik's family was sent to Siberia. I lived in Siberia, after all, it was a good place. I had heard about Soviet labor camps; they were a place where people who made mistakes were sent so that they could redeem and purify themselves through hard productive work. This was one of the things that made the Soviet Union great— instead of sending people to prison, like in the West, criminals were given the chance to help contribute to building the nation through their work.

But I thought about my mother and father being sent away, like Pavlik's, and the idea sent a shiver of fear through me. I no longer felt flattered by the serious way our teacher spoke to us. For the first time I sensed that the shape of my future was a never-ending progression. My adulthood would be regimented by society and, should I choose not to comply, I would have no place. There was another subtext to Pavlik's story: if I didn't behave myself, I might meet the same fate as his family.

I didn't want to live like a soldier anymore, and I didn't want to begin every day by swearing allegiance to the Party. I didn't want to agree with everything I was told. I watched the birds outside the window, flying free against the billowing clouds while inside the school building the Soviets were trying to kill my spirit. I was starting to grow up.

Now that my studies had become more serious, I had less time to myself and less time to spend at the theater. School took over my life. The teachers made no secret that this was their goal.

Communism should be all you think of, they would say during class. Your other thoughts are dangerous and idle. Your time is best spent on study and labor. Everything else is decadence.

Winter deepened into the time of year when everyone spent as much time as they could indoors. The smells of tea, tobacco, and pickled cabbage filled the apartment. In the afternoon the light of the sun low on the horizon faded into early darkness. I came home one afternoon and saw my mother's sewing machine on my family's huge wooden table, looking as though it was waiting for me to arrive.

In my mind's eye I could see the simple gowns I had sewed as a child to wear for my parents' entertainment. In an instant I reviewed all the years I watched costumes being sewed at the theater, the careful stitches and bursts of wild imagination. Next to the sewing machine was my mother's cache of fabrics and thread. I was wearing my school uniform, my regulation dress and apron, and I held fabrics up to my body in the mirror, straining to find the individuality that the school was trying to take from me.

I had worn homemade clothing all my life. As a child my mother had clothed me from head to foot, including my shoes. It was more affordable than buying clothes with what little cash we had, and since I was beginning to grow taller, many of the clothes in the state store didn't fit me.

The apartment was quiet until I broke the silence with the mechanical rattle of the machine. Each fabric had its own color, its own texture. Outside there was only gray sameness. The Soviets had used concrete, steel, and words to kill the passions of millions. But my hands and mind could express my emotions and fantasies through cloth and thread.

I found a carefully wound ball of yarn in my mother's collection. The weather had turned colder that week, with wet snow collecting on the sidewalks and fields. My calves were wet and frigid, which gave me an inspiration. When my parents returned from work that night, they found me huddled on the sofa knitting long tubes to cover my legs. In the West they were called leg warmers. I had seen a photo of them in a tattered Russian magazine in the school library. I stayed up late for a week, working and growing more excited. They took shape in bright colors of red and blue. But they would be warm and functional, so I hoped the administrators would allow me to wear them in addition to my uniform.

I walked up the school steps the next morning. The girls in my class admired my creation. They're so nice, I heard a girl say. Such pretty colors. Can you make some for me?

Of course, I replied. I knew it would make me happy to see them wearing colors as well.

Even before our first lesson of the morning the teacher called out my name and made me come to the front of the class. She told me to stand still and, for what seemed like a couple of minutes, she looked at my legs as though they were nearly beneath her comment. I watched the floor, looking up only once to see my classmates staring at both of us with anticipation.

You know who you look like? she finally said. She looked out over the class with a smirk, inviting them to share the joke. You look like Pinnochio.

The class laughed, encouraged with a look by the teacher to break our usual tense silence.

Pinnochio is a book by a subversive foreign author written to corrupt young children into the ways of greed and capitalism, she added with acid seriousness. These things you are wearing, they make you look foolish. Never come here again wearing anything other than your uniform.

She made me stand there a few more minutes, soaking in her ridicule and disapproval. Then I removed the leg warmers, rolled them up, and stuffed them deep inside the pockets of my winter coat.

Today you are wearing these clothes, she said to the entire class. Tomorrow you are helping to bring down your country. This is an important lesson, and I trust that you will remember it.

I made a hat from bright yellow fabric, then a scarf from silky green. I wore them when I walked to school and took them off when the building came into sight. I put them on again when the day was over. I walked home trying to catch a flash of color in the windows of the buildings I walked past. The air grew so cold that sometimes it froze my eyes shut when I blinked. I made another hat and scarf so that I could have variety. The next week I wore them until I had seen the school for thirty seconds. The next day I wore them until the building had been in sight for a full minute. I wondered if the teachers could see me from inside. With breaths that condensed in the air I said, over and over, It is only clothing. What can they do to me?

In class I found myself staring at the teacher. I tried to see the reality of who she was underneath her shield of Leninism and strictness. I realized that she was nearly as old as my grandmother. When she walked she often reached behind, massaging her aching back. I wondered why she wasn't at home with her family. The power of her political beliefs kept her glued to the school.

You must listen to the word of the Party, she said. The destiny of the people is represented in its commands. A word against the Party is a word against the State, and either is a crime. Always remember the lessons of the Revolution and the teachings of Lenin.

I stiffened in my chair. Maybe these things were the truth, maybe they were lies. I was too young to say for sure what was the difference. Yet her words were always the same, merely arranged in different combinations.

The Party has given me the power to mold you into citizens, she said. So you must do what I tell you to do. You will believe my words, and your every action must reflect that belief.

I stood up. Why? I asked in a clear voice.

She acted as though she hadn't heard me, barely glancing my way as she said, Irina, I have not called on you. Sit back down in your seat.

Why should I believe that your way is the only way? I asked, still standing. I pressed my hands to my side to keep them from shaking. My voice sounded sure and strong, like a woman's. Why should you be the only person in the world who I listen to? Why should I have to live in your world?

The room fell under such a silence that I could hear the wind outside. The other students didn't even dare to look at me. I felt a hot trembling inside my chest.

The teacher folded her lesson in half and laid it against her leg. She looked out over the room with a haughty expression, as though daring anyone else to join me in my rebellion. No one did.

Lenin spoke of the antirevolutionary impulse, she said, turning to look at me. It lives inside all of us, and we must be strong to fight it.

I started to say something else, but she raised her hand to silence me. Our eyes met. In that instant I saw her as I never had before. She was weary and old. She was tired. She didn't want to fight me. But she would destroy me if I gave her no other choice.

Irina, you have been warned, she concluded. She opened her lesson and started teaching, not even bothering to see if I had retaken my seat or not.

Something inside me snapped. In class my arms and legs tapped the desk and floor with nervous rhythm. I sewed to fill my free time, riddling my fingers with cuts and pricks as I struggled to master more complicated techniques. I dreamed that I could take a pail of magic paint and throw it over the world to banish the tedium and blandness.

I worked hard on my lessons and my grades were still high. But now I pushed against my teachers with my replies. The square root of thirty-six is six, I said one morning. But maybe you want me to believe it is seven.

There were thirty children in my class; two or three were Buryats. I felt the other students distance themselves from me when we were inside the school doors, even though some of them still spoke to me on the streets. My body was growing tall and I felt a cool strength also developing in my soul.

I wore a blue scarf into the classroom, breaking the uniform rules for the first time since the leg warmers.

Take that off, the teacher said.

Excuse me, I said. I forgot that it is a crime to wear a scarf.

That afternoon we were talking about politics. The lesson was about equality under communism.

I agree with you, I said. We are all equal under communism.

Very good, Irina, the teacher said. It's nice to hear you give a politically mature answer.

And since we're all equal in the Soviet Union, then I no longer have to listen only to you, I added. We are equal as people, so now it is time for you to listen to my ideas about how to live and what to think. This is what equality and freedom mean to me.

She shook her head and wrote down something in her classbook. In that instant I felt a pang of sadness. She was old, she was simply doing what she believed in. I didn't dislike her personally; if she were my grandmother, I thought, I might love her.

I will report this to the administration, she said. In the meantime, if you cannot talk like a good communist, then just keep your mouth shut.

Of course I would never win, I realized. My teacher would have been in deep trouble if she had ever allowed me to speak my mind freely; she would have been considered a subversive corrupter of the youth. But fighting against her kept my soul alive. I wondered if my resistance drove her even deeper into the closed world of her communist beliefs.

As I walked home from school that afternoon the wind blowing between the apartment blocks made my eyes water. I passed the open window of someone's apartment and heard a song playing on the radio inside:

My native country is so wide
It has many forests, fields, and rivers.
I do not know of any other country like mine
Where a man can breathe so freely.

I dreamed about throwing myself into a wall that never yielded. I had visions of the Soviet Union as a great rushing river; I was a tiny twig in its irresistible current. The days of my initial *Why* turned into weeks. I felt pressure like a fist balled in the middle of my body, from the moment I awoke until the time I fell asleep in the night.

I had always been different. My parents were artists while the other children came from families of factory workers and bureaucrats. Now that I was growing from a girl into a woman I was taller than nearly all the boys. I looked like no one else in my class. I thought like no one else in my class. All of my jokes and displays of strength, which had always helped me to fit in, were no longer enough. I sensed myself becoming separated from the other students; my little rebellions entailed a level of risk that none of them wanted to take.

During the daytime I tried to concentrate on my studies. During political discussions my teacher and I eyed one another like fighters in a ring, wondering who would strike the first verbal blow that day.

Walking home at night, I started to feel a strange blackness in my soul. Each day I felt as though my soul had moved a bit farther away from the system. But I had only words, while they had the power of a nation. There had always been whispers of the camps, the prisons, the special schools where they sent troublesome children for reeducation. I began to wonder if those places would be my fate.

Few of my outbursts in class were openly hostile; instead, I picked at the edges of my teacher's logic and legitimacy. One afternoon as the year neared its end, my teacher asked me to stay after class. After all the students had gone we met at her desk. Shadows filled the fields of snow and half-covered trees outside the tall windows.

I've tried to be very patient with you, Irina, she said. She straightened her papers and averted her eyes. You are a bright girl, a nice girl. Because of this, I have allowed you time to correct your conduct on your own.

I understand, I replied.

She glanced up at me. You're setting a poor example for the others, she said with sudden harshness.

I am only trying to express what I believe to be the truth, I said.

She shook her head; in that instant I realized that she had tried to provide me with an opportunity to apologize and promise to change. But I continued to speak as I did in class. To her it was like a slap in the face.

You are almost an adult, she said in a tired voice. You will learn that there is more to the truth than what you think. Who are you? A little girl.

But I have a mind, I said in a low voice.

Her face reddened. The truth of communism is greater than individual truths, she said, each word emerging through clenched teeth. It is a collective truth. It is a historical truth. It is a cosmic truth. I have tried so hard to make you understand, girl. Communism has granted you the freedom not to listen to the voices that would lead you to evil.

She stared into my eyes, letting the impact of her words penetrate the silence. Outside in the hall I heard someone sweeping the floor. They sang softly in a high voice.

I can't believe that my heart is evil, I replied.

Something seemed to break within her. She had shared her views with me, revealing her beliefs on a more profound level than she ever explored in class. And I had rejected them.

In that case, she said, then you will find that you are on a collision course with history and our people. And you will have to live with the consequences of this. One day you will curse yourself for your ingratitude.

By the time the thaw arrived, my little bedroom was full of clothes I had made. With each creation I grew more self-assured with the eccentricities of the sewing machine as well as the complexity of creating patterns. I worked with the most colorful fabrics I could find, caressing their textures with fingers still cold from the outside. A few girls from school began to stop by my apartment after school to see what I was sewing. We drank tea and played dress-up. I knew my teacher would believe that I was corrupting them if she found out.

In the morning I could hear the birds outside that had survived the winter; I imagined that they sang songs of perseverence that they had composed especially for me. The days grew longer and moods lifted everywhere: at school, in the theater, on the slushy streets, in the lines, in my teenage heart.

A month before, my parents had told me that they had been invited to Leningrad to work for a few months in a traveling production. This was good news, because they would be making extra money, but I was disappointed because my upcoming examinations would keep me at home alone. I went with them to the airport, helped them load their suitcases into the baggage hold, and kissed them good-bye and embraced the members of the troupe who were going along.

I walked home feeling that something had changed. The sun was shining higher in the sky, no longer skulking low on the horizon. I would be responsible for myself during the entire time my parents were gone, and I felt a sense of self-confidence that filled me with strength and possibility.

I returned to the apartment, which was still and quiet. It was morning, the entire day lay ahead. The sun shone through the curtains. Because I wanted to be mature and responsible, I pledged to myself that I would spend the day studying after a trip to the market for food.

The market was new to Ulan Ude and was by far the brightest and liveliest part of the entire city. We heard talk about the reforms of *perestroika* in Moscow. Political reform had yet to filter its way into the provinces, but permission had been granted to rebuild the market in the center of town. It had appeared like something out of a dream; the lines still operated for clothes and other goods, but now there was a place to go to buy a variety of food.

The market was only ten minutes by tram from our apartment, and I knew if I left soon there would be plenty of time to study. This would be my first trip to the market alone, though, and I wanted it to possess a special quality to match the feeling I had awoken with.

I would make something new to wear. I knew what I was doing, it wouldn't take long. I picked a few bright pieces—thinking the fabric matched the reborn sun in the sky—and sketched a design on the back of a school assignment. I cut the fabric with my mother's big, sharp, professional scissors. The cloth would become a short summer jacket in what I imagined was a very modern style. Within the hour I was finished. I turned back and forth in the mirror, crouching so I could see my entire body.

The mirror revealed to me what seemed like a new person. She was smiling back at me, a sight I hadn't seen in far too long. Her clothes were vibrant, the look of someone having a love affair with her own life. She held a shopping list in her hand. She looked like a girl who moved through her days with confidence and spirit.

The market was crowded as always. People moved under the bright lights with quick purpose, as though they secretly believed the Soviets would close the place down any minute. Some wandered from one aisle to the next without selecting anything, their ability to choose diminished like an unused muscle by years of standing in line and accepting whatever lay at the end.

Like nearly everyone else, I focused on picking out the greatest variety of food with the limited amount of money in my purse. I lingered over the vegetables, which were so abundant that they would create a painful memory when winter returned. I gripped a tomato in my hand and wished I could step through time and bring it to my family in January when there was little to eat.

Someone touched my arm as I dropped the tomato into my basket. I hadn't noticed the pretty woman in her thirties who had been standing next to me.

I'm very sorry for disturbing your shopping, she said. Though she was older than me, she spoke in a quiet and shy manner.

My name is Larissa, she said, holding out her hand.

I am Irina, I said, trying to sound very adult as we shook.

What grade are you in at school? Larissa asked.

The eighth, I replied. I'm nearly finished.

Larissa looked surprised. You're very tall to be so young, she said. You know, I approached you because I'm a clothing designer. I have a fashion house here in the city.

I put down my basket, searching for anything to say in return. She seemed like such a fascinating person. I couldn't imagine why she had chosen to start a conversation with me. Larissa seemed so sure of who she was, so adult, like the woman I searched for in the mirror and hoped to one day become.

She reached out and gently touched my jacket. By the way, this is very interesting, she said, looking at my stitching with what I hoped was approval. The colors are beautiful, she added.

It's me! I blurted out. I made it myself, just this morning.

Very impressive, she said.

My heart swelled in my chest. I looked hard at Larissa, wanting to memorize every detail of her face so I could replay this conversation over and over in my mind. Her hair was black, shoulder length, parted in the middle. Her brown eyes sparkled at me, and her small mouth was made up in a sophisticated shade of lipstick. I felt a deep attraction to her, and sensed that in just minutes she had forever changed my life.

I have to go, Larissa said, lifting her own food basket. She

handed me a slip of paper. This is my address, she added. I
would like you to come visit me at my fashion house when
you have some time.

I took the paper. Yes, of course, I said, trying to imitate her
calm, warm, grown-up way of speaking.

She left me standing there among the fresh produce, my
hands shaking as I read the address over and over again until
I knew it by heart.

That night I drew designs in my room until my hands ached
and my fingers were blistered. I lay back and closed my eyes,
trying to imagine myself wearing an elegant gown created by
a glamorous designer. I didn't know how the fashion business
worked, or what modeling was, but I had a vague sense that
somewhere in Ulan Ude people made a living by creating
clothes. The idea was like a revolution in my mind.

I opened my mother's old case full of fabrics and thread. In
my mind's eye the swatches of cloth transformed themselves
into the shapes of human bodies, altered by a magical unseen
hand. Colors blended with each other like a dream ballet. I
strained against the limits of my imagination to depict the appearance of a warrior, a jester, a princess.

By the lamp in the living room I tried to concentrate on my
studies. It was nearly impossible. I could have stayed up all
night, fueled by excitement. I finally slept only because I
wanted to be rested the next day when I went to see Larissa.

In the morning the sun shone down on the city stronger
than the day before. I opened our apartment windows now,
and I drank my tea on the balcony, looking out in the direction
of Larissa's address. The street below was dusty, and the bright
light exposed the cracked cement buildings and their drab colors. Somehow I minded it all less than before.

On the tram I rocked in my seat, wishing it would move
faster and knowing it wouldn't. I rehearsed some of the things
I would say, like an actress preparing for an audition. I would
show Larissa that I was strong, that I was mature and creative.
I was wearing a new dress that I had just finished sewing that
morning. I imagined what the place would look like, what sort
of people would be there. I almost cried out aloud when I

allowed myself to think that they would accept me and let me join them.

The street was familiar to me, though when I found the address I realized it was a small building that I had never noticed before. It almost looked as if it was hiding among the larger offices and apartments to either side.

I pushed open the door and walked inside, trying to appear confident yet free of arrogance. My first sight was of a small group of young women dressed in silk embroidered evening dresses. They were all tall and beautiful, and they looked up at me as I stepped in the room. All around me were bolts of colorful fabrics and half-sewn dresses, along with mannequins wearing blouses and jackets. It was as though the door I had stepped through was a portal that had transported me from the familiarity of Ulan Ude into a world tailored to my fantasies.

Can I help you? an older woman asked, looking up from a sewing machine.

I'm here to see Larissa, I said. She invited me.

The woman went into a back room and, moments later, Larissa emerged with a big, open smile that instantly relaxed me. I'm so glad you could come, she said, taking my hand.

I watched the way the women in the room reacted to her; the atmosphere in the place was very calm and friendly. I realized that Larissa was always as warm and easy as she had been to me in the market, and I decided that I very much wanted to be her friend.

Here are some of my designs, she said. She walked me past tables with dresses, blouses, accessories, then showed me a scattered stack of her drawings. Her pencil lines were fluid and easy, as though they had been created without effort. We joined the models, who introduced themselves to me casually, as if we were equals, even though they were all a few years older than I was. Larissa had them turn this way and that so I could examine the delicate embroidery on their gowns.

Hold still, Larissa said as I traced my finger over a bolt of fabric. She pulled out a tape and began taking my measurements. You know, she said, we have plenty of things that would fit you well. You have a very nice figure, very slender with long legs.

The other models said they agreed. I felt a hot flush of

warmth in my cheeks. It was as though the world had suddenly decided to start spinning in the opposite direction.

Larissa searched through a rack of hanging dresses until she found what she was looking for. Perfect, she said with satisfaction. She handed me a short blue dress with a high neck and short sleeves. Go in the other room and put this on, she said, then we'll have you model it for us.

The dress fit me perfectly, flowing around my body as though it had been made for nobody else in the world. Larissa gestured toward a tiny makeshift stage that had been set up in the corner of the work space. I stepped up and stood heads taller than everyone else in the room.

I . . . I don't know what to do, I said. I don't know how.

Two of the models immediately stepped up with me. They corrected my posture, moved my arms into position, framed my face with their hands and told me to hold it there. They walked back and forth the few steps the stage would allow, turning, demonstrating to me how to bring out the best in the dress. Their words and their touch were firm but kind. They were treating me, a young girl who walked in off the street, as though I were their friend.

Then they left me up there alone and I saw Larissa watching me and nodding with approval. When I was done she found another dress that fit me, then another. I tried on long gowns, summer dresses, and skirts that could have been worn by an office worker.

You see, one of the models said to me from the foot of the stage. Each dress makes you feel different, like a character in a play. Each piece of clothing has a personality that you have to discover and then communicate to the audience.

This was one fact that I didn't need to be told. In my heart I had returned to my family's living room, with my parents sitting on the sofa anticipating my newest production and latest costume. My mind filled with scenes from the theater, fabulous ways of being and thinking. I felt as though a part of me that had been pressed down by my teachers was now being allowed to live.

Come on down from there and have some tea with me, Larissa said. You've worked hard enough for one day.

We sat together in Larissa's office, which was filled with

stacks of designs and worn-out fashion magazines that looked as though they had each been read by a hundred people. Larissa poured tea and asked me to tell her about myself. I told her about my parents, about the theater, about school.

So it's not so great, but you're a good student, right? she asked me. I told her I received high grades, and she nodded with satisfaction. I hope you don't mind my telling you this, she said, but when I saw you yesterday I thought you were a special girl. Very bright and pretty. And now I'm sure that I was right.

What about you? I said. Her compliment had filled me with the urge to jump up and dance around the room, but I stayed calm. I remembered my childhood, when the actors spoke to me as if I were an adult. Feeling this affection and respect was something I had almost forgotten after years of verbally fencing with my teachers.

I grew up here in the city, she said, sipping her tea.

The nonchalant way she spoke thrilled me. My parents had taken me to Leningrad and Moscow once when I was a girl, during a short tour for their theater troupe. Though I had been too young to absorb much besides the fast-paced atmosphere and imposing architecture, somewhere in the back of my mind I now realized that my destiny might lay in such places.

One of the models, Sophia, stuck her head into the office to say good-bye. The models were beginning to drift away, going to work or home or school. From the workroom came the steady hum of a sewing machine.

How did you think to start a clothing business? I asked when we were alone again. My mother makes clothes, she is a great sewer, but I never thought you could design clothes to sell to people. At least not here.

This was always my dream, she said. I went to Leningrad for design school when I was sixteen, then I came back here and started working at a local atelier. I started developing contacts with private clients. It had never really been accomplished here in Ulan Ude, not the way I've done it.

She spoke with pride mixed with an attractive humility. My mind reeled. To have a dream in the Soviet Union was no small matter. It meant holding that dream close and protecting it from a world that would do everything in its power to smash it. My own dream had been to live and express myself somehow without having to constantly fight against the system. And in one day this dream had turned into something more tangible, shaped by an unfamiliar surge of hope.

So, Irina, what do you want to do when you grow up? Larissa asked. She sat back in her chair and looked me over.

I want to be you, I said quickly. I mean, I want to be like you. I want to be a fashion designer, I want to make clothes.

Well, okay, she replied. Did you make the dress you're wearing today?

I did, I said. I designed and made it myself.

You are a surprising girl, Irina, she said warmly. I'll tell you what. You can come here as much as you want. Spend some time with us, see how the business works. Then you'll know if this is really your future.

My future, I thought. I repeated the words to myself over and over.

For the next month I endured school by counting the minutes remaining until the final bell. I took my exams and did well, and in class I found myself fighting less with my teacher. She could say what she wanted. My life, my future, had nothing to do with that sterile room and the endless repeated lessons of Lenin. When called upon, I simply answered the question I was asked. I noticed my teacher cock her head once when she looked at me, probably wondering what had changed. Perhaps she felt that her teaching was finally succeeding.

When classes ended I raced to Larissa's design house every day, coming through the door breathless from running. Every second I spent there seemed impossibly precious. I took in information with endless hunger. Each day I watched the entire process of making clothes: the initial design, the choice of fabric, the sewing of the components, then the casting of final stitches. I followed Larissa from worktable to worktable, asking question after question. I sat with the women who sewed and stitched, observing their meticulous technique and memorizing their methods.

One afternoon I sat with Natalia, a seamstress in her fifties. You have a lot of questions, she said, not looking up from her stitching.

I paused, not sure how to react. I'm so sorry, I said. I must be bothering you. I don't mean to be thoughtless.

She smiled, still staring with total concentration at her work. It's good to have questions, she said. It means you really want to learn.

Soon I knew everyone there, the workers and the models. They all followed the tone set by Larissa, and the place was nearly always full of kindness and happiness. It was like an oasis to me, a sanctuary. Every minute spent there gave me more strength for what lay outside.

Larissa came out of her office and looked around the workroom, counting the models at her disposal. I watched her number them on her hand and, when she glanced at me, she added another to the total.

Everyone listen, she said. The weather's turned warm. It's time for the annual show. I've arranged the hall and notified the buyers and clients. Now I need to know how many models I have to work with.

The fashion show was scheduled for the next weekend. Larissa went around the room to Sonia, Nikola, Alexandra. They all could come. When she reached me I said yes before she could even ask the question.

I arrived early for the show, too nervous to stay at home and finish my homework. The hall Larissa had hired was normally used for musical performances, and I walked across the stage a few times until I felt at home. A small runway had been constructed for the models, and I stepped to the end, picturing in my mind the audience that had yet to arrive.

Backstage I found the models putting on makeup and laughing. Nikola was telling a story about her boyfriend who worked in a food-processing plant. He brought bones home for his dog, whom he treated better than his own friends.

I told him, Why don't you marry the dog, then? Nikola said.

The other models roared with laughter. I said hello and sat with them, though I barely heard what they were saying. I breathed deeply. My nervousness was nearly gone, replaced by a deep core of calm. What I was doing was right, it was good. I was certain that I would perform well and that the audience would enjoy me. Like the actors before a performance at my parents' theater, like Alexei wearing his costume and performing voice exercises, I was home.

We heard a murmur of voices beyond the curtain as the hall began to fill. I reviewed the material we had rehearsed and the program that Larissa had created. With each new outfit we would express a new theme. Our show involved as much theater as fashion; we performed choreographed dances instead of walking to the end of the runway and returning backstage. I joined the other models in a final rehearsal.

I slipped into my first dress, one of the embroidered gowns I had seen my first day at the fashion house. Silence came over the hall and the music started. I felt its sensual rhythm and allowed it to control my body. I stepped out of the curtain and into the lights.

My dress was sophisticated and pretty, something a woman would wear when she wanted her husband to fall in love with her again. The music was smooth, but a horn played a melody of longing and desire. I began to dance, counting off the steps as I became the woman who wore the dress.

I felt the audience watching me. I felt them love the dress, I felt them love me. They worked along with me to express the fantasy. They wanted to believe it as much as me. I felt them encourage me without words.

Larissa's voice echoed from speakers beside the stage. These dresses are very elegant, but they are also affordable, she said. The quality of the stitching is excellent, and they will last for years if properly cared for.

I felt as though every woman in the hall wanted my dress, and that every man wanted one for his wife. I switched from one outfit to the next as though they were also masks that changed my face and soul. For the next hour I lived one dream after another.

After the show the models gathered backstage. We embraced each other like little girls. Without saying so, we each exulted in the memory of the freedom we had just experienced. We tried to keep it from ending by pressing close and repeating every detail of the show to each other.

Larissa had stayed in the hall speaking with her clients. She came backstage with a handful of orders and telephone numbers written in her notebook.

You all were great, she said. You were beautiful.

And how about this young one? Nikola said, nudging me with her shoulder.

I nearly turned away with embarrassment. I was watching you, Larissa said to me. You looked as though you've been doing this for ten years instead of just one day.

I began to applaud—for the other models, for Larissa, for myself. I rode home in a car one of the models had borrowed, feeling the warm breeze caress my face. The entire night I saw the lights of the hall and heard the music. I remembered the characters I had created as though I had lived an entire lifetime inside each of their bodies. I was flying.

I returned to school Monday morning. The birds sang in the flowering trees. I thought about summer vacation, which was coming soon, and how I would travel to my grandparents' village.

Waiting for me at my desk was a note from the director of the school. In a few words, it said that I was to appear at her office at ten that morning. My mother had been notified. She would be there as well.

I took out my papers as the teacher began that morning's lesson on the Russian Civil War. The groundswell of support for the Bolsheviks in the cities and in the countryside during those years was very powerful, she said. Again the lesson of history is that capitalism and monarchy are not only wrong but are part of the painful history of man's errors. Communism is an advancement in thinking every bit as great as the invention of the wheel.

I began to tune her out. Why would I be summoned to the director's office? I had been there before, of course, for arguing with my teacher and talking during class. But lately I had been agreeable and quiet. My grades were still high, among the best in my class. I must have done something to displease them. It didn't matter what I had done, because I didn't care what they thought. One day soon I would be a woman, and I would work at Larissa's fashion house and I would be happy.

I repeated these thoughts in my mind as though they were armor that would protect me from anything the director might say. I noticed that I was gripping my pencil so hard it was about to break.

At five minutes until ten I got up from my seat and showed the teacher the note from the director. She barely glanced at it, then motioned for me to go. Of course she had read it, of course she knew everything.

My mother was waiting outside the director's office alone in a row of wooden chairs. Her face was taut with tension, and she greeted me in a whisper.

Do you know what this is about? she asked.

I don't, I replied. She stared at me. Truly, I don't know, I insisted.

The director's assistant ushered us into the director's office. The director sat behind a huge wooden table, her arms folded. We sat down, and she greeted my mother.

A portrait of Lenin stared down from the wall. A map of Eastern Europe hung on another wall, the Soviet Bloc countries shaded red. On the director's jacket were pins and medals attesting to her communist fervor. She was a big woman, with big hands and a broad chest. Her hair was pulled back into a bun so tight it seemed to pull at her face. She stared at me for a long moment, her expression revealing nothing.

Then she stood up and extended her hand across the table.

I know that you are a good girl, Irina, she said in her grave, husky voice. That is why I am extending my hand to you. This is my hand of assistance to you, and it is your salvation. Take it, girl.

I don't understand, I said. I . . . this is very nice of you, but I truly don't understand what you're talking about.

She thrust her hand closer to my face.

You know what I am talking about, she said.

I don't mean to be disrespectful, Director. My voice caught in my throat. But please explain to me what's happening.

Don't say another word, she commanded. Just take my hand. You will be happy again, and you will never forget me for this gift.

My mother coughed. What has my daughter done? she asked.

The director moved around the table, hand extended, until she was very close to me. She took a deep unsteady breath and I saw red blotches appear on her cheeks. I realized that she was trying to keep her temper under control. She seemed as though she wanted to scream, and each moment I sat still and didn't take her hand made her more incensed.

The director was much like my teacher. Her world was regimented, everything was explained and planned in advance. Another student probably was due in her office at ten-fifteen. I was probably throwing off her schedule by refusing to break down in tears and accept her help.

She pulled her hand away and, though I thought she was ridiculous, a part of me felt that I had forever lost an important opportunity.

You have been at this school eight years, she said. Haven't you learned how to behave? Don't you know what to say to me?

I don't mean to upset you, I said.

This made her more angry. She slapped the table. I can't stand this anymore, she moaned. Go get your teacher.

I glanced at my mother, whose hands were tightly clenched in her lap. Go, she said, in a voice I could barely hear.

I returned to my classroom, where the teacher stopped her lesson in midsentence. I looked down at the floor when I saw that every eye in the classroom was focused on me with curiosity. This was different, this was out of the ordinary. With a voice that sounded strange to my ears, I asked the teacher if she could return with me to the director's office.

We walked together down the hall. My teacher's face was hard with disapproval and, I thought, anger. She took her place at the director's table and greeted my mother.

I thought you were improving your conduct, Irina, and now this, she said. I cannot understand how a nice girl like yourself could come to this. You are a very attractive girl, that is your good fortune. But you have to know that this is an unacceptable way to live your life.

We cannot tolerate it, the director added.

I realized what they were talking about. They had found out about the fashion show. They wanted to condemn me, but they could find no words to describe what I had done.

It's a terrible thing, being a prostitute at your age, my teacher said. Her voice was thick with disgust.

If you continue, we cannot keep you in this school, the director said.

I glanced over at my mother, whose eyes were wide with shock. She knew that I wasn't a prostitute, but she also knew that the facts would not matter if the director and my teacher turned me in to the authorities.

I am not a prostitute, I said slowly. You have heard about the fashion show in which I was a model. I can see that. But it was only showing clothes and dancing. To me, it was an artistic endeavor.

You are too young to show your legs, my teacher said. To show your body in that way incites decadence.

Somebody told us that you were taken away in a black limousine, the director said. And that you were seen with an older man. You are only fourteen. Who is this man? Doesn't he realize that it is immoral and against the People's law to be with a woman as young as you?

Black car? I said. There was no black car. And—

We have to be like Lenin, the director said. Remember the words of Lenin, remember the pronouncements of the Party: *Today you are listening to jazz, tomorrow you will sell out your country.*

I did nothing wrong, I said.

We brought you here to speak to you nicely, the director said. Her anger had transformed into something else, something more dangerous.

Irina is a good girl, my mother said weakly. She looked as though she had stepped into a dream from which she knew she could not awaken.

There are special schools, the director said. They are for children who are a danger to themselves and to our society. If you are sent there, you will not return until your mind is completely changed.

There's no need to send her to any school like that, my mother said, fear entering her voice. Irina is a nice girl. She won't do anything wrong.

I haven't done anything wrong, I said. I wanted to repeat it over and over until they all stopped.

Perhaps we should speak about this matter again at a later date, the director said, looking at the wall clock. But we have made an entry in your permanent file, Irina. I hope you understand that it would be sensible of you to change your behavior.

My teacher stared at me, suddenly dejected. I have tried so hard with you, she said.

The director shook her head and turned away from me, waving her arm for me and my mother to leave her presence.

I offered her my hand, she muttered under her breath as we closed the door.

I started to borrow clothes from Larissa, colorful designs with short sleeves that I wore in the warm afternoons. I also began to design more and more clothes for myself, changing as soon as I could after school and folding my uniform into the deepest recesses of my bag.

Walking home from Larissa's fashion house in the afternoon, I wore a thigh-length black dress with no sleeves and a collared neck. It was a simple design, comfortable and made to last.

I crossed the street a half mile from my home, pausing to let a bus pass. The heat had turned the city dry, and dust kicked up from the intersection. When I reached the other side I saw an old man staring at me. He was dressed in laborer's clothes, and his face was lined and creased. Some of his teeth were missing. He probably was an old war veteran.

He moved away from the spot of shade he had occupied under the portico of an apartment building. His eyes remained locked on mine, and I stopped to see what he wanted. I thought he might need help with something.

When he was near me he spat on the ground at my feet. Now I could see the anger in his eyes, twin pools of hate under his greasy mop of tangled hair.

Whore, he said, his voice a hiss.

I took a step back, so shocked that his words had the impact of a physical blow. He looked up and down at the outfit I was wearing, then shook his head with complete disgust.

Dirty whore, he said. He spit on the ground again, then walked slowly into the building.

In the West my dress would have been considered modest; I knew that, even then, from Larissa's fashion magazines. But in Siberia I was a whore.

*   *   *

A week passed. My teacher and the director took no action against me. During our ideological lessons she leaned on her desk and stared at me as she spoke. I knew her actions were designed to signal to my classmates that her words applied to me.

One of the students asked me recently about the word *stylaga* and what it means, she said.

I knew she didn't specify who had asked because no one had. Still she stared at me as she talked.

A *stylaga* is a decadent fifth columnist, an imperialist thug under the spell of America and England, she continued. They are people with low morals who are interested only in themselves. To them, the achievements of communism mean nothing. The struggle of the People means nothing.

She went around her desk, opened it, and pulled out a magazine. It was one of the journals read by Party members, and it was folded to a specific page.

Look at this picture and pass it to the student next to you, my teacher said.

I waited for the magazine to come to me. Still she stared at me. The other students had started to notice this, and I heard gasps of surprise move through the room as the picture worked toward me.

The *stylagi* listen to Western rock music, she said. They wear Western-style clothes. They care about fashion and not the State. They are sexually liberal, and they carry sexual diseases. They are scum.

The magazine reached me. The boy who handed it to me avoided my eyes. The folded page depicted a detailed drawing of two men and a woman lying in bed together. They were nude, covered by sheets. On the floor were their jeans, leather jackets, and motorcycle boots. Their hair was long. A rock 'n' roll record jacket lay tossed on the floor. One man was sticking a hypodermic needle in the woman's slender arm; the other man lay back on his pillow, taking a long drink directly from a bottle of vodka.

The caption read: Stylagi *at home. They seek their pleasure while the rest of society strives against the evils of the West.*

We must guard against the influences of capitalists, the

teacher said. She surveyed the room then let her gaze rest on me again.

Today you are listening to jazz. Tomorrow you are selling out your country.

Gorbachev was in power now in Moscow. At the dinner table my parents talked about rumors they had heard, that a real shake-up was going on in the Kremlin. On television we watched Gorbachev moving through Russian crowds, smiling and shaking hands. He was young and vital, a completely new kind of man than all the Soviet rulers my family could remember.

But none of it mattered in Ulan Ude. Moscow might as well have been on another planet. My parents received letters from friends in Moscow saying that everyday life was easing up there. It was now not completely impossible to get a Western magazine, or to buy blue jeans and other clothes not made in Soviet factories. But for us nothing substantial was different. It was as though the changes in Moscow were stuck at the Ural Mountains and would take years to make their way across.

People are starting to talk, my mother said as we ate a dinner together of potatoes, cabbage, and squash. She looked up from her plate and met my eyes.

Why is everyone always looking at me? I asked. I haven't done anything wrong. I haven't bothered anybody.

You've bothered people, my mother said. People are talking. They say you are having sex with older men. Today someone said they heard that you are going to be sent away. I can't listen to this anymore. You must stay at home and stop going to that fashion house.

You can't keep me here, I said. It's not fair. I've finally found something I care about.

It's wrong, she said, her voice suddenly bitter. What you are doing is wrong because it's getting you in trouble. I can't take this kind of trouble.

Forget about the director, I said. She's ignorant. All she knows is communism. She doesn't know anything about art or culture. She thinks modeling clothes makes a girl into a prostitute.

My mother put down her fork and pushed her plate away. Neither of us had an appetite.

Don't you think I understand? she asked. Of course they're ignorant. Don't you think your father and I have had to deal with the same thing at the theater? They've recommended to him in the past that he stop writing Buryat music. And he fought them. But we never have any money. Who knows what they might do to you? I can't stand having you sent away to some prison. You'd never come back.

I got up and walked to the open window. A soft rain had begun to fall.

They won't win, I said as much to myself as to my mother. Maybe they don't understand enough to know they're wrong. But they won't win this time.

I continued to go to Larissa's fashion house after school, watching and learning. There were no fashion shows scheduled before the end of the school year, so all my modeling was confined to fittings inside the closed doors of the house. The end of the school year arrived and I was not thrown into a prison for ideological undesirables.

The neighbors in my building had begun to look at me strangely. Some men smiled at me in ways that made me uncomfortable, making me quicken my step to pass them. I imagined I heard whispers in the halls at school when I passed. My mother still complained and sometimes threatened to force me to stay at home. My father worked on his compositions, tidied the house, and generally kept out of the arguments. I took his silence as a form of limited approval.

After a week of summer holiday I packed my things to visit my grandparents in their village. I hated to be away from Larissa, but part of me ached to escape from Ulan Ude. The city had stifled me. My neighborhood felt like a small town in which everyone had decided that I was an evil person.

The bus reached the limits of the city and moved into the countryside. I pressed my face to the window and lost myself in the ocean-blue sky. The sun shone down on the newly green fields and I stared at the blurry edge of the horizon. I began to let down my guard, feeling my tension vanish like the unclenching of a fist. Soon I was asleep.

I awoke with a dry mouth and feeling as though the sun had

pressed its heat deep inside my body. I had reached my stop, and I disembarked the bus alone. My grandmother was waiting there for me, smoking her pipe as she always did. We walked together along the lane, talking about my parents and how well I had done in school. If she knew anything about my troubles she didn't mention it. By the time we reached her home I was able to pretend that I had no problems.

I found my grandfather in the fields taking care of his horses. He smiled with his eyes when he saw me and waved for me to join him. I walked over a small rise, smelling the air full of grass and hay. When I reached him, he pulled out a strip of leather which he was carving into a belt. He had carved the handle of his knife himself; its pattern depicted deer, a team of dogs, birds. We sat together for an hour, and as he carved patterns onto the leather he held it out for me to see, so that I would learn.

When the sun was lower on the horizon, he nodded toward one of his horses, a sign that I was allowed to ride it. In the weeks to come this privilege would be permitted me only after I had finished my household chores, but this first day was special. He helped me onto the animal and affectionately patted its rump. I rode the horse across the field, hurtling us as fast as I could toward the ends of the earth. The horse ran so fast it might have had wings. The wind filled my ears like a moaning voice and burned my face, and I felt the animal beneath me revel in the same elemental freedom that was now releasing me from myself and my life. I was not upset, happy, sad, angry about anything: I wished everyone in the world could feel as I did in that moment.

Finally the horse tired and I guided it into an empty field. It filled its stomach with grass while I lay back on the cool ground. The sky was so empty that I imagined I could see the stars through the sun's luminance. I heard the songs of the insects, the crackling of heat on the earth. I put the side of my face down to the ground and smelled the dry vegetation, imagining that I could see the grass growing. No one could reach me there.

The Buryats say that Lake Baikal starts to move again in the first week of June. Once frozen over, the vast water began to thaw and break. Many times in the spring I had stood on its

banks watching glaciers of white ice colliding as though waging
battle against each other. They looked like floating mountains,
and when they smashed together the noise echoed through the
hills. Splinters of ice plunged into the water and resurfaced. A
fine mist of vapor covered me, including me in the game.

The trees that covered the hills again showed their greenness; above them the cloudy sky trailed off into infinity against
the mountains far in the distance. Streams melted and released
their water into waterfalls that crashed down rocky hillsides.
A fine mist hung low and passed through the hillsides in the
yellow morning sun.

By July the lake had melted and temperatures rose into the
eighties. The summer would last about six weeks, followed by
a short autumn before the long freeze. I spent my days helping
Grandmother in the house, then helping my grandfather with
his horses. I learned more about caring for their animals: the
lambs, chickens, horses, dogs. I felt my spirit begin to relax,
and when I lay down at night I drifted quickly into dream-
filled sleep.

My mother arrived on the bus when the lake was fully
melted. I walked with her down the lane, asking about my
father and my uncle. She said nothing about our fights or about
my teacher's threats. It was as though they existed in a lower
world that would be pointless to discuss.

In the city the air is full of dust, she said as we neared her
parents' home. It's hot and noisy. I couldn't wait to come here.

I couldn't, either, I replied. Our eyes met in a wordless
understanding.

My mother and grandmother walked together around the
land. They stopped to spend time with Marie, my grandparents'
cow who was pregnant with a calf. I walked several feet behind
them, listening. At the edge of the lane the forests were bloom-
ing with a speed and urgency driven by the knowledge that
soon they would again be covered in snow and ice for nine
months. I could sense the energy of growth around me, above
me, under my feet. In the wind was elation mixed with desperation. Two yards below the ground, the earth was still frozen
solid.

In the morning my mother, my grandmother, and I journeyed to the lake with the small wooden boat that my grandfather had crafted by hand. The lake's surface was smooth and

blue, and other fishing boats dotted its surface. I put my hand over my eyes to block the sun and strained to see the lake's dimensions. At its greatest length it extends nearly four hundred miles, and I looked out over the watery expanse that seemed like an endless ocean.

We got into the little boat, our knees touching, and began to row. We didn't talk for a while, except when my grandmother told us to steer more to the left or right, or to speed up or slow down. We bobbed up and down in the gentle waves, and the boat seemed to shrink as the waters expanded. Soon we could no longer see the shore.

This is fine, my grandmother said. This is far enough.

She knew the lake as though she had placed it on the earth and shaped it with her own hands. She knew exactly what to do at every moment, and in her presence the enormity of the water was no cause for fear. In some places Lake Baikal is more than a mile deep, the deepest lake in the world. My grandmother stood up in the shaking boat and looked around with an expression that told me the world was good. Her gray hair was tied atop her head, and she held her lined face up to the sun.

In her features I saw my mother's, and mine in both of theirs. My grandmother's generation had survived the war. They had endured the Soviet campaigns to drive the Buryats out of their villages into cities and towns, where it would be easier to mold them into communists and make them forget their culture. In our three generations of women was symbolized the journey of the Buryats from the green fields and crystalline lake into the concrete drabness of urban Soviet life. There on the water I felt as if I had finally come home.

We pulled together at the fishing nets, made of thick twine that forever needed mending. The nets splashed quietly into the water and sank. My grandmother tied the lines to the boat and sat down again, looking at my mother and me with quiet patience.

She began to sing. At first the sound seemed unearthly, like another voice of the wind. Her voice came full and clear from deep inside her. After a few words my mother joined in.

Powers of the water, we come to live in harmony with you. We bless your shores, we bless your depths. Please bless us with your bounty. Please help us to live, so that we may live with you.

I joined in the song, since this was one to which I knew the words. Our three voices joined together to ask the forces of nature for a good catch that day. The songs were ancient. They had been passed down by generations now lost to history, from ages even before Russians had come to Lake Baikal. With our voices we created a melody that cast a spell over us and the infinite water beneath us.

Gentle waves caressed the boat and sprayed our faces. When our voices trailed off we sat in silence. I imagined the fish below us, swimming in harmony to the last watery echo of our song, reaching out to the nets to sacrifice themselves so that we could live.

When the quiet had enveloped us like a blanket my grandmother spoke.

Irina, when the sea was as big as a puddle there lived a man named Zerdalamergin, she said to me.

It had been years since Grandmother had told me a story, and I knew this one by heart. Her voice reached into my heart and filled me with calm.

He was killed by a dragon, she added. But he had a sister named Zeherulanbashalai. When the dragon came to take her brother's horses, she fought it and cut his head off. It was then that she gathered her brother's bones and decided to travel deep into the forest, where there were three heavenly girls who were said to have the power to bring the dead back to life.

I closed my eyes and listened to her hypnotic voice. Again and again the Buryat stories returned to Lake Baikal. It was the birthplace of our people and our myths, the center of who we were. Floating on its ancient waters I felt time slip away. Myth was life. The past was the present. Running through it all was the lake.

Our muscles strained and we yelled out together with effort when we hauled the nets back into the boat. The catch that day was good, and while we rowed back to shore my grandmother sang songs of thanks.

On the shore we unloaded the nets full of *omul,* fish common only to the lake. I stacked the fish while my mother arranged and folded the nets. Grandmother built a fire out of dried wood and leaves. Within minutes she had pierced a few fish on a long stick which she held out over the fire. The smell of cooking fish permeated the air as juice ran down the wood and sizzled in the flames.

Here, Irina, my grandmother said as she held out the stick for me. Take one.

The taste of the fish was like the flavor of eternity.

The hottest days of summer coincided with our annual festival holiday. The village Buryats conducted a ritual dedicated to thanking nature and the universal forces for granting us another year of survival on the earth. This concept was the basis of our shamanistic faith, and the ancient rites had survived invasion by both the czars and the Soviet Union.

Our conception of shamanism embraced nature. We recognized the obligations between people and the world in which we live. Everyday life was holy and spiritual to us. We were reverent to nature and thankful. Buryats also had historical ties to Lamaist Buddhism, and combined the two through a belief in reincarnation and an eternal cycle of life. But the Soviets had made Lamaist Buddhism a target of their antireligious campaigns, and Buryats gradually focused more on nature-based shamanism. To me these systems of thought were the underpinnings of the universe. I could sense the eternal cycle of death and rebirth. And all around me was the boundless power of the natural world.

The villagers walked together to a nearby sacred field. We walked under the sun, barely speaking. At our fore was a small, old man, his skin wrinkled and his eyes cast to the clouds. He wore a sacramental tunic in bright cloth and carried handmade sacred objects in his hand. He was my grandfather.

One of the village elders knelt down on the ground and began sparking kindling with a flint stone. The flames slowly came to life, fed by the dry vegetation of the forest. When the bonfire was as tall as any of us, the villagers gathered around it. The elders were in the front, the adults behind them, and so on until the youngest children took their places in the rear. Carved wooden seats were occupied by those too old to stand.

I looked at the faces around me, familiar since my childhood. Most of them had never lived in the city and didn't particularly like to visit. They lived in tiny dwellings heated by wood stoves, and endured winters that were as deadly as they were long. Their lives were formed by the vast power of Siberia, its long sleeps and frantic summers.

One of our neighbors in the village brought their baby boy and placed him in Grandfather's arms. The baby was wrapped in lambskin, and my grandfather stood straight as he recited ancient prayers with roots both in Buddhism and shamanism. He sacrificed a cup of milk, with butter and sour cream, to bless the baby with a long life.

My grandfather stepped closer to the flames.

May the wind accept our humble gifts, he said. May the rain accept our humble offering. May the earth accept our thanks.

He cast bread and milk into the fire, where it hissed and burned. Still he recited and gave thanks. The prayers had been passed down from the previous shaman and were as ancient as our people.

May the sun accept our thanks and continue to bless us, he said.

My eyes followed his to the east, the sun's birthplace. The voices of the village rose up to repeat his prayers, the words of the old blending with those of the young. Our offerings of thanks were essential to our survival. Our well-being was granted only by the generosity of the great forces which surrounded us. Our thanks and prayers asked those forces to allow us to survive another winter, by granting us food from the ground and water from the sky. Grandfather and the people of the village hung strips of colored cloth from the branches of trees and between wooden poles. The cloth swayed lightly in the breeze and marked off the sacred site and the importance of our ritual.

When the prayers were concluded my grandfather stepped away from the flames, his face locked in solemnity. The villagers stepped back from the flames and turned away, all of us newly aware of our delicate yet glorious place in creation.

The horses were untied from their leads and brought out into the fields. First the men mounted them, riding hard through an obstacle course of trees and barrels. Our mood turned to celebration, and the children were allowed to join in the contests. The horses' hooves kicked up clouds of dirt, and they snorted and sweated in the heat. I joined the other young adults in a foot race while our parents cheered for us. I lost, but at the finish line were prizes of candy for everyone.

Igor, an elderly man who had fought in the Siege of Stalingrad, took the youngest children aside to give them the same lecture I had heard years before. He leaned on an old wooden cane, and his voice was rough and breathy.

Life is like these games, he said. You have to work hard for your prize, with all the sweat and labor of your body. It will be hard to work and gather food to survive when you are older. Your prize then will be your survival.

I watched the villagers separate into two opposing lines, one of men and one of women. They began to shout at one another, hurtling insults and taunts.

One man stepped to the front of his group. Anya is very pretty, he said, but I can't say much for her cooking.

That's because she saves her special cooking only for handsome men, one of Anya's friends shouted back.

I had watched these verbal contests as a child and marveled at the wit of the adults. Now some of the men and women facing one another were just a few years older than me. And I sensed a change within myself, in the way I ached to return to Larissa's fashion house and in a greater longing which I couldn't have named.

I spent my days working in the village. The time would soon come to gather hay to feed the animals through the winter. I counted the days that remained until I returned to the city.

Across the plains the sun turned the land green, which receded into blue and violet as my eye wandered to the mountains that ringed the horizon. The waters seemed to slow in anticipation of the winter that would soon come.

The young people who lived on my grandparents' road gathered outside under the stars every evening when the day's chores were finished. Insects buzzed to punctuate the silence. The boys and girls arranged themselves in a circle and told each other stories. I talked about city life, the high-rising apartments and industrial smoke. I recounted the stories of the plays that had been staged in the theater. I made up tales about young lovers separated by evil magic who eventually were victorious and spent their lives together in the cool winds from the lake.

A boy would pick up a guitar and we would sing about the mystery of the world around us:

The starry lilac shines at the window,
The night burns up the summer.
Two winds were dealt to me by fortune at the crossroads,
One in my favor and another against me.
The Milky Way is resting on my shoulders,
Two events happened this crucial day.
One was our coming together, the other our separation.

One night the air was warm and thick. Lights from outdoor fires flickered along the lane. I sat in the cool grass with my friends making up a story.

A princess and a knight were very much in love, I said. Which angered the magician who lived in a mountain high over their valley. He created rains that split the land into islands. The princess and the knight could no longer find each other.

A few young men and women approached us and quickly took places in our circle. They were from another road, and I didn't see them every day. Yet they were familiar faces.

The knight found a witch who lived in the hills beside the lake, I continued. He asked this witch what he should do. She gave him a piece of crystal and told him to put it in the waters when the sun appeared in the east.

My friends listened quietly to me. Some of them closed their eyes, trying to picture the witch's haggard face. I glanced at the newcomers to the group, and my eyes fixed on a young man.

The knight did as he was told, I said. He put the crystal in the waters, and suddenly they began to freeze. Soon he was able to walk on ice from island to island, calling out the name of his love.

He was about fourteen, my own age. His dark hair hung close to his ears. His features were strong and refined. He listened to me with his hands folded over his knees. For an instant he looked at me, and when our eyes met he shyly looked away.

The evil magician heard the knight's voice echo through the hills, I said. When he looked down and saw the ice, he grew very angry. He cast a spell that began to melt the ice. Steam rose from the ground, and soon the ice began to crack and the waters began to flow again. But now the knight was closer to the princess. She was on the very next island, and when he looked hard he could see her waiting on the shore.

I looked at the boy as I spoke. I was captivated by his eyes, by the curve of his chin. I had seen him before, but we had never spoken. He looked up at me again, this time daring to hold my gaze for a few instants longer.

The knight found the witch and asked her again what to do. She told him to find the crystal and, this time, to place it in the sky. She gave him a golden thread which he could toss up into the heavens, where it would catch. He could attach it to the crystal and send it up to the sun.

His eyes shone in the light of the fire. He looked at me and I felt a warm hand pass through my body.

The knight did as he was told, I said. And the crystal burned in the sun. It became so hot that the waters turned to steam. The knight walked across the muddy land and found the princess. They built a castle and lived there forever, protected by the good witch.

That was a nice story, my friend Lusya said. Very romantic.

Still the boy's eyes were on mine. When he left with his friends I asked who he was. His name was Alexsandr.

Alexsandr had lived in the city until two years before, when his aunt became ill and he had to move to the village to care for her house and animals. He was quiet and shy, I was told, and didn't speak much except to his closest friends.

I sat on the ground outside my grandparents' house playing with my young cousins. They were one and two years old, and I let them crawl through the grass and kept them from straying.

I looked up from the children, feeling eyes upon me. It was Alexsandr riding a bicycle. His head turned to watch me as he slowly passed. I lifted my head slightly in greeting. A moment later he was gone. I returned to the children, burning with the wish that he would have stopped.

The next day I received a note delivered by one of the village children. I opened it in the green pasture under the high sun.

Irina, it read. *My name is Alexsandr. I wished to write you because of how I have felt since seeing you. Yesterday when I rode by you in the field I felt such a strong emotion inside me. Seeing you in the green grass, beautiful and gentle, playing with young babies, was like a vision from a dream. I could not keep from letting you know how I feel.*

I folded the note and put it in my pocket. For the rest of the day I felt a radiance filling my chest. I pictured his face, his lips. I heard his words in my mind though I had never heard his voice.

I sent a message through the local children that I would like to meet with him. In the city we could have gone for a walk in the city square, but there was nothing of the kind in the village. Instead we met in the village under a full moon near a copse of trees. He was waiting for me when I arrived.

I offered no words of greeting, nor did he. He sat with his arms folded around his knees, looking at the incandescence of the stars. I sat a few feet away and did the same.

I studied the profile of his face, the slenderness of his fingers. He turned to look at me, his mouth turned into an almost imperceptible smile. Still he said nothing.

After an hour we rose together and left. We had said nothing. Our bodies had not touched. I lay awake that night burning with love for him.

He wrote love notes to me nearly every day, full of poetry and innocent desire. I did the same, pouring out the intensity of my emotions and trying to explain my soul to him. We met nearly every night in the grass by the trees. We said nothing, we did not touch. It was as though we experienced the silence of eternity together, our hearts one in a wordless perception of our mutual feelings.

It was time again to return to Ulan Ude. I packed my things and spent a final afternoon with the cow and the horses. I walked over a gentle crest with my grandfather, both of us entranced by the cool wind that whistled through our ears.

That night was my last in the village until the winter holidays at the end of the year. I walked into the shadows of twilight and looked across the road. My group of friends was there talking in soft voices. Though the air was still warm, the evenings were cooler than a week before. The arm of winter had begun to reach for us.

I went to the spot where I always met Alexsandr and waited, watching the flicker of lights turning on and off in the tiny houses. I had written him a note asking him to come see me that night. I rocked back and forth in the grass, feeling my inner heat turn blistering. I thought that I might not see him before I left, and the idea made my eyes burn with tears.

The night deepened. Lights were turned off and not illumined again. I listened to the songs of insects and the rustling of the trees. Finally I saw a figure approach. It was him.

Alexsandr sat next to me, a bit closer than usual. Our recent notes had talked about our ideas of love. I had said that love was like food for me. Without it, I withered and would die. Alexsandr's love was my sustenance. He had said that his love for me was like the sun, warming him and making his life possible.

He moved closer and our hands brushed together. It was the first time we had ever touched. I shifted toward him and looked into his eyes, which reflected the moonlight.

His face turned to meet mine and our lips met. I felt his hand encircle my back and pull me to him. I shut my eyes and felt the warmth of his body against mine. We kissed until I could feel the power of his soul colliding with my own.

Soon he took my hand and stood up. Your grandparents will worry, he said. I should take you home. Promise that you will write me, my love.

We kissed again, then walked together in silence. Before he disappeared into the night he kissed my hand, holding onto it for a moment longer to feel my skin against his cheek.

I walked slowly back to my grandparents' house. The stars seemed to shine brighter than before, as though they reflected what had happened. I felt the wind, the trees, the grass, the black sky all speaking to me in a single voice. They congratulated me for holding Alexsandr in my arms, for loving with the passion of my heart. I went back to the city the next day.

*   *   *

Back in Ulan Ude I made my parents an offer. School was over for me now unless I attended an institute. But a girl from the provinces with a stained ideological record had little hope of attending one of the fashion and textile universities. My parents weren't Party members, and I knew that I would never be a communist. Only bribery or connections could have gained me a place, and I had neither.

I sat my parents down on a late summer night. My brothers were in the next room arguing with each other and watching television.

I want to work two years at Larissa's fashion house, I told them. I can see the practical side of the fashion business and make a little money at the same time. Then maybe I will be able to get into an institute, because of my experience.

There are other institutes, my father said. Ones that aren't so difficult to get into.

We were lucky they didn't give us any more trouble over that show of yours, my mother said. You're becoming a woman. You have to learn that if you keep pushing they're eventually going to push back.

I see, I said. And deciding to become an artist isn't pushing? Or never becoming Party members, or never getting officially married? So you want me to live a conventional life and do what they tell me to do?

Loud laughter came from the next room. Sergei turned up the volume on the television, oblivious to our conversation.

My mother shook her head. She's right, she said in a quiet voice.

My father glanced at her. All right, he said. Two years. You can learn about the profession and then we will talk. The other institutes will still be open in two years.

The next morning I woke up early. Larissa had said I could start as soon as I had my parents' permission, and as soon as I was absolutely certain I wanted to work for her.

You know I like you very much, she had said. But you're still very young. I don't want to be blamed later if you decide you've made a mistake.

I took the tram to the building where I was a full-time worker for the first time in my life, carrying a lunch of bread and smoked fish from the village in my cloth bag. Inside the little building was the usual rattle of sewing machines, the normal faces tight with concentration. I put my bag and jacket on a small wooden rack by the door and stopped. I was now a part of things, no longer a young girl merely observing. My world expanded like the concentric rings running gently out from a stone tossed into still waters.

Larissa was overseeing the final stitches on a black jacket with a model and a seamstress. She stopped what I was doing when she saw that I had arrived.

You're on time. Very good, she said, putting her arm around my shoulder. You can come and go as you like during the day. All I ask is that you complete your work.

She led me over to Natalia, who was sewing a blouse seam by hand, her fingers moving almost too fast to see.

Natalia's going to be your boss, Larissa said. Just do what she says and learn from her. She's very good.

Natalia looked up from her work. Her short dark hair framed her stern, severe face. This girl has been watching me long enough, she said. It's time for her to take on assignments of her own.

She handed me a design and a roll of fabric. Cut this to the specified measurements, she said, handing me a pair of big cloth cutters.

Natalia returned to her work, and I began mine. I cut the fabric with concentration and precision, and when I was done Natalia handed me a roll of heavy thread and a sharp sewing needle.

Welcome to your new job, she said. Now sew.

I worked with Natalia into the winter. Every morning I found her at her worktable, focused intently on her sewing, a cup of tea steaming next to her. She always greeted me with the same curt hello, but soon after I had started, she began to warm to me. She taught me every variety of stitch, and techniques for assembling all kinds of clothing from patterns and designs. Some days it was so cold inside I had to wear gloves. At night I drew my own designs at the dining table at home.

Aleksandr and I exchanged love letters, fewer and fewer with time. My heart still ached with the thought of him, and I concentrated on my work with greater fervor with every day that he didn't come to visit me.

After six months I was awarded with a certificate awarding me the rank of master seamstress, second class. I pinned it to the wall. It had more meaning to me than all the Pioneer and Octobrist prizes I had ever won or wished for. I had done this for myself. Almost imperceptibly, the black void of my future had transformed into a life where I could work, live, and, perhaps, be happy.

In the evenings I brought home tea and bread from the market, which I paid for with my own money and shared with my family. My father and mother were quietly appreciative, because for the past year the value of the ruble had descended while salaries remained the same. Though I couldn't have named the Moscow policy that was affecting our lives in this way, I could see and feel all around me a growing insecurity and fear.

Inflation was never a word I had heard used until then, and now it was spoken all the time. The price of bread rose from one day to the next, then rose again. There had never been enough money. Now there was even less. In the market people asked each other how this could happen in a communist country. They assured themselves that it would all soon end. Moscow had taken care of everything in the past. Surely this couldn't go on; otherwise, one day we would all be penniless.

It hasn't been the same since Brezhnev, my father said one evening to my uncle. The snows were piling in the streets and the sun sank lower in the sky every noontime.

Maybe things weren't good then, he added. But they didn't get worse. Now life is getting better in Moscow, less repression, but the money isn't worth anything. And what do we have here? The same politics, and the money still isn't worth anything.

I don't pretend to understand it, my uncle said. He lit a cigarette and watched the smoke curl around his long-fingered hands.

I listened intently. Money was money, there would never be enough of it, I believed. But whenever information came from Moscow, usually from a friend of a friend, it seemed that life there was less fearful. People were gradually being allowed to speak more freely, to create art without the threat of being thrown in prison or being castigated by other citizens.

It was so far away. I imagined myself there, in the company of artists and writers. I thought of my new friends, the cafes, the streets full of sophisticated and interesting people. Then I remembered that I had never lived anywhere but Buryatia. I wondered how much a room would cost to rent in Moscow, whether there was a job there that I could do. My fragment of thought fell to pieces before it could become a full fantasy.

I walked from the tram stop to the fashion house with my hands shoved deep inside the pockets of my coat. Underneath I wore three thick sweaters. My ears stung in the wind even though I had pulled my hat down over them. Each breath I took made my lungs sting. I peeled away my layers by the stove and shook the snow off my boots.

Natalia waited in her usual position, scratching her head and staring at a diagram for a long-sleeved dress. She motioned for me to join her and pushed all the work to one side.

We have an offer for you, she said. Something for you to try.

Part of me clenched in irrational fear. I had dreaded the possibility that Larissa might have to fire a worker because the economy had turned so sour. Because I was the newest seamstress, I knew that it would have to be me to go.

Why do you look like that? Natalia asked with uncharacteristic warmth.

I'm nervous about my job, I admitted. I don't want to lose it.

Natalia laughed. Don't worry, girl, she said. I'm talking about sending you to a two-month program of design courses. Larissa thinks you have potential. She wants you to learn more than we have time to teach you here. This is a business, after all, not a school.

A program? I asked. At an institute? Where?

Vladivostok, Natalia said. The big city.

One of the models' brother lived in Vladivostok, on the Pacific Ocean. She went there to visit him twice a year, and always returned talking of how vital and cosmopolitan it was compared to Ulan Ude.

Larissa walked through the front door, cursing the weather

in her cheerful manner. She sat on a stool in the corner and began unlacing her boots.

So? she shouted toward us. Did you tell her, Natalia?

She told me, I said.

Did she tell you that we're going to pay for the course? she asked.

No, I said. Larissa bent over to knock a wedge of ice from the sole of her boot. I thanked her quietly, feeling humbled. I wanted to tell Larissa that she had changed my life, that she was beautiful and generous and that I still wanted to be just like her. But every time I began to say these things she would make me stop.

It's a big city compared to here, Larissa said. And it's a good program. Concentrate on your studies, and when you come back you'll do even better work. It's an investment for me, as well.

I had less than a week before classes began. I finished all my pending work at the design house and packed days in advance for the journey. My mother was impressed that Larissa was willing to pay to send me to school.

They must think you have real potential, she said. She had told everyone in the theater about it.

The night before I left, a woman from our block came to our apartment. I recognized her from the food lines, and I had always said hello to her when we passed on the street.

I hear you're going to the design institute in Vladivostok, she said. I didn't ask how she knew. In my town, people simply knew things about each other.

My daughter is there, the woman said. She's older than you, and she knows her way around. Her name is Valya. When you get there, ask for her and tell her I said to take care of you.

After she left my mother and I went through the fabric chest and talked about the potential of some new swatches she had taken home from the theater. We spent time and talked in a way that we rarely did. That night I dreamed of the city, the sea, and as always, the penciled outline of the woman that I was trying to become.

The train took three days to reach Vladivostok. I passed through the hills and spectacular landscapes east of Lake Baikal to the lower woodlands of eastern Siberia, where towns and villages appeared from seemingly endless stretches of trees. Then we finally rode through the outskirts of the city, where small farmhouses gave way to wooden homes in disrepair, then the monumental brick facades of Soviet apartments. I had invented a picture of Vladivostok as shining and perfect, but I saw the same drab colors and cracked concrete as in Ulan Ude.

But there were differences. The town was bigger, its streets more curving and unpredictable. Flashes of color appeared more and more as we neared the city center. There I saw the usual monuments and statues glorifying Lenin and Stalin's victory in World War II. It wasn't the city of my dreams, but it was not Ulan Ude. In its face I thought I saw more imagination, more wildness, an intangibly stronger hold on life. Great navy and merchant ships docked close to each other in the harbor, returning from and embarking for places with names I had never heard of.

The institute was a series of aged and cracking buildings off a quiet street. I walked with my bag through the campus. The students all seemed older than me, and if they noticed me at all, it was with momentary curiosity about my appearance. I pulled a woman aside and asked her how I could find the girls' dormitory. She pointed at a rundown building with small windows and kept walking.

It was cold and most of the students were inside. In the entry hall my nose filled with the smell of cigarettes and cooking food. Music blared from radios behind closed doors. The ceilings were low, the halls were narrow, and some of the light bulbs had been burned out and not replaced. I pulled my bag close to my chest, feeling young and lonely.

A woman of twenty sat in a wooden chair near the front doorway. From the noise coming from down the hall, I assumed she had chosen the quietest indoor spot she could find. She was pretty, with long auburn hair, and she looked up from the sketchbook in which she had been slowly drawing.

You just arrived? she asked, looking at my bag. Do you need help finding your room?

I'm looking for someone named Valya, I said.

Her eyebrows raised a fraction. Upstairs and down the hall, she said. Room 211. I don't think you'll have too much trouble finding it.

Without asking what she meant, I thanked her and found

the stairs. My bag felt heavier than before as I walked. My eyes burned, and this small exertion made me feel weary with hunger. The train ride had been long, and I had been so excited that I had barely eaten anything.

Room 211 was at the far end of the corridor. I dragged my bag and looked inside a couple of rooms with open doors. I saw beds stacked along the walls and tiny desks crammed together. Inside the girls' dormitory, I learned, we would sleep five to a room.

I stood outside Valya's room and knocked. I had heard music from halfway down the hall, a noise that grew louder and peaked from behind this door. Men's and women's voices shouted over one another to be heard. The smell of cigarette smoke had escaped through the crack under the door. I pounded louder until the conversation stopped and the door was hurtled open.

Clothes, papers, books everywhere. Unmade beds, ashtrays. A low table in the center of the room was full of glasses, vodka bottles, loose tobacco, fruit, dried meat. The radio blared from the corner of the room, its tiny speaker distorting the sound. I peered through the cloud of smoke at the faces of four or five women and as many young men. They lay back on pillows on the floor and leaned against the walls in the beds.

I'm sorry to interrupt, I said, unsure if they could hear me over the music. I'm trying to find Valya.

In the corner, on a small stuffed chair, was a woman in her twenties with straight dark hair and piercing eyes. She was big, as tall as me and with shoulders probably twice as broad as mine. Young men sat to either side of her, drinking and smoking. She looked up at me as through just noticing that someone had knocked and entered the room.

Who the hell are you? she said.

I gripped my bag tighter, feeling that I could cry from tiredness and hunger. She shot the question at me so fast that I didn't know how to answer it. Everyone in the room looked at the two of us. Our eyes locked, and I decided I would stare back at her until she either looked away or said something more. It was like being in the wilderness, surrounded by animals that would attack if I showed weakness.

She slowly looked me up and down, at my clothes, my hair, my shoes.

Where did you get that skirt? she asked, pointing at the fabric peeking out from under my coat.

I made it, I said in a determined voice.

She took a handful of nuts from a dish at her feet and started to chew. I knew now that this was Valya. And I could see that she was the queen of the room. Her chair looked the most comfortable, and the others waited for her cue before deciding how I would be treated.

Not bad, she said.

Valya slapped the boy nearest her on the back of his head. Move it, stupid, she said. The boy found an empty spot near the door.

I know who you are, she said. Irina. My mother has told me. Come on, you can sit next to me.

Her words had the effect of a royal pronouncement. I felt the others relax, and the boy I had dislodged took my bag from my hands and stored it under a chair. I sat down hard next to Valya, weariness running through my legs. At least I had passed my first test.

Valya put her arm around me and I felt the heat from her body. This is a good girl, she announced to the room. She's from my town.

She grabbed a vodka bottle from the table and poured me a tall glass, then replenished her own.

Now we drink, she said, tossing back hers in a single gulp.

I had seen adults do this before. They poured tall drinks for guests who were then expected to drain them in a single swallow. It was very Russian, part hospitality and part challenge.

I had never drunk before, other than a glass of watered-down wine. But I understood already that Valya was essential to me. I had to study, sleep, and eat for two months more than a thousand miles from home. I took the glass and, trying to look as though I had done it a hundred times before, poured the vodka down my throat. It traced a fiery path down my chest and I coughed, but I was able to smile and put the glass back on the table.

Valya clapped her hands and squeezed me close to her. I told you! she said to her friends. She is one of us.

My days were spent in classrooms, hearing lectures on the practical aspects of clothes design. I was taught how to format designs at a professional level and how to draw complex patterns. I learned fabric costs, where fabrics were made, their strengths and weaknesses. My certificate would not be as valuable as the ones earned by the three-year students, but I hoped it would help me gain entry to another institute.

I was one of the youngest students in my class, and I watched the young couples with curiosity. During breaks I walked with Valya, who had decided that I needed the benefit of her instruction in life.

Men are like dogs, she announced in a loud voice as we left the communal dining hall. They're nice to look at and nice to pet. And you can bear being around them as long as you teach them how to behave.

It was like having an older sister. Valya introduced me to everyone at the institute, informing each person that I was from the same town as her and that they had better treat me nicely. She was liked by the other students, who were also a little afraid of her strength and the will of her personality. She became like a mother bird to me. When we ate together she piled food from her plate onto mine, telling me that I was too skinny.

Men like big girls they can hold onto, she said. She pointed at her breasts. And they like these, too. So eat.

When she introduced me to boys she would ask them if they thought I was pretty. Some said yes, others were embarrassed and said nothing. My forehead would burn and I would shuffle my feet. I was too young and naive to think romantically about the older boys around me.

I think that one likes you, she said after she introduced me to a handsome boy from Novosibirsk. He had shook my hand, introduced himself, and walked on without another word.

Why do you say that? I asked. He's not interested in me.

You just don't understand men, she said. Spend a little more time with me. Then you'll know the world better.

*   *   *

A week remained in my program before my exams and the long train ride back home to Ulan Ude. Valya was around always, lecturing me, prodding me to speak with boys, criticizing the way I did things. I began to understand the drawbacks of having a big sister.

Valya organized a group to walk across town to the birthday party of a friend she had met somewhere. Valya knew more people than anyone, and I had a hard time remembering where she had met them. It will be a real party, she said. Lots of drinking and men.

The small house was full of people pressed into loud smoky rooms. I didn't know anyone other than the people I had come with. It was long past midnight and I found myself in a room full of unfamiliar faces. I had asked Valya if we could leave, but she had shrugged me off. We'll leave later, when I'm ready, she said. Just have a good time.

It was too late for me to walk home alone. The institute administrators had warned us about the streets of Vladivostok at night. There are sailors and criminals, we were told. Always travel in groups.

I sat on a sofa talking to a girl who worked in a canning plant. She left, and someone turned off the light, leaving only a small lamp to illuminate the room. I started to get up, but a man in his early twenties sat heavily next to me. He pressed against my arm to keep me seated.

No one introduced me to you, he said. What a beautiful girl.

I smelled vodka on his breath and in the sweat that soaked his shirt. I told him I had to leave, but he pressed me down harder. In his eyes I suddenly saw a wave of darkness pass through him from somewhere deep in his soul. A wordless voice commanded me to get away, that he wanted to hurt me. He rubbed my shoulders then began to caress my breasts. I yelled out and, surprised, he let go for an instant. I pushed him off me and staggered to the door. In the kitchen I ran into a group of strangers, sending them reeling into the walls and cabinets.

Where is Valya? I asked, breathing hard. Stabbing pain racked my chest, and I struggled to calm myself. I heard loud footsteps coming down the stairs from the second floor. Valya ran into the room, her drink splashing onto the floor. I told her what had happened.

Where is he? she asked.

I pointed toward the room I had just left. A moment later I heard a man's voice saying, It was nothing. I just wanted a kiss. She's a pretty girl, I didn't mean anything.

Get out! she yelled at him. Look at yourself in the mirror, you monster! Who do you think you are, trying to molest my friend? She's a young girl! I should throw you through this window!

He left, realizing that Valya was capable of making her threat reality. She found me in the kitchen, where tears had begun to burn my cheeks. I had been under Valya's domination for too long. I blamed her for what had happened. She had gone off and left me alone. I had felt helpless and out of control.

This is too much, I said. I wanted to leave, but you wouldn't let me. You know I couldn't walk home alone.

Shut up, don't be a baby, she said.

I don't care who you are, I said, suddenly angrier than I could remember being. You've been very good to me, and I appreciate it, but—

When you got in trouble tonight, whose name did you call? she said.

Yours, I replied. And I thank you again. But sometimes you act like you're the only person in the world. I can't stand it anymore.

Listen to me, she said, her hands on her hips. It was her usual position when she was about to begin a lecture.

No, not anymore, I said. I'm tired of it.

Maybe you need a good fuck, she said. Maybe that's what's bothering you.

She smirked at me. I'm not playing any more of your games, I told her. You think being a friend means telling someone what to do. Well, it's over. I'm leaving.

I turned my back on her, the tears coming faster. Go on, then, little bitch, Valya yelled out as I opened the door. You'll see how far you get without me.

I slammed the door behind me and walked quickly into the night. When the tears cleared from my eyes I saw that it was nearly completely dark. There were no houses or apartments around. The wide concrete road was empty of cars. I didn't care; I remembered the way back to the institute, and I would go back alone. I didn't need Valya or anyone else. Anything was better than returning to the party and to Valya's gloating face.

My steps echoed in the night. From far away I heard the sound of a car, but there were no headlights and the noise receded. I moved faster and tried not to think of all the warnings the school had issued. The entire walk home would take about forty minutes, a little less than the walk to the party because my pace alone was more rapid than the group's had been. I counted off steps as seconds, which turned into minutes. I tried to convince myself that I wouldn't be harmed.

A man's voice called out from behind me. I kept the same pace. I hadn't heard what he had said. Maybe he was shouting at someone he knew.

Hey you, stop, he said. I want to talk to you.

I looked behind me. He wore a jacket zipped up to his neck and had one hand stuck in his pocket. On a long leash at his feet was a slavering dog, a big mixed-breed whose teeth shone in the dark.

Come on, don't be afraid of me, he said. He moved faster. I heard his dog panting hard with the quick excitement of the hunt.

I knew that to show fear would mean that I would be his. He crossed the road and walked alongside me, several paces behind. I heard a frightening intensity in his voice. When I glanced back again I caught him peering all around us, trying to make sure there was no one who could see us.

I think we should go back to my apartment, how about that? he said, half insinuating, half commanding. A beautiful girl like you shouldn't be alone at this time of the night.

I said nothing. I tried to walk faster without making my fear noticeable. I imagined both the dog and man could smell my terror.

I have a nice apartment. You'll like it, he said. His steps matched mine; between them was the clatter of the dog's claws on the pavement.

Irina! a woman's voice yelled out.

I dared to turn around again. He had moved closer but remained behind me. The street was deserted all around.

It's me! I said. Who's there?

He turned to look. His dog whined and performed an agitated dance of excitement. Jogging behind us was a woman I had met at the party. She worked in one of the government offices downtown, and we had shared a friendly conversation before the tide of her friends had pulled her away.

What's going on here? she yelled as she drew close. Is this guy following you? What, are you some kind of pervert or something? He looked around and licked his lips nervously. His dog did the same. He shot an angry, frustrated look at me and jogged away until he reached a cross street. He disappeared without a glance back at me.

I've been trying to find you ever since you left the party, she said. Never walk alone around here. This town is full of creeps.

We walked back together; she smoked and kicked at the road as she walked. Don't be such a bumpkin, she said when we approached the house. The world is nothing like some little town in Siberia.

I took my exams, passed them, and received another certificate for my wall. In the few days that I remained in Vladivostok, Valya never warmed to me in the same way she had before—by questioning her authority I had undermined our entire relationship. She regarded me with distrust and uncertainty. When I left for the station, though, she gave me a small tin of sweets for the long train ride, as well as an extra tin for her mother. I kissed Valya's cheek and we embraced.

When I came back to Larissa's fashion house she made me tell her everything that had happened. She nodded with approval when I described the curriculum, and she chided me when I told her about my long walk alone in the night. I tried to describe Valya but couldn't. She was the first friend I had made while on my own. She was impressed on my memory like a seal on wax, like a first lover.

You're ready to have your own clients now, Larissa told me. They'll place an order and your job will be to fill it. You'll be making more money than before.

I shook Larissa's hand very formally. You won't be sorry, I said.

The cold night sky hung close and cloudless over the city. I maneuvered through snowbanks as high as my waist, stopping as a tram disgorged a load of people in my path. The public clock in the city square read a quarter-hour until seven. I pulled my scarf tighter against my head and walked on.

The dense monumental apartments and bureaucratic offices of the city center dwindled gradually. Smaller buildings spotted the street, little stores and nongovernment offices. If I kept walking another twenty minutes, the city would end and I would trace my path on a road leading into the deep countryside.

A tiny building huddled between a brick apartment and a dentist's office, small and featureless. I threw open the door and jogged in, hoping that I wasn't late. The tram ride and long walk from my atelier typically took forty-five minutes, longer when the snow hadn't been shoveled from the streets.

Music played for a Spanish *Baski* dance, a complicated rhythm to accompany difficult movements. I began to peel away my layers of clothes, smelling sweat and cigarettes lingering heavy in the air.

How was work today? a voice said behind me. My laces had frozen completely over during my walk, and I looked up from the difficult job of releasing them from the ice.

Great, I said. I completed an outfit for a picky customer. She said she's asking for me specifically next time.

Lena took a long sensual drag on her cigarette, considering what I had said. She tugged at her dancer's tights.

Party member's wife? she asked.

Don't ask. I rolled my eyes. Of course she is. Who else has the money these days? I'm getting to know them all.

Lena stamped out the cigarette on the floor. It's changing in Moscow and Leningrad, she said. It was a phrase she repeated often, like a mantra. Gorbachev's opening it up. Freedom of speech, elected government. I'm telling you, the artists won't have to suffer forever.

Lena studied choreography at the arts institute. She constantly lectured me on the importance of culture. She had described for me the cracks that were appearing in the edifice of communism. Her fellow students returned from Moscow wide-eyed with talk of the small freedoms that were being granted there.

She clapped her hands for attention. All right, men and women, boys and girls, she yelled. Let's take our places and begin with the first act. Our last rehearsal was excellent, but I know we can do even better tonight.

I barely had time to say hello to the other dancers as we walked onto the hard floor of Lena's studio. We danced ballet to warm up. The music began again, and I concentrated on the challenging series of moves which were assigned to me in Lena's program. My arms ached from a long day of sewing, and my back was sore from bending over my worktable. Yet I could ignore my body's complaints. Lena had taught us that between the music and movement was the essential act of creation, that each of us in that moment was like a loving and beneficent god.

She had showed us books of art and told us the life story of painters. She taught us about music and about the great orchestras in the West. She instructed us in ballet and modern dance, taught us about choreographers such as Pina Bausch, leading us through programs which she wrote for her university degree. Our troupe had performed once in front of an audience, and I had seen tears in a grown man's eyes over the beauty of our work.

Several of our dancers had spent time in the juvenile jail for stealing, fighting, speaking back to a policeman. Most of them hadn't graduated from high school. Many were unemployed and saw no future for themselves in the Soviet system. Before they joined Lena's troupe they smoked and drank and tried to look tough on the streets. They were the people I might cross the street to avoid.

When we began dancing we were all the same. Lena shouted out instructions and we moved as one.

I raced from the fashion house to Lena's studio every day. It was winter and I woke before seven in the morning, worked until six at night, then rode a bus for more than an hour to the dance studio. I left before the sun rose and returned after it had set. I was chasing life, running after experience. Though I was often fatigued I never felt truly tired; I loved dance so much that the sacrifice was worth it. I danced the lead in a ballet called "A Toy"—a Japanese story about a little girl who lived in Hiroshima; she held onto her doll after the atomic bomb destroyed her city, and my dance followed her into her teenage years.

When I reached Larissa's fashion house one morning I kicked the slush from my boots. I opened my sewing box at my worktable and began stitching together a simple black blouse.

I thought that was you, Larissa said, emerging from her office. Have you seen this?

She handed me a clipping from the newspaper about a beauty contest. It was to be the first of its kind in Ulan Ude, an event that would have been impossible just a few years before.

You should do it, Larissa said. You should enter.

Me? I asked. No, I—

Look, she said, pointing at the clipping. They want beautiful young girls. I think you would have a good chance. And the winners get prizes. Why not?

I don't want to, I said. It isn't for me. I don't want to compete.

I looked into Larissa's eyes. There was an expression there that told me she would not stop insisting until I did as she said. I folded the paper and put it in my pocket.

All right, I said. But you'll see. This is a silly thing.

The contest was held in a drafty hall in the center of town; a stage was set up with bunting, and the judges sat at the foot of the stage. The winner would become "Miss Ulan Ude."

I sat backstage in a simple dress that I had borrowed from Larissa. From the stage I heard music playing on tinny speakers. I reviewed the program in my mind. I wanted to do well now that I was there, but there was an imposing variety of areas in which I was supposed to compete.

First I had to dance with a partner, a sandy-haired young man who led me through the lights. When we were finished I danced on my own, performing steps that had been imprinted on my memory by long nights at Lena's studio. When I finished I heard applause from the darkness beyond the stage.

Then the competitors were led to a series of tables equipped like individual kitchens. I had to cook a meal and decorate the table. I chopped potatoes, onions, and carrots into thin slices and arranged them in a symmetrical pattern on the plate, imagining an almost mystical pattern. A middle-aged woman came to my table with a clipboard and a very serious expression. I pinched the back of my hand to keep from laughing, caught up in the absurdity of it all.

Finally we were quizzed on Russian history. *What was the name of the last tsar?* Nicholas II. *Name three plays by Chekhov.* Three Sisters. The Cherry Orchard. Uncle Vanya.

When it was over I sat backstage waiting for the judges' verdict. Images spun in my mind from the competition: dancing, cooking, answering history questions. It had all seemed so odd and disconnected, as though each piece had struggled but failed to relate to the one before it.

The other contestants and I were called back to the stage and arranged in two long rows under the lights. I looked around at the other young women, their faces expectant and anxious. I realized that I shared their feeling, that I wished to be rewarded for my effort with victory.

They read off the name of the winner. I started to clap for her, ready to congratulate her. I looked around to see who she was and realized that everyone on the stage had turned to look at me.

Me? I asked silently, my mouth forming the word without a sound.

I stood still under a spotlight as a young girl put a crown on my head. One of the judges handed me a bouquet of flowers. Then the grand moment came: my prize. The smiling judge handed me a small *magnetophone,* a tape recorder. I held it up for the audience to see.

Thank you, I said to everyone.

I had become Miss Ulan Ude. I turned from one side to the next as a couple of photographers took pictures of me. I began to laugh until the crown nearly fell from my head.

The bunting was taken down from the stage by burly men carrying armfuls of lighting cable. I chatted with one of the other contestants, a girl my own age who lived just down the street from my apartment building.

Excuse me, a voice said from behind me. Can we talk for a moment?

I turned and saw a woman in her thirties wearing a knit sweater and sophisticated eyeglasses that hung from her neck by an embroidered cord. She carried a thick book that burgeoned with pieces of paper and photographs.

Contratulations on winning the contest, she said, nodding toward the tape recorder in my hand.

I thanked her.

I'm with Gorky Studios in Moscow, she said, speaking very fast like someone from the big city. I'm a casting director. I came here specifically for this beauty contest because I'm looking for exotic girls for a film.

I see, I said, trying to keep up with her train of thought.

Turn to the left for me, she commanded. Now the right.

She paused, evaluating my face. How old are you? she asked.

Sixteen.

She nodded, apparently satisfied. Have you ever acted before? she asked.

No, I said. But I know about the theater. I grew up with it.

She seemed to grow bored with my answers. She jotted my name and address in her book and said she would call me later if she had any additional questions.

I went to Lena's studio that night and danced hard after answering my friends' questions about the beauty pageant. I concentrated on choreography and thought nothing more about what had happened earlier in the day. A role in a movie. It was something that happened to girls in Moscow, or young women with Party connections. Such a thing would never happen to me.

The next afternoon when I came home there was a phone message waiting for me. Gorky Studios wished for me to make arrangements to go to Moscow. I was under consideration for the lead role in their next production.

I landed at Sheremetyevo Airport in the morning. The Aeroflot plane descended through the gray dirty haze that perpetually blanketed Moscow. I had slept through almost all of the night flight, waking only when the pilot hit a pocket of turbulence and the plane rattled and moaned in protest.

We descended through the murk and I saw Moscow from the air for the first time. It extended before my eyes like a part of the land itself. Individual buildings began to appear, gray and stolid. Roads divided the earth into grids that wound to the limits of my vision. It was impossible that a place could be so vast yet so dense. I pressed my face to the window and felt the plane fall to earth. I was like a spirit plunging to the world from the heavens.

A car had been sent for me by Gorky Studios. The driver cursed and gestured as he careened recklessly through broad streets to the highway. We drove for a half hour and the city continued to reveal new parts of itself. It was a kingdom forged out of concrete, asphalt, steel, and stone. I pressed back in my seat, suddenly overwhelmed by a vivid sense of my own smallness.

I took out the folder that had been given me by the studio. I hadn't prepared much for my visit because I barely understood what would be expected of me. I was just a girl, a nobody from the remotest part of the country. I couldn't envision what I could contribute to the Soviet Union's movie-making apparatus in Moscow.

I started reading the materials inside the file to distract myself. There was a letter and a rough pamphlet. Gorky Studios was the second-largest studio in the USSR, after Mosfilm. Gorky Studios specialized in movies for Soviet children and young adults. Whereas Disney in America made capitalist propaganda disguised as innocent children's stories, Gorky Studios made films that explained and promoted the history and ideology of Soviet communism. Normally they told stories of young martyrs of the revolution, such as Pavlik Morosov. Occasionally the studio produced Russian folktales, or fairy tales from the Soviet Republics.

The latest project was to be titled *The Adventures of Hadja Nasredin,* the story of a folk hero from the Asiatic USSR. Hadja Nasredin was much like Ali Baba, the letter said. He was clever and resourceful. He battled an evil sorcerer in order to rescue and win the love of a beautiful princess. I was to be considered for the part of the princess.

I put the letter back in my pocket and gripped the doorframe. The driver swerved the car into the next lane to get around a slow-moving sedan. We nearly hit the car behind us, which squealed its brakes and pulled hard to the left to avoid us.

The driver glanced at me in his mirror. Damned slowpokes, he said with a harsh laugh. If you can't drive, you should stay off the road.

The city gave way to intermittent emptiness along the outer ring road. The driver jerked the car hard off an exit, and we drove fast through an area of decaying industry and warehouses.

We're early, the driver announced. They told me to take you to the museum first, until they're ready for you.

I received no further explanation, and I stopped myself from asking who *they* were. This was another world, full of busy people living in the great city. If I was told to stop at a museum, then I would stop at a museum.

I got out of the car and promised the driver that I would be back in forty-five minutes. He lit a cigarette and pulled out a newspaper. I noticed that it wasn't *Pravda*. This man was reading a slim paper with a cover proclaiming that it contained debate about Stalin. I had never really thought of such a thing. Under Brezhnev, we had been taught that Stalin was the great leader who had vanquished the Nazis. My teacher's face had glowed with pride when she remembered those years.

I walked along a quiet gravel drive, listening for the songs of birds but hearing nothing. Maybe the studio was delaying me for an hour because they didn't really want me for the part of the princess. But then why had they paid to fly me to Moscow? A few tourists milled around, looking stunned and flattened as they slowly strode away from the museum park.

Their expressions made sense to me what I saw where they had just come from. The exhibition park was a series of individual museums, each more ambitious and monumental than the one before it. They rose from the ground in odd shapes, like cakes made by a crazy baker or the product of a sculptor burning with fever. A plaque explained that they had been ordered by Stalin himself to celebrate the achievements of the Soviet Union. The grass between the buildings was sparse and choked by weeds. The structures themselves were cracked and peeling. I wondered whether no one cared to fix them, or whether money was as hard to come by in Moscow as it was in Ulan Ude.

One building was dedicated entirely to the history of farming grain. It contained maps and charts and photographs of peasants working on collective farms under the bright sun. A picture of Mikhail Gorbachev accompanied a recorded voice enumerating his achievements in agriculture while serving on the Politburo. The next building was filled with exhibits detailing the USSR's dominance in steel making. Another showed models of Russia's energy production, from the massive electric generators of Moscow to the oil fields of Siberia. I picked out Ulan Ude on a textured map, feeling the gentle slopes of Buryatia with my smallest finger.

I walked in the park between the museums. Everything the Soviets designed had the intent of making the individual citizen feel small and helpless. The massive buildings, the individual's life subsumed by the long march of history. The historical breakthroughs of Soviet scientists and engineers were the collective pride of our people, one display touted. And for a moment part of me sympathized. I had grown up feeling communism pressing down on me like a giant hand, but the system had also left positive marks on history that would never be forgotten. The old pride of my Octobrist days flickered through my heart. I hated the conformity, the uniforms, the fear. But it hadn't all been for nothing. There was a meaning to everything.

A young man said hello and walked alongside me on the path. His skin was pale and his eyes were lined and tired. He explained that he was one of the caretakers of the museum. We walked without saying much, and I understood how bored and starved for company he was.

In the back of the park was the first Sputnik, which the Soviets had launched into space even before the Americans. Next to it was the first rocket to send a man in outer space. They were the greatest pride of the nation. Their paint was peeling, and spots of rust corroded their surfaces where they met the cement pedestal.

Far to the right from the park's entrance were twin colossal figures, each more than three stories tall. A woman grasped a sickle. Next to her was a working man holding a hammer. They stared into space, seeing a vision of the future.

What's happened to this statue? I asked. The man and woman towered over us like the parents of a political idea. I pointed at their knees, which were cracked and starting to bow. Pieces of their metallic clothing had worn away and fallen off. It looked as though a strong wind would dash it to the ground.

It wasn't built the way it was supposed to be, the young guide said. His hair was cut short and already starting to thin. He shoved his hands in his trouser pockets with embarrassment.

Someone should fix it, I said. It's too big to just let it rot. It could fall down and hurt somebody.

The sculptor who created it is dead now, the guide said, looking away from me. No one knows how to fix it, I suppose. Or no one cares.

The driver pulled through an open gate toward a compound of long, low-lying buildings that hugged the earth amid birch trees and rough patches of grass. He opened the car door for me and pointed toward an unmarked door in the building. I gave the security guard a sealed letter which had been sent to me in Ulan Ude. He looked it over for a second, not long enough to really read it, then waved me inside.

On the walls were posters of past movies, each more enthusiastic than the last in their patriotic fervor. There were stories of the Revolution and the war, tales of children who had bravely resisted the capitalists and the fascists. Each was emblazoned with slogans and excited descriptions of each movie's plot and historical significance.

The place was like a maze or a warren. I started to fall in love with it even before I had spoken with anyone there. Hallways branched off into new secret places, offices for decision-making and editing. I glanced inside a door and saw an array of dials and microphones and electronic panels. The people moved with quiet confidence. It was a factory producing fantasy and expression instead of steel and glass.

I didn't care if the fantasies existed in the service of the communists. The films were dreams, and I felt that dreams could be bent and corrupted only so far. I remembered the films of my childhood. No matter how hard the Soviets tried to instill their beliefs in me, I had been preoccupied with the sights of other places and other lives. They had tried to leave me feeling dedicated to working for the betterment of communism at home, but I had usually stepped out of the theater filled with visions of the world and a burning need to see more of it.

An escort took me to a set of production offices. Two men and a woman were waiting for me in a room full of charts and schedules. They examined my letter and told me to follow them down the corridor.

We're the production staff, I was told. Do you understand what that means?

I think so, I replied. You're in charge of the movie.

That's close enough. Let's go to the studio stage, the woman said. Her hair was short and stylish, her steps quick and light. We followed the men, and she caught my eye and gave me a small secretive smile.

The filming studio was vast, like a train station. Bright lights ringed the center of the room, where a circle of projectors were wheeled around under the orders of a tall man wearing casual slacks and a button-up shirt. Their movements were quick and efficient. I had the impression that they were used to working in a hurry.

Please wait here, the woman told me. They're preparing for your screen test.

I realized that all of this activity was for me alone. I wanted to tell them to slow down, not to rush, that it was only me. It was impossible that I would get the part. I was a princess only in my own mind. I pulled the thirty pages of script out of my suitcase and folded it in my hand. I had memorized what they had asked me to learn, and though I didn't need to look at the pages their weight felt reassuring.

The director pointed at a young woman. You there, he said, move those wires. I don't want to trip over them. He was impatient, a man accustomed to having his orders obeyed without question. He looked across the stage at me and the production staff.

This is her? he asked. He motioned for me to step into the lights. An assistant pulled out an expanding white screen that was about ten feet tall.

Stand in front of this, the director said. When I say go, recite the lines that you were sent. Remember, you're a princess. I want to hear that you are a princess. I want to see it.

He left me standing under the lights, which were so bright they made it impossible to see anything else. I heard a camera begin to run and footsteps all around me. I felt like a blind person in a crowd.

Now, the director's voice issued from the darkness.

Hadja Nasredin, I recited. For so long I have waited for someone to return me to my father and his kingdoms—

No, no, the director said. He clapped his hands once. The sound echoed in the high ceiling. Still the camera whirred.

You're just reciting the lines, he said. You know them by heart, fine. Good. That's not enough. I want you to feel that you're the princess. I want you to convince me who you are. Don't just say what's written on the page. Anyone can do that. I need you to *live* it.

The studio was silent for a moment. I was shocked deeper

into my shyness, felt like a young girl from the provinces who had come to a place where nothing she knew would be good enough. I tried again.

No, stop! the director yelled, even more agitated. Think about who you are. You are the princess, you will be rescued soon by Hadja Nasredin.

I heard a second voice say something quietly. All right, the director called out. Take a minute, think about it. Then start again.

I breathed hot air under the lights and thought about the theater in Ulan Ude. I remembered the fresh snow on the ground as I walked to the opening of a new production. I heard my father's music, pictured the poise of the actors on stage. I could sense all the eyes in the room focused on me. I willed myself to enter those eyes like beams of light, to occupy their spirits with a transcendent reality.

I began to speak my lines. I envisioned my young, handsome rescuer before me. He had suffered so many trials for my happiness. I felt the rhythm of the words and swayed gently on my heels. After a few minutes I had finished.

Silence, machines vibrating. All right, the director said. If that's how you see the part, then fine. Now let's try it again for the camera.

I blinked. The sound I had heard was some other device, not the camera. They had been rehearsing me before expending precious film on my screen test. Somehow I had to revisit that elusive moment in which I had become somebody else.

Camera ready? the director barked. Go.

I said the lines again, trying to feel the pain of my captivity and the hope my rescuer gave me. I almost couldn't dare to hope that my life would change, that I would escape the wizard. I couldn't bear the disappointment I would feel if Hadja Nasredin failed.

When I was done I heard the director rise from his chair. Cut, he commanded. That's it. Print it.

He stepped out of the blackness and took my hand. Thank you very much for traveling all the way from Siberia, he said, his voice kinder now. My assistant will notify you about what will happen next.

The director informed the cameraman that he wanted my

test film developed as soon as possible. His steps resounded as he left. I didn't feel that I had done well, or that I had failed. I didn't feel anything, just vague relief that it was over.

The director's assistant, a young nervous woman, escorted me through the building. I wanted to ask her if I had pleased the director, but I didn't have the nerve. She walked me out into the fresh air, where the sun had cut through the haze and now beamed down on the vast parking lot.

Why don't you take the car and have a look around? she said. Have you ever been in Moscow before?

Once, I replied. When I was a girl.

Things have changed a lot since then, she said. Try to relax, then meet us here later in the afternoon. By then we should be able to tell you what comes next.

I asked the driver to go straight into the heart of the city. Now that I had left the studio I felt my heart beating fast with the strain of what I had done. Part of me wanted to order my driver to keep going, to push the car as far as it would go and never stop.

I returned to the studio and was told that the director hadn't made his decision yet. There was another girl in consideration who had flown in from Uzbekistan. We weren't allowed to meet or speak with each other.

I was provided with a room in a hotel on the outskirts of town. I walked around the street outside until it was dark. All day I had searched my memory for what Moscow had been like a decade before. Surely it hadn't been like this. There was an openness on the streets, in the way people walked and talked. There were more cars, more goods for sale. The buildings and streets were shabbier than I thought they would be, but my eyes were now met with colors other than cement gray and Soviet red.

In the morning I returned to the studio and again presented my official letter. I was ushered through corridors that seemed familiar to me now. I belonged there. Surely they wouldn't ask me to leave.

The director's assistant came for me in the waiting room. She looked at the clock on the wall. I have time for a break, she said. Let's go for tea and something to eat.

We rode to a nearby cafe, where she ordered tea and a big

piece of apple cake. She ate greedily, and forced me to order a slice as well.

This is better than anything you'll get in Siberia, she said, not insulting, merely stating a fact.

I tried to eat the cake, but my stomach was knotted with nerves. I wondered, Why is she doing this to me? Am I the mouse and she the cat?

She ordered a second cup of tea and looked over every contour of my face. You're a lucky girl, she said.

Does that mean—

You know, we've looked at three hundred girls for this part, she added. We were starting to wonder if we would ever be able to fill it. But now we have. The director has asked me to tell you that we want you in the movie.

I took a bite of cake, trying to imitate her serenity. She acted as though it was all an interesting game. My mind began to flood with images from the script and of cameras aiming their searching eyes at me.

Thank you, I said.

Don't thank me, she replied. You were very good.

Can I start right away? I asked.

She finished her tea and leaned back. Of course, she said. We start measuring for costumes this afternoon. We have to make you look like a genuine princess. Someone the people will believe in.

I spent the next week at Gorky Studios, returning to my quiet hotel at night. The head of the costume department showed me the gowns, veils, and jewelry I would wear in the film. I offered suggestions—perhaps this collar could be embroidered, or that sleeve could be shortened. My youth and inexperience earned patronizing answers, but still they listened to me. I began to feel part of their world. I slowly stopped fearing that one day, without warning, they would send me back to Ulan Ude.

I sat at a long metal table in the production studios. Anya, the woman I had met my first day in Moscow, led the meeting. The director, Ivan, sat silently in a turtleneck sweater. Giorgi, the boy who would play Hadja Nasredin, sat next to the director. Giorgi was young and handsome, and rarely spoke to anyone. He was from Moscow, and he had appeared in two Gorky

Studios pictures before this one. I sensed him watching me and waiting to see whether I would meet his standards.

You all have the script, Anya said. It's been approved by the government propaganda offices, and any further changes will have to be submitted there directly.

I leafed through the pages of the script. I didn't know who had written it, nor had I ever been asked if I would like to make any changes in it.

You have all been given an itinerary, Anya continued. It takes us through August and September. First we will travel to Tadjikistan, then Uzbekistan.

In the script I befriended Hadja Nasredin, who later rescued me from the evil magician. I helped Hadja in his struggle and returned safely to my castle. The plot was designed as an allegory about the struggles of the Soviet people, and working people around the world, against Western imperialism and capitalism. I thought the writer had also managed to tell an interesting story.

I examined our traveling schedule. I had learned about the Asiatic Republics in school but had never considered visiting them. In my imagination they were harsh, wild, mountainous. The world of the princess and Hadja merged with the unknown lands of the faraway republics. I stacked my papers neatly, prepared to do whatever was asked of me.

I learned how to behave like an exotic princess after a hot two-hour bus ride on an unpaved road up a steep mountain. I pretended that I lived in a castle, though I stood in front of a two-dimensional set that had been constructed out of wood and nails on a windy hill. I moved from person to person on the set—the director, the set and costume designers, the cinematographers, the sound recorders—asking questions until I felt the end of their patience was near.

I woke early. I sat for makeup, watching in the mirror as the cosmetician accented my eyes and painted my lips. I watched Giorgi filming his scenes and waited for the time when my character would appear on the shooting schedule. Everyone but me had done this work before and knew what to expect next.

The summer turned more hot as we traveled and worked

through the production schedule. The sun-baked barren hills of Tadjikistan burned with the heat. We found shade under rocks jutting from the slopes. We drank water constantly. By the middle of August I felt as though I had been living on another world, one that orbited the sun much closer than my own.

The crew built the last set for the scene in Uzbekistan. It wasn't the final scene of the movie, but we had shot out of sequence so it was our last scene left to film. The movie would soon be completed. I sensed the cast and crew turn tense.

We haven't had any real problems on this film, I heard one of the cameramen mutter. That means we're probably going to have them all at once.

The director stalked around complaining about the corruption of the local authorities. They wanted bribes for everything and had even threatened to shut down the production. It didn't matter that we had clearance and orders from the government. It was as though they no longer respected Moscow's authority.

We waited for two days in our small camp, sleeping outdoors. We have become Gypsies, went the joke that passed among the crew.

I woke up under the morning sun. I heard that we would finally drive to the location that day. It would be a long ride, more than sixty miles into the sun-blasted hills. I paced near the bus, reciting my lines to myself over and over. Hadja Nasredin and I would come together that day to face the evil forces that only we could defeat. It was a pivotal moment in the film. I pictured it in my mind like a waking dream.

Giorgi appeared, looking nervous. I tried to ignore him, willing myself to become the brave princess who defeated wizards. Other crew members joined us by the bus, smoking and drinking water out of little plastic bottles. Soon they began to comment that it was getting late, that we would lose the good light if we delayed much longer.

I left the world of the princess. Ivan kicked his shoes in the dirt, cursing softly to himself. As the director he would be held responsible for any further delays, and now it looked as though it was inevitable.

All right, enough is enough, he said. He spat on the ground. Where's the driver? Why haven't we left yet?

He dispatched his assistant to find our driver, a local man who maneuvered roads that made our crew gasp with fear. I closed my eyes, trying to find the princess again. I needed to fight off the growing anxiety around me.

The assistant returned looking pale and stunned. She whispered in the director's ear. His eyes widened, then he stroked his chin as though trying to find the greater meaning in what he had heard. He swore, with less enthusiasm than before, then held up his hand for silence.

Listen to me, everyone, Ivan yelled. Voices gradually silenced save for a few crew members who started to complain.

The light will be bad, someone said. We've already lost two hours.

The driver is dead, Ivan said, and now no one spoke. He went to sleep and didn't wake up this morning, the director added. This day is over. We'll have to find someone to take us up there tomorrow.

That night the set-design crew returned to the camp with complaints of their own. The wind was too strong and was blowing the set away. The paint chipped in the harsh sun. Local people were hovering around, ready to steal anything they could. A few members of the crew had decided to stay there overnight so there would still be a set in the morning.

I slept under a tent canopy, the soft breeze warm but not unbearable. The voices all around trailed off until the night was still. The open black sky seemed to reach into infinity. I counted stars and watched the moon, wondering if it looked the same in Buryatia. Sleep wouldn't come to me. Though I hadn't known the driver well, his face eclipsed the stars in my vision. His death became all I could think about. His passing felt like a warning to leave that place and never return again.

We hired another driver in the morning and rode to the set. The day was cloudless, it was almost ninety degrees before ten o'clock. Ivan worked fast to arrange the lighting and cameras. Giorgi and I waited in full costume and watched the curious crowd of local citizens who pushed and shoved for a look at us. I imagined strange mists and castle moats until it was time to shoot the scene. Instead of my kingdom I saw the jagged hills and baked dirt around me. A fear gripped me that I couldn't explain or describe.

You cannot vanquish us, I said to the wizard and his evil helper. We have the power of good on our side, the will of the people. You cannot enslave the strong.

The words sounded unbelievable even to my own ears. Ivan yelled out to stop the scene and gave me a moment to relax before I would have to try again.

I tried to block out the driver, the hills, my fear. I felt my legs tremble beneath me, and I hoped that someone would catch me if I lost consciousness.

The next time I was able to say my lines better, though not well. Giorgi, however, stuttered and forgot what he was supposed to say.

Ivan sat in his director's chair biting his lip. His chest rose and fell beneath his khaki shirt. Our eyes met, and I sensed he shared my anxiety. Invisible electricity ran up from my legs into my abdomen. I felt I was surrounded by powerful evil from the earth beneath me. It wasn't a safe place. I wanted to run away.

I think we're in trouble here, I blurted out. The driver's death was a sign. We can't stay much longer.

The crew stared at me, this young girl talking nonsense.

Thanks for warning us, Irina, Ivan said. As soon as you finish this we can all leave. The only danger is that we are going to spend the rest of our lives here trying to get it right.

We worked into the afternoon. Some of what we shot was adequate; much of it wasn't. We returned to camp depressed and exhausted. The food tasted odd, the water stale. No one spoke much, and we slept again in the open air. Before the last fires were put out I sank deep into dreamless sleep.

On the set the next day we started the scene from the beginning. We were ordered to attempt the crucial scene again from beginning to end. The characters' words still sounded tense and unconvincing. Ivan jumped from his chair and ordered the cameras to stop.

This is the last day we can be here! he shouted. The money is running out! This movie is nothing without this scene!

The cast looked away. Giorgi kicked the ground, scuffing his elaborate boots.

It's this place, I said. It's dangerous to be here, and it's affecting everyone. I want this to work, but I think it's impossible.

Ivan's features dropped. He took my arm and led me away from the set to the shade of a canopy.

Look, maybe you're right, he said so that only I could hear. Everything's been screwed up since we got here. I won't argue with that.

You know I want this movie to be good, I said, emboldened by his intimate tone. This is a great opportunity for me. But I think this place is more powerful than all of us.

Then you have to save us, Ivan said. A small smile played across his lips, but I could tell part of him was very serious. This is your great scene. If what you think is true, then it's up to you to make it possible for us to leave. Between you and me, Gorky Studios won't let me leave this place until the movie is finished.

We returned to the set and tried again. I felt trembling in my limbs, heat in my chest. Again it didn't work. I could feel the irritation of everyone around me. I began to feel guilty for failing them.

Ivan threw his script on the ground. That's it, he said. We camp here tonight, and tomorrow we start early.

He looked at me, waiting to see how I would react. I was certain we had nearly lost our last chance to get away from this place. Every minute we lingered brought us closer to disaster.

A half hour, I yelled to him. Give me a half hour by myself. I promise we can finish today.

I ripped the pages from my script and left. I found a shady seat under a rock formation and rubbed my eyes. A delicate breeze came down the hill, and I tried to make myself part of it. I remembered my grandfather's words: *We are of the sky, of the wind.* I touched the ground at my feet and tried to understand why I felt as I did. Slowly I calmed myself. When I returned to the set I announced that I was ready.

Instead of my lines, I repeated to myself that I had power. Power conquers evil, I repeated. I handled the thought gently with invisible hands and melded it with the scene like pouring milk into a bucket.

I recited my lines. The people have suffered at his hand, I said, of the wizard. But no more. He will lose today.

Giorgi stepped forward. Our power is greater than his because it is good, he said in a clear, courageous voice.

We worked like a perfect machine together. Hadja Nasredin, I said, you have showed the people the way. Our love showers you like the beads of the morning rain.

Your domain will again be ruled by good and righteousness, Hadja promised me. I swear it, upon my life.

We embraced. There were no more lines. Still the cameras kept rolling. I looked up at Ivan, who was staring at us as though he barely understood what he had seen.

That's it, he said calmly. Cut and print. Let's start taking apart the sets, and then let's get the hell out of here.

In Moscow I returned to Gorky Studios and made arrangements to go home to Ulan Ude. There was no guarantee that I would appear in another movie after *The Adventures of Hadja Nasredin*. We would have to see how the people responded and whether the government liked it.

I sat with Anya and reviewed my itinerary back to Siberia. I had made a few friends on the crew, and three women had invited me to spend an extra week in Moscow at their apartment. Anya honored my request to push my flight back to next week.

I heard there was difficulty in the final days, she said as she handed me my travel papers.

A little, I said.

Anya sighed. We don't need more trouble, she said almost to herself. Things are bad enough.

What do you mean? I asked.

You're a young girl, you don't have to worry so much about politics, Anya replied. Things are changing for the better, but none of us knows how long that will last.

What do you mean? I asked. Are you talking about the studio?

I'm talking about everything.

The women I stayed with were a few years older than me. One worked on the set-design crew at Gorky Studios and the others had done makeup and hair for the movie. They had a break before the next movie was due to start, and they showed me around the city. I saw the red stars shining above the Kremlin towers and walked for hours in the pedestrian mall that had been created out of the Old Arbat district. The hand of communism was still firm, but in the mall there were street musicians and a few small restaurants. This was when I first heard the name Boris Yeltsin. He was the one responsible for Old Arbat, I was told.

I relaxed on the sofa at the apartment and watched television for hours, soaking in the exotic images of the new shows that had been permitted by the Politburo. This was because of Gorbachev, I was made to understand, because of *perestroika.*

Still, it was not an entirely new world. On the state-run information program a man dressed in a drab brown suit read that day's news approved by the Party. My mind wandered. My new friends were in the kitchen boiling potatoes for dinner.

I saw brief news footage of Boris Yeltsin. I examined his features and listened to his voice as he responded to a Moscow reporter. From the tone of the report I understood that he was currently considered undesirable by the Politburo. Why was that? And why was he allowed on television? The Soviets had never permitted such dissent.

That evening the four of us ate together. The television was still playing in the next room, and we heard it low as a background to our conversation.

Wait a minute, be quiet, Ina said. She was the oldest among us, and had worked ten years at Gorky Studios.

What is it? I asked.

Ina left her fork on her plate and got up. Did you hear that? she asked us. On TV. There's a special news bulletin.

The rest of us joined her in the living room. Ina turned up the volume. On the screen was the same plain man who had read the Party news broadcast.

There has been a powerful earthquake in Uzbekistan, he began, reading with even more solemnity than usual.

Uzbekistan? Ina said. We were just—

Wait, be quiet, the set designer said.

Though reports are not complete, it is estimated that this event has been catastrophic, the announcer continued. The earthquake was severe. The death toll is expected to be in the hundreds. Preliminary reports indicate damage to homes and buildings.

Turn it off, someone said. I can't listen to any more of it.

We were just there, Ina said in a frightened voice. Three days ago we were there, shooting the final scene of the movie.

All of us remained standing in the living room, our dinner forgotten and left to grow cold. My legs began to tremble beneath me, a vibration that spread up into my body. It was the same sensation that I had experienced in Uzbekistan.

Ina turned as though seeing me for the first time. You were frightened, she said. Everyone was angry with you for delaying the shoot, but I could see how upset you were.

I don't know about it, I said.. I don't understand.

I went into the apartment's back room and lay down in the dark. Nausea and panic gripped me as they had just days ago. I pictured the awful earthquake in my mind, the ground giving way, people dying.

An hour later I came out into the apartment again. Leonid, one of the camera technicians from the film, was there with the women. They were all staring at the television, where footage of the disaster was beginning to be aired for the first time.

Irina, did you hear what happened? Leonid asked when I joined them.

I couldn't speak. I simply bowed my head to make him understand that I knew about the earthquake.

You were telling us to get away from there, Leonid said. I remember it. How did you know?

I knew nothing at all, I said. My voice was louder than I meant it to be.

Come on, you were shaking like crazy that day, Leonid insisted. He glanced at the women for support, but they all looked away. They had seen my face when the news had first arrived.

It was wrong to be there, that's all I remember, I insisted. I never said there was going to be an earthquake. I just knew I wanted to get away from there.

It's all right, Irina, Ina said. There's no reason to get upset. It's all over now.

I spent the night awake on the sofa staring at the low ceiling. I fretted that my new friends would think I was crazy. To them

I was a young girl from the end of the planet. None of them had ever met one of my people before me. And now it seemed to them as though I had predicted that disaster.

I wasn't crazy. There was nothing special about me. But that night I also made a vow to myself. If my feelings were ever again as strong as they were on the film set, then I would act on them. I had never calculated much in my life, instead I had just acted. And that was how it would always be.

In Ulan Ude I saw the autumn green fields as never before. They were beautiful in their struggle for life against the first insinuations of winter, but they also seemed static and unchanging. My home city now seemed provincial. I returned to my family's apartment and unpacked, burning to leave again, to travel and explore.

It seemed as though nothing was different. My parents' theater was staging a new Ibsen production. In the evenings after working at Larissa's I went there and watched rehearsals. The actors all asked me about the movie studio, whether it was as grand or as terrible as they had thought. It was neither, I responded. It's like a factory. It's what they create that is incredible.

The next morning was warmer than usual, and I was able to wear a sweater instead of a coat. I got off the tram at my usual stop and walked around fresh mud puddles through the streets to Larissa's. At my usual worktable were a pair of simple evening dresses that I had designed for one of Larissa's favorite clients. I planned to start my day by checking the work I had done yesterday, making sure the seams were tight and strong.

I folded my sweater and poured a cup of hot tea. In Larissa's office I heard her speaking to two unfamiliar men.

We're very impressed with your collection, one of them said in an accent that was vaguely familiar. Very stylish. A very nice variety.

Absolutely, the other agreed. I guarantee that we can make money for all of us. All we need is your commitment.

I need to think about it, Larissa said, her voice neutral. This is a big jump for me. I can't agree to anything right now.

We understand, the first man said. But times are tough here. We both know that. I'm sure you need the money.

Of course I do, Larissa answered. But I still need to think about it.

Don't misunderstand me, the man said. I don't mean to sound vulgar. But times such as these require creative measures in order to make a profit. You supply your collection and models, I supply the connections. Mister Chang here will help you with the language and culture. We'll all make money. It's very easy to understand.

I'll tell you what, I'll contact you this evening, Larissa replied. Is that good enough?

I wondered if the men heard the hint of irritation in Larissa's voice. Probably not. To someone who didn't know her well, she sounded completely composed and businesslike.

The three of them came out of Larissa's office into the workroom. I pretended to concentrate on my work, and Larissa didn't offer to introduce me. I glanced up and saw that one of the men was Chinese, the other Russian. They both wore business suits and carried themselves as though they were very important. They both shook hands with Larissa before leaving.

Larissa stood by the window and watched them walk away. Very interesting, she said.

I put down my work. Who were they? I asked. What did they want?

Two other women had also arrived for work. They ignored what had happened, probably assuming that the men had been typical buyers. I sensed something was different. They were slicker, like men from Moscow. And I could see that they made Larissa nervous.

Come on back to my office, she said. I'll tell you about it.

Larissa's desk was covered with her latest designs. One of the rolling clothes racks had been wheeled in and occupied almost a third of the room.

You were showing them the entire new collection? I asked. Normally a buyer saw a range of items, but almost never did they ask to see everything that Larissa had.

They wanted to see everything, Larissa said. She sat behind her desk and looked at a card one of the men had left.

Are they buyers for a big clothing store? I asked.

I wish they were, Larissa replied. They want me to take the collection to a town in the north of China. They'll stage some shows for me at a hall. They say I can sell plenty of clothes there because there are no real designers in the entire region.

Have they done anything like this before? I asked.

They say they have, Larissa said. One of them worked in Novosibirsk and the other in Peking. The Russian is acting as a go-between for the Chinese man, Chang. They'll pay me to bring the clothes there and to hire eight or ten models. All they want is a share in the profits.

This could be a great opportunity, I said.

Or a disaster, Larissa answered. I don't know anything about China. What if something goes wrong?

But somebody might discover you there, I said. You might meet some new partners and financial backers, and I'm sure you'll sell plenty of clothes. If you want to do it, I'll come with you.

Do you think so? Larissa asked. I could tell she was almost convinced. For both of us it would be our first trip outside the Soviet Union. China to our south had always occupied our imaginations, a close second-best to Europe. The more we spoke about it, the more certain I became.

I met some girls in Moscow, I said. Some very pretty girls with experience in modeling. I'm sure I can get them to come if there's money in it for them.

All right, then, Larissa said, looking again at the business card one of the men had left. We'll go to China.

Larissa worked deep into every night preparing her collection for the trip. She had five huge trunks, and she calculated that the space inside them would carry her entire new collection plus some duplicate items. She asked the seamstresses to work fast and stay late when they could. Now that Larissa had reached an agreement with her two new backers, she wanted to take advantage of her opportunity. With every day that passed in Ulan Ude it seemed that the ruble was worth less. Hopefully things were better in northern China.

I made expensive long-distance telephone calls to Moscow from my parents' apartment. Four of Larissa's models had agreed to go on the trip, which left four spots to fill. I dialed the Moscow phone extensions, and each time I reached one of my friends the conversation was almost identical.

It's a free trip to China, I would tell them. All of our expenses will be paid. When will you have another chance like this?

Well, fine, they would reply. But are we going to be paid? The travel expenses are nice, but I don't model for free.

Larissa's backers had told her that the models, myself included, would be paid from a share of the profits from selling tickets to the shows. I knew that Larissa's clothes were beautiful. Any woman would love to wear them, Russian or Chinese.

That's why we want to go there, I said over the scratchy phone line. To make money. We're all going to be in it together.

I hung up after the final call. Larissa would have her models, including four from Moscow who would arrive in a few days. I had found an old geography lesson book left over from high school, and I sat at our dining table tracing our route through Mongolia with my finger.

My father watched me from the kitchen. China, he said, as though to hear how the word sounded. You're sure that everything checks out? It's a very different country from ours.

It's going to be fine, I said. We'll be back in three weeks.

Just don't feel worried if everything doesn't go according to your plan, he said. Long voyages rarely do.

Didn't you tell me that Buryats once rode to Moscow on horseback, I said, six thousand miles to address a grievance to the tsar?

My father scratched his nose to hide his smile. I might have mentioned that story, he said.

Well, it's not that far to China, I said. And I'm not going on horseback.

When the models arrived from Moscow I introduced them to Larissa's regular girls. I watched them silently examining one another, the brash young women from Moscow with their Siberian counterparts. The meeting might have gone differently in Moscow. In Ulan Ude, some of my Moscow friends' flash quickly started to fade. The voyage was just a few days away, and we all realized we had to bond in order to survive in a foreign land.

The money came for our travel passes. We loaded Larissa's

five trunks into the bus at the city terminal and boarded together.

For the first hours it felt as though we were a rolling party. Larissa and Masha, her assistant, sat at the front looking over maps and travel plans. In the back were the models. Nadia and Alexsandra, the polished Moscow girls, were sharing makeup with Sonia and Nikola from Ulan Ude. I sat with Natasha from Moscow and asked her for stories of artists and writers and musicians. Soon I realized how much I missed Moscow.

You should come back, Natasha said. Life isn't easy there, but when was life ever easy for Russians?

The familiar landscape outside the bus windows gradually changed from the familiar landscape south of the lake to rougher, more barren land. We stopped for passengers in Kyakhta, a town I knew of only by name. My father had traveled there on one of his winter theater tours. He had said the people there were even poorer than in Ulan Ude. Looking out on the shabby station, then the wooden shacks beside the road driving out of town, I saw that he had been right.

Within a half hour we crossed the border into Mongolia. The women from Moscow began to talk among themselves, asking each other if they knew we had been so close to the border. None of them had.

The bus stopped in Altanbulag, a little border town. We were ordered by soldiers to step off onto a platform. We remained quiet and calm. Surely this was just a formality. None of us had ever left the country. We assumed that this was what happened whenever you crossed a national border.

Outside the shelter of the bus was a different planet. Wide flat space stretched into nothingness on all sides. The sky met the land, and each seemed to mirror the other in its featureless desolation. The station was the size of a tiny house. Its windows were cracked and repaired with sealing tape. The outside walls were caked with dirt and mud. The wind seemed to whirl at us from all sides, with nothing to block it.

Larissa was talking to one of the soldiers, who spoke broken Russian.

There's nothing to worry about, she said to the group. They want us to go inside the customs building so they can check our travel papers. We have to leave our things inside the bus.

The driver walked around the bus and laboriously opened the cargo bay. The soldiers, grim-faced and silent, began to remove Larissa's trunks and deposit them on the platform.

We were seated at a long table inside. I sat next to Larissa to help her talk to the soldier in charge. He looked over our papers with a look that mixed boredom and hostility. After examining them, he started to shake his head.

Nyet privivki? he asked us. *Zaraznjie?*

I replayed his words. His accent was heavy, but he was speaking about vaccinations and infections.

Larissa leaned close to me. We don't have the right shots, she whispered. We can't get in without them.

When we had arranged our travel permits we had been told about the injections for cholera and other infections we would need before we could enter the country. But such rules were always lax in Russia, and we had assumed Mongolia would be the same.

Outside the window the soldiers were going through our bags. They dumped the contents of a suitcase onto the platform and sifted through its contents with the barrel of a gun.

I don't think I can do this, I said to Larissa. My aunt worked in a hospital. She told me what can happen if you're injected with a dirty needle. Look at this place. Do you think they have clean needles?

One of the soldiers appeared from a back room with a small medical kit. He opened it to reveal needles, syringes, and small vials of serum.

I gripped the table. My aunt had told me horror stories about people seizing up and dying hours after a bad injection. In Ulan Ude, one of the most thriving businesses was buying and selling syringes. No one trusted the hospitals anymore, and anyone with enough money brought their own to the doctor's if they became sick.

Larissa asked the soldiers for a moment to think. We huddled together in the corner and Larissa explained what was happening.

I understand if you don't want the shot, she said. But we can't go on without it. We're in the middle of nowhere and I can't think of anything else to do. Probably if we take the shot nothing will happen, but I can't say for sure.

This place is so dirty, Nikola said.

Natasha from Moscow folded her arms. No way! she said. If this was Russia, maybe. But this is Mongolia.

Larissa nodded sadly and said she understood. I want to protect you girls, she said. But I'm taking the shot because I have to go on with this trip. Each of you has to decide what you want to do.

Larissa sat down at the table and rolled up her sleeve. The soldier with the medical kit swabbed alcohol on the inside of her arm.

I looked away, trying to control my fear. I knew this trip was crucial to Larissa. She had invested a lot of money putting together the clothes, and she had to at least break even to stage the next season's fashion show in Ulan Ude. It was also the first time she had left Siberia since she was in school, and she would never forgive herself if she stopped before she reached her destination.

What should we do, Irina? Natasha from Moscow asked.

I had called Moscow and invited my friends all the way to Siberia, first the long flight to Irkutsk then the long bus ride around the lake. All of us were hoping for an opportunity to bring money back to our families. We could either take the shots or wait for the next bus back to Russia.

I unbuttoned my sleeve. I'm doing it, I said. The rest of you have to make your own decision. No one will be angry if you turn back.

Larissa got up from the table rubbing her arm. Her eyes were ringed with red. The soldier motioned for me. I sat down and closed my eyes. The needle pierced my skin like a wasp's stinger.

Thirty seconds passed. I felt the same. The soldier gave me another shot, and I waited for my heart to stop or for my blood to boil from within me.

Nothing happened. I got up and turned around. Everyone else in our group was waiting with their arms bared.

We boarded a train and left the dismal station behind. The soldiers hadn't taken anything from our bags that we noticed, but they had emptied everything and put our possessions back almost randomly. We spent the first hour trying to put our own things back into our own suitcases.

Again we were stopped, this time for a customs inspection. I waited under the endless sky, looking out on a land that gradually turned from dirt to barren desert as it unfurled to the edges of my vision.

Larissa called to me. She was in a heated conversation with a customs agent, another soldier dressed in a worn uniform. He waved our stack of papers in the air as though they were completely worthless.

No stamp, he said. If you bring this here, you have to have the right stamp. Didn't anyone tell you?

It has to do with the clothes we're bringing into the country, Larissa explained to me. They say the collection is worth too much money, and we need special permission to travel any further.

Where would we get this permission? I asked the soldier.

Before you come here, he replied angrily. You can't get the stamp here. You have to leave everything or go back.

Larissa took the papers from the soldier and handed them to her assistant. All right, you win, she said to the soldier.

What do you mean? I asked.

Larissa pointed at the clock on the wall. The train is leaving in ten minutes, she told me. You have to be on the train or you'll lose your tickets. You have to go. Masha and I will wait here.

What about you? Sonia said, panic entering her voice.

I don't know, we'll do something. Larissa sighed. We'll call home. Maybe somebody can come by car and bring this paper we need. You go on ahead and we'll meet up with you.

We can't leave you here, I said. I looked at the trunks full of clothes. Larissa and her assistant, two women alone, couldn't protect such valuable merchandise in that remote train station. They would be robbed before morning. Larissa's features fell with disappointment.

We have nine minutes left, I said. You can't stay here.

I grabbed Sonia's arm. Can we talk to your supervisor? I asked the soldier.

No, no, he said. It's impossible.

I took him aside. You can see we're good people, I said to the guard. We didn't know we were breaking any laws.

I don't care, he said. He looked across the platform as though something else had already attracted his attention.

It's just a little stamp, I pleaded. Surely nothing will happen to you if you let us go on.

Sonia put her hands on her hips and smiled. You're such a handsome man, she said. I'm sure you have women asking you for favors all the time. But can't you help us just this once?

He glanced at Sonia. These are the rules, he said, as though it were now him asking for help.

I smiled at him as warmly as I could. Would it be possible to pay for the stamp here? I asked. You know, informally.

In our luggage we had brought soap, vodka, and cigarettes that we had planned to barter with in China. I pulled out a few items and showed them to the soldier. He shielded the sight from the other soldiers with his body.

Perhaps I can help you, he said, staring at Sonia.

She took a pack of cigarettes and a small bottle of vodka from the suitcase. The soldier stuffed them into the pockets of his uniform, glancing around to make sure nobody had seen.

It's all right, let them go, he called out. It was just a technicality. Let them board the train.

He passed me a little slip of paper authorizing us to continue traveling into Mongolia. We boarded the train seconds before it left the station. On board the conductor told us that the next train would have left in three days.

I woke up feeling as though I was sleeping in a furnace. My eyelids swelled with sleep and heat. My lungs burned with hot, dry air. The motion of the train continued on, trying to seduce me back into the world of my dreams.

I stood up and looked around. Most of our group was asleep. It was dark outside, and the moon was high in the sky. We had been on the train for almost two days and nights, and time had begun to lose all meaning. I realized then what had awakened me: the sound of a strange language spoken very fast. Chinese men and women looked for familiar landmarks in the dark rural landscape outside the window.

I got out of my seat and found Larissa. She was deep asleep, her head bouncing with the train's rhythm. I nudged her several times until her eyes fluttered slowly open.

I think we're here, I said. We're in China.

Larissa shook her head and rubbed her face, trying to wake up. She looked around and listened as I had moments before, then burst into a smile.

We did it, she said. We actually made it.

I woke up the other models. After three days traveling together we had begun to feel open and comfortable around each other. Sophisticated, conceited Moscow girls were sleeping with their heads on Siberian shoulders. We crowded around the windows to catch a glimpse of the foreign night speeding by in a blur.

I never thought I'd see China, Nikola said. We were all silenced by her comment. We had all entertained dreams, but in our hearts we had wondered whether we would ever see the world outside Russia.

The train stopped at the first station inside the Chinese border. We were pulled aside by a pair of stern guards who asked for our papers and told us, in Russian, to return in two hours to board the train again.

That will give us plenty of time to examine your travel clearances, said one of the guards. He sounded as though he hoped to find something wrong.

I hope everything is all right, Sonia said. I don't think I can afford another stamp.

We walked together in a tight circle into the station. Though it was late, the town was still alive and awake. Heat pressed down on us, from the air and from bodies. Outside was a street of colorful lights and soft music emanating from a shop window. I listened to the language being spoken all around, trying to hear a familiar word or sound. Eyes followed us. Soldiers who looked like young boys dressed up to play in costumes stared at us as though we had descended from another planet.

I began to laugh with happiness. The people, the sounds, the wind, were so all different from our experience. I felt a surge of intoxicating romance with the country.

I want to see the markets, Nadia said. She pointed to a row of brightly lit shops across from the station.

I felt a hand on my arm and looked down. A short woman

with gray hair pulled her hand away and smiled. Encouraged by her bravery, a young boy touched Larissa's hand. A small crowd gathered around us, watching, laughing, touching to make sure we were real. They followed us across the station, talking and commenting. We smiled and nodded at them, their opinion of us a complete mystery.

The markets were open into the night; in Russia they were open sporadically. During my entire life I had to stand in line for food; the Chinese shops' shelves were full of food. We separated from each other, calling out across the store when we discovered something new.

Cookies! Sonia called out. And so many!

I wandered down a row of sweets wrapped in plastic. I saw bottled juice for the first time. It was like a museum, an exhibition put on for our amazement. I touched everything I could, cellophane, glass, cardboard. I wondered if the people in the town understood the abundance in which they lived.

The shopkeeper watched us with a mixture of amusement and wariness. His eyes followed our movements when we picked up something to show off. I wished I had the words to tell him that we wouldn't steal, and that his small store would become a legend among us.

A small crowd started to gather again. They stared at the Russian girls, who seemed all arms and legs in comparison to the Chinese people. I remained enraptured by the things I saw in the store. Toilet paper. Salt. Soap. Packets of dried meat. I wanted to buy something to take home after our trip, but I couldn't understand the signs that listed prices. Within minutes the store had begun to feel cramped with curious people. We nudged our way through them and found our way back to a long bench in the open part of the station.

For the next two hours we watched everything and everyone around us, barely saying anything to each other. The people we watched were full of life, their movements quick. Strangers addressed each other in loud open voices that seemed full of complaint. The Chinese language hovered in the air with its elongated vowels and clipped consonants.

I think I might go back to the store, Nadia said. I'd like to buy some tissue paper and soap.

I'm staying right here, Natasha said in return. I'm not moving a muscle until it's time to get back on the train.

We moved closer together, feeling the press of cramped and hectic life moving into the space we occupied. It was like a whirlwind that could have swallowed us into its turbulent swirl without even noticing.

The next afternoon we rode closer to the town where Chang, Larissa's backer, was supposed to meet us. The train was tightly packed, and the air grew stale and heated. Each mile south into the country's interior seemed to raise the temperature another degree. We stopped in little villages and towns to let off and take on passengers. In between was endless country, with poor farms and dirt roads that seemed to lead nowhere.

We reached another stop, a little station in a small town. The doors opened and only a few people stepped inside. I closed my eyes, trying not to feel the press of suitcases and humanity all around.

The conductor burst into our compartment and pointed at us. His voice was harsh, and he slapped his book of tickets and pointed at all our things. Our luggage filled the compartments above our heads and at our feet, boxes and crates full of dresses and hats and shoes.

I can't understand what he's saying, Larissa said to us. Does anyone have any idea what's going on?

The train doors closed. This was a short stop, only a few minutes. The conductor called up to the next compartment as the engines moaned in anticipation of leaving.

We have tickets, Sonia said. There's no problem.

The conductor slapped his hands together, growled in frustration, and started pulling our boxes out of the storage compartments. I stood up. Everyone in the cabin was watching.

What are you doing? I said to him. Do we need to move our things?

The conductor yelled at me in a high-pitched voice. He pointed first to me, then the ticket in my hand, then to our luggage, and finally to the platform outside. The doors opened a second time.

Wait, I said to Larissa. This is our stop. That's what he's trying to say.

I looked at my ticket, then at the little station. I couldn't decipher what anything said or meant.

That can't be right, Larissa said. This place is too small. Chang said we were going to a city.

I grabbed suitcases and trunks as quickly as the conductor passed them to me. The other women joined in, their arms filling with heavy luggage. The conductor pushed and pulled at us, his face tight with tension. The moment we stepped onto the platform, the doors closed behind us and the train left the station. We watched it recede into the distance.

This can't be the place, Masha said.

This wasn't a city, it was barely a town. No wonder the stop had been so short. We were nearly the only people who had disembarked there. The street I could see from the station was filled with little two-story brick and wood buildings. The people around us moved with a slow country pace.

Do you see Chang? Larissa asked me.

We stood alone on a concrete ramp leading into the station. No one was waiting for us, no one noticed us save for a few soldiers smoking cigarettes in the afternoon heat.

Is something wrong? Natasha from Moscow asked. Are we supposed to take a bus or something into the city?

I guess this is the place where we're supposed to meet Chang, Larissa said in a small voice. I don't understand why he isn't here.

Can't we just buy tickets to return home if he doesn't come for us? Sonia asked. I mean, it's a long way, but it's not as if we don't have a way home.

I said nothing. There was no more money because Chang and his Russian had refused to give us an advance. Our entire fee was to be paid to us in China after the shows of Larissa's collection. It had seemed like such a small detail. Now I wondered if there would be any shows at all.

I could sense the models looking to me for some idea what to do. I had encouraged them, I had recruited them. I had seduced them with notions of adventure. The girls from Ulan Ude turned silent. They weren't as far from home as the Moscow models.

So what now? Natasha from Moscow asked. The old arrogance was back in her voice. Her tone made me feel as though I had led her into disaster.

Irina, what have you done? Alexsandra said. Where have you brought us? Where is the car to take us to our hotel?

Their voices blended together into a single complaint. They circled me, forgetting Larissa, seeming to place me in charge of everything.

I looked through my bag for Chang's telephone number. It was useless. I didn't have any change. I didn't know how to work the phones. I realized I didn't know how to even get food in China.

Let's get off this ramp, I said to them. We'll find someone to answer our questions. It can't be as bad as it seems.

We carried and dragged Larissa's collection into the station. I felt the close presence of humanity occupying almost every inch of the floor and every available place to sit. This town seemed much poorer than the one that had amazed us with its market. Men and women walked barefoot. The children were dirty, some of them half-naked. They carried their possessions in stained bundles of rags and twine clutched close to their chests.

I looked around for an administrative office or a police booth, anywhere that I might find someone who spoke Russian or Mongolian. I clutched Chang's phone number tight in my hand. There was still a chance that it was all a mistake. I imagined myself and my friends a few days in the future, on a stage before an adoring audience.

This is it for us, Irina, Larissa said, pressing close to my side. I should have known better. I should have known Chang and his partner were cheats and liars. I should have been more careful.

What is she talking about? Nadia said in a loud voice. Are you two hiding something from us?

It felt as though everyone in the entire station, hundreds of people, were staring at us. We walked slowly with our luggage. It was taking us a long time. I could see no one who looked as if they could help us. A young boy surged from the crowd and tugged at the bag I was carrying. I pulled away and he disappeared around a corner.

Look at them, Nikola said. Everyone's coming closer and

closer. What do they want from us? Will they chase us if we run away?

Stop talking nonsense, I told her. We have to stay relaxed. We don't want these people to think we're scared of them or that we're dangerous in any way. They're simply curious.

I smiled at this crush of strangers. Children tugged at my clothes. A woman with nearly all her teeth missing reached out and stroked Nadia's blonde hair. I felt cornered. The people could have kept coming closer, they could have devoured us.

Does anybody here speak *Russki*? I yelled.

Faces were lined up around me like paintings in a gallery. Tired, lined foreheads. Crooked grins. Eyes that seemed greedy in their thirst to take in every detail of our dress and appearance. The chatter of Chinese continued, voices echoing in the low ceiling, merging into incomprehensibility.

A little bit, a voice said. I looked and saw a man in a straw hat and a shirt with the seams tearing at the shoulders. He smiled at me warily.

Can you help us? I said in Russian. We need to find a man— I have his phone number. I need to make change and use the telephone.

The man shrugged. He couldn't understand. I heard Russian words emerge from the chaos: *Pretty girls. Big city people. Where? Welcome.*

Our group began speaking back to them. *Thank you. You are very nice people. You have a very nice town. We are very happy to be here with you.*

We chattered at each other for several minutes, at least ten Chinese men and women for every one of us. The dialogue soon degenerated into laughter, and gradually the townsfolk began to drift away and leave us space to breathe, both us and them reassured that no one meant any harm.

A young man almost my age lingered close to us. He singled me out and asked if I spoke Mongolian.

You look Mongolian, he said. Is that where you're from?

No, but not far from there, I said in a mixture of Buryat and Mongolian; the two languages had similarities, with enough shared words to conduct a simple conversation. I need a phone, I added.

He pondered this for a second and grabbed my arm. Let's go, he said.

Come on, I told my friends. He wants to show us something.

I had no idea where he was taking us or what would happen there, but I was making something happen. I had learned that people in China didn't stop to explain their behavior or to reason with you. They simply acted, and you were expected to do the same.

The young man had short-cropped black hair and a narrow face. He wore a Western-style T-shirt with words in English that I couldn't read. He led me to a chipped wooden stall where there was an aged phone with frayed wires.

Phone, he announced in Mongolian. Call here.

I made him sit down with me and explain how to work the phone. I gave him paper money. After disappearing for a moment, he returned with change. I let him keep some as a reward. Speaking half Mongolian, half sign language, he explained how to get a phone line. I dialed the number and listened to it ring, tapping my foot on the dirty floor. After ten rings, a woman's voice answered.

Oh, I'm so glad you picked up, I said in Russian. Can you understand me?

A little bit, she said.

Good, good. I signaled to Larissa that everything was going great.

I need to speak to Chang, I said. In the clothing business. We arranged to bring a fashion collection here, and he is supposed to take us to our hotel and set up meetings with buyers. Is he there right now? Did he forget?

Silence. I don't understand, she said.

Chang, I repeated. Clothing? Fashion show? Theater?

That is not what we do, she said. I don't know who you are talking about, and I don't know who you are. I'm very sorry, but I can't help you.

Wait, wait, I said. I could feel hot tears beginning to burn my eyes.

We are not a clothing business, she said, starting to sound annoyed. We fix the roofs on houses. There are two men working here, neither one is called Chang. I think you were given the wrong phone number.

She hung up. I stared at the number. I knew I had dialed correctly. There was no point in calling back.

Why are you crying? the young man asked me. He wore a relaxed and happy grin that seemed never to disappear from his features.

We're lost, I admitted. We have no place to stay and nothing to eat. We have no money and no friends.

Why did you come here? he asked.

To sell clothing, I said, pointing at my blouse then at our trunks and bags to make sure he understood. We were supposed to meet a man to sell clothes, but now we think he is either a thief or a liar.

This is not a bad place, he replied. You shouldn't worry so much. If you have something to sell, then maybe we can make a deal. I know plenty of people around here.

He held out his hand for me to shake. Call me Sing, he said.

Let's go with Sing, I said to our group. I think it's a good plan.

Plan. Alexsandra snorted. You're very liberal in your use of that word.

Sing found rooms for us in a little wooden publican house off the town's main street. We gave him a couple of cotton blouses to show to his friends and family, and in return he arranged for the owner of the house to feed us bowls of thin soup for dinner. The Ulan Ude girls stayed in one room, the Moscow contingent in another next door. Through the thin wall I could hear their voices complaining.

Larissa went through her trunks of clothes, refolding items that had been wadded together by the customs inspectors. Masha joined in while the models lay back on the small creaking bed.

It's not the end of the world, Larissa said in a soft voice.

I want to go home, Natasha said, staring up at the ceiling.

I looked out the window. The town's lights had come on, multicolored strings on storefronts and in shop windows. The townspeople crowded the sidewalks, everyone seeming to be in an incredible hurry. Part of me shook inside at the sight of so many individuals who knew nothing about me, and whom I imagined had no regard for my fate. I tried to force my heart to beat slower and my breaths to come more evenly.

There was a knock at the door. Larissa and I looked at each other, then I crossed the room to answer it. It was Chang, standing alone with a creased hat held tight in his hands. He nodded and smiled and stepped past me into the room. He smelled of sweat and cologne.

I'm so sorry I missed you at the station, he said in his mixture of Mongolian and Russian. His gaze lingered on the models as he looked around the room.

What happened to you? I demanded of him. You arranged the schedule. You know we've never been in China before.

But you're fine, he said. He gestured over the room as though it had been his magnanimity that had obtained it for us.

No thanks to you, I said. But never mind. What's happened to our deal? You said you would introduce us to people and that we would have shows in a big theater. Take one look at this town. There's no big theater or concert hall here. It's too small.

Chang smiled and looked down at the floor. His shoes had been stylish once, but now they were worn and frayed. In the light of the hotel room he looked shabby and untrustworthy. His was a different face than I had seen before, with darting glances and an air of insincerity.

There's no need to be upset, he said. I promised you could make money here, and I told the truth. You and your friends are very beautiful, very precious. If you are able to dance, and if you're friendly, I can use my connections to make us all a good deal of money.

His words echoed in my mind. I see, I replied. You think that a fashion model and a whore are the same thing.

Chang held up his hands as though that would calm me. No no, he said, you misunderstand.

You've lied to us enough, I said. Has anything you've said been true?

I paid for your train tickets, he said.

And we're here, I told him. Find us a big theater and the clothes buyers from Peking that you talked about. Then we'll do business.

Be sensible, Chang said. You're in a strange country. You have to be flexible.

Larissa was standing next to me, listening. As I explained

what Chang had said, her face turned red. Tell him to go to hell, she said.

I know this isn't Ulan Ude, I said to him. The next time we're there, we'll meet and we'll speak differently. We know this is your country and not ours.

Good, Chang said. He looked over the models reclining on the bed, as though making plans in his mind.

But we're not dancing for you, and we're not meeting any men, I continued. I don't know what you thought, but we're here to do legitimate business. If not with you, then with someone else.

You'll find it difficult, he said in a neutral voice. This is a small town.

I understand small towns, I said. They don't frighten me.

Just tell him to go, Larissa said, shaking her head.

We'll speak later, Chang said. Your train tickets home are only good a month from now. I think you'll change your minds before then.

In the morning there was a small crowd beneath our windows, talking and pointing up at us when we opened the curtains. There seemed to be hundreds of people, most of them wearing conical hats; families of four or five people rode single bicycles, the children wedged tight between the husband in front and wife in the back. Everyone had heard about our arrival and who we were. The owner of the public house fed us breakfast in exchange for a skirt out of Larissa's trunk.

Sing arrived on his bicycle and found us in the kitchen.

Did you sleep well? he asked. I couldn't tell if he was making a joke.

Ask him if there's any way we can make some money, Larissa said. I can't keep exchanging my designs for rent and food. I owe the fabric seller in Ulan Ude and I owe the workers wages for their overtime. I'll go bankrupt if we don't find a way to earn some money.

I looked away. More than ever I felt responsible for everything. My encouragement and planning had helped bring us to this town at what seemed like the end of the earth. The streets outside were packed soil and tattered asphalt. It seemed impossible that anyone there had enough money to buy Larissa's designs and make her a profit.

We need to work, I said to Sing.

He frowned. This is a poor region, he said. What are your skills?

I can sew, I said.

I can't help you, Sing replied. But what about these shows you were going to perform? Are you singers or dancers?

We can do anything, I bluffed.

Sing scratched the sparse stubble on his chin. Let me introduce you to some people I know, he said.

He left on his bicycle and returned an hour later with a man in his early twenties and a younger girl. With Sing's help I learned that she was a dancer and he was a singer. They had formed a small performance troupe and performed for free in town a couple of times. Another friend of theirs played guitar, and another had a home-made drum set.

Larissa joined us, along with Masha. The girls are very upset, Masha said. They want to sell the clothes and buy tickets home right away. I tried to talk them out of it, but they just got more angry. They're up in the room now, yelling at each other.

We can't sell your clothes, I said to Larissa.

Chang said we might make it all the way to Peking, Larissa said sadly. Can you believe it? Peking. We might as well go all the way to New York while we're at it.

She looked out at the dismal street. Look, I'm willing to sell the collection, but only if I have to, she said. My honor and my reputation would be destroyed in Ulan Ude. But maybe we've reached the point of desperate actions.

I introduced her to Sing's friends, trying to distract her. Her worries showed in her pale cheeks and heavy eyes.

We might be able to arrange something better, I said. Maybe Chang was right, in his stupid way. We have to be flexible.

I wore a skirt and matching jacket in black with tasseled trim. I waited behind the curtain while Natasha from Moscow twirled on stage in a green silk dress. She was accompanied by a guitar and two women singing Chinese lyrics in high-pitched voices.

I hate this, she said to me as she walked off stage.

We're seeing the world, I said to her. And you look beautiful. Your modeling is an inspiration to me.

Her expression softened. I walked out to the stage, dancing with gentle arm movements to the music. The small audience looked up at me with rapt amazement. They had never seen such a show.

Our program included fashion, dancing, and singing. The hall was really a community meeting room, with a stage that raised only a couple of feet above the floor. Communist Party signs and banners hung on the walls, demanding allegiance to the system that was crumbling in my homeland. Masha waited outside the front door, charging whatever the people were willing to give.

We had played a stage in another town fifteen miles to the south, where we performed under a mural depicting the marching Red Army. The people had sat on the floor in orderly rows, clapping and commenting in loud voices with the arrival of each new outfit or song. Selling tickets had earned us enough money for our rooms and meals at the public house. Larissa's collection remained unsold.

After the show we worked together folding the clothes and replacing them in Larissa's trunks. A few women from the audience filtered backstage and joined us. They ran their fingers lightly over the fabrics and spoke to each other in reverent, hushed voices. The sound of the language was no longer completely strange to my ear, and I was able to understand that they thought Larissa's designs were gorgeous and exotic.

Larissa held a small pile of coins and bills in her hand. She went from performer to performer, giving each an equal share.

I'm rich, Nadia said sarcastically, waving the money in front of her face.

We have food and a place to stay, I said. We're having new experiences. I don't know why you're complaining.

Nadia and I stared at one another. Every day I felt my anger rise, along with my guilt and frustration. Now I looked at my own tiny portion of money. Nadia reached out and mussed my hair affectionately.

Maybe you should become a tour guide, she said. You've found your calling.

We held onto each other's shoulders to keep from falling over with laughter.

I met with Chang at the train station the morning we were due to leave. He wore the same suit I had seen him in before, and he sweated in the early heat. He glanced all around him as we spoke, as though worried that someone was looking for him.

We had an agreement, I said. You were supposed to find backers for shows and pay us for our work. We held up our end, and for what? None of us has even had enough money to call home and tell our families that we are alive and safe.

I knew Chang wouldn't pay us; everything that came out of his mouth was a lie. But I felt obliged to at least try to get some money from him.

Well, it hasn't worked out the way I expected, he said. For one thing, you have not been very nice to me. You have hurt my feelings.

I looked away, unable to believe what I had heard. My friends sat together in the shade of a dirty canvas canopy, all our luggage spread out at their feet.

Maybe you will return to Ulan Ude on business, I said. Then this conversation might have a different conclusion.

His eyes narrowed. This is my country, he said. I will do what I want to do. You have no power to change that.

The heat rose from the concrete platform in waves that blurred my vision. I felt sweat trickle down my back. It was hopeless. Chang went to Larissa and shook her hand before leaving. She swore under her breath as we watched him blend into the crowd on the street.

When the train arrived the porter stepped onto the platform, yelling at us to hurry. We dragged all our luggage inside and the doors slammed behind us. I found a seat and fell into deep sleep. On my closed eyelids played images of villages and teeming streets, of wooden shacks and communist posters, like a movie without end. I slipped in and out of consciousness, watching villages pass outside the window, bathed in golden sun.

We stopped again for customs the next morning before leaving the country. Again our bags were searched, our papers examined by skeptical-looking soldiers. After we replaced everything in the train compartment we had a few minutes in the station. I walked through the shops again, taking snapshots in my mind which I would describe to my family when I was home again.

The train left the station, gathering speed. With each mile that passed I felt myself drawing closer to Buryatia. I pictured the hills around the lake, the apartment blocks in the city. It would all seem beautiful to me, I thought, when I saw it again.

I noticed Larissa walking back and forth in the aisle, looking at all the passengers. When she turned toward me her face was full of worry.

What is it? I asked her. Did you lose something?

Have you seen Sonia and Nikola? she asked.

I got up and looked around the car. All the faces were Chinese save for our group's. I counted off the models from Moscow. In the back of the car two of the Moscow women were asleep. Sonia and Nikola were nowhere.

I saw them at the last station, I said. They were going into one of the food shops.

Larissa opened one of the storage compartments. Look here, she said. Here are their bags and their papers and passports. Do you think they could have been left behind?

Outside the train, China passed by as though it were running away from us. We were already at least ten miles beyond the station.

Maybe they got on another car, I said.

You're probably right, Larissa replied. Anyway, there's nothing we can do. If they aren't on the train we'll wait at the next station. They'll catch up.

Neither of us sounded convinced. We sat down together and rode for hours in silence. I pictured Sonia and Nikola in my mind, both safe, laughing as they caught another train. With all the force of my will I tried to make this vision come true.

The next stop was called Dzamin Uud. When the train pulled to a stop we were no longer in China. I felt like celebrating, but by then we all knew that Sonia and Nikola were missing. When we got off the train together we looked all around the platform, as though hoping they had magically arrived ahead of us.

The station was tiny and old; shingles hung in disrepair from the low roof, and the cement under our feet was cracked. A solider examined our passports and tickets, pulling us to the side.

What is your business in Mongolia, and how long do you plan to stay in the country? he asked. You have none of the proper authorizations.

But we're not staying, I replied. We're going home to Ulan Ude.

The solider shook his head. This ticket doesn't go that far, he said. It runs out here in Mongolia.

His words made my spirit go numb. Chang had bought us enough of a fare to get us out of China and no farther. It felt as though he had reached out from across the border to strike us with one final blow.

We're stuck here, I said to Larissa. We don't have tickets.

Her mouth dropped open. We don't have any money for new tickets, she said. We spent every penny on our room and food.

The other models gathered around. At the latest news their faces registered the same tired shock I had felt. No one had any money. No one had enough energy to become angry or complain.

We have to talk to the police, I said. We'll tell them about Sonia and Nikola. Then we'll figure out how to take care of ourselves.

On the street outside the station was a small cinder block police headquarters. Inside a few officers sat at their desks, smoking and talking lazily. When we walked in their conversation stopped. I told our story to the supervisor, who kept his eyes focused on Nadia and Alexsandra.

Your friends won't be on the next train, he said when I was done. They won't let them leave without passports.

Then we have to send them the passports, I answered. Can you do this for us?

The officer shrugged. That isn't our job, he said. You'll have to take care of it yourselves.

We carried our luggage back into the station. I found an older couple waiting together for the next train south. They agreed to take Sonia and Nikola's handbags with them, then leave them with the police at the station in China. When the train came I helped them board it.

Afternoon passed into night. We stood on the street outside arguing what to do. The soldiers wouldn't let us sleep in the station, and they had told us the Soviet embassy was closed until the next morning. There was nothing for us to eat. The Mongolian economy was even worse than the Russian, with bread rations down to three hundred grams a family. We were all dizzy with hunger, but buying food required a ration card that was available only to Mongolian citizens.

We could sell some clothes, Natasha said. Or maybe exchange them for food somewhere.

People had stopped on the street to watch us, staying distant but examining us with curiosity. The apartments on the street were aged, their exteriors falling apart. I wondered if anyone in the town would possibly have extra food to share with us.

You'd better not do that, a voice said from behind us. Selling goods on the street isn't permitted. You'll be thrown in jail.

A tiny woman with long hair and deepset eyes reached out and felt Larissa's blouse. This is nice, she said. I make clothes at home, but I've never seen anything like this.

She designed it, I told her, pointing at Larissa.

Really? the woman asked, seeming impressed.

We're returning to Ulan Ude from China, I said. We put on a series of fashion shows there.

The woman was wearing a frayed green tunic and pants. Her expression warmed when I opened one of the trunks and showed her a few of Larissa's creations. She sighed at the fabrics and colors. Now the last light was nearly gone from the sky. The few streetlights in the town started to switch on.

So why are you out here? the woman asked. There are no more trains leaving tonight.

The woman said her name was Ona, and I instinctively knew that I could trust her. I told her that we were stranded until tomorrow when the embassy opened. I told her we were hungry. Her eyes widened with worry when I told her about losing Sonia and Nikola.

We're very poor here, she explained. There's not much we can do for you.

I understand, I replied. We just need someplace to sleep tonight.

Ona thought for a moment. My sister just moved out of her

apartment, but she still rents it, she said. It's empty, no furniture. But you could stay there for one night.

I explained to Larissa what Ona had said. We all shook her hand and thanked her again and again. Without her help we would have been forced to sleep in a doorway. I felt certain that we would have either been arrested or robbed.

Ona took us to the empty apartment, where we made beds out of our jackets and coats and lay down on the floor. Ona left for an hour and returned with bread and yogurt. Larissa tried to repay her with a blouse or dress, but Ona refused.

I lay in the dark that night on the floor, looking through a window at the deep black Mongolian sky. There were no light fixtures in the apartment, and our conversation gradually abated until there was complete quiet. I lay there contemplating the stars and wondering if there was a cosmic principle that placed on the earth one Ona for every Chang.

When the embassy doors opened in the morning we were waiting there. Larissa started to explain what had happened to us, but soon we all joined in, embellishing and supplying detail. It was as though we needed to explain everything that we had experienced to assure ourselves that it had all been true. Two clerks from the embassy joined their supervisor to listen, all of them shaking their heads with dismay.

You were naive, the supervisor said. He had a thick face and a brush mustache. He looks like Stalin, I thought.

You could have been killed, one of the clerks added. People disappear in China, and there's nothing we can do about it.

I started to explain that the Chinese people had been very gracious and kind to us, but there was no use. As far as they were concerned, we had returned from the dangerous hinterlands. He asked Larissa for names of people to contact who could vouch for us. She gave him one of her backers' telephone numbers, a regular customer who might be able to send the small amount of money needed for the train tickets.

Sit down in the waiting room while I make some calls, the supervisor said. You've really got yourself in a lot of trouble.

In the waiting room was a real Russian samovar. Our thirst for a familiar taste was so great that we nearly emptied it of tea. The supervisor poked his head into the room, seeming to disapprove of us somehow.

More than two hours later he returned. We found the friends you left behind, he said. But the next train doesn't leave until two days from now. You'll have to go home without them.

Do you mean we have tickets home? Larissa asked.

The supervisor sniffed and nodded, as though he felt we were escaping from our predicament too easily.

It's taken care of, he said. Your financial backer has made arrangements.

Incredible, Larissa said. We can go home.

I don't think you understand, the supervisor added, rising to leave. You simply can't travel to places like China as if there is nothing to it.

But apparently we could.

When I opened the door to my family's apartment I found my parents watching television together. They both gasped and stood up, grabbing my arms and touching my face as though to make sure I was real and not a ghost.

Why didn't you call? my father said angrily.

I couldn't, I said. There wasn't enough money.

Not enough money? my mother said. But I thought you were going to be paid.

It didn't work out, I said, too proud to explain the entire truth.

The telephone rang. My mother answered and handed it to me. It was Larissa.

I'm sorry to call, I know you probably want to sleep, she said. But I have a problem. It's Sonia's husband, Algor. He's calling and threatening me because Sonia hasn't come home yet. Don't be surprised if he calls you as well.

The phone rang again minutes after I hung up. It was Algor.

Where is my wife? he yelled.

In Mongolia, hopefully, I said. She'll be home in a day or so. Don't worry, she's fine. The embassy took care of everything.

I'm going to sue you and Larissa! he yelled. You're both responsible for this. How could you leave Sonia?

We had no choice, I said. Please, Algor, you'll see Sonia soon.

Damn it, he said, his voice lower. I knew this would happen.

I asked him what he meant. She's found someone else, he

said, almost crying. I knew she would. I could never hope to keep such a beautiful woman.

Algor, please, I said. Do you think she's eloped with Chairman Mao?

I listened to him complain for nearly half an hour, trying to reassure him. When I hung up I walked to the window. Nothing had changed in our apartment or our town. The dull street below slumbered in the afternoon sun. I grasped the windowsill, wishing that my legs were strong enough to propel me into the sky. Into another world.

Centuries ago Buddhist monks traveled into southern Siberia, spreading the teachings of Gautama Buddha. They stopped just thirty miles short of Lake Baikal. My maternal grandfather, who lived close to the lake's banks, didn't practice Buddhism. But my father's family, who lived in southern Buryatia, grew up with the Lamaist Buddhism that reached their part of our land. As a result, I always linked my deep feeling toward Buddhism with my father's relatives.

In school we had been taught that religion was the opiate of the masses. The new Soviet citizen was supposed to be sufficiently evolved to see the truth of dialectical materialism, so the Russian Orthodox Church was repressed, along with Buddhism. And when Buryats were moved from their villages into the city, they were supposed to leave behind their language, their customs, and their religion.

There were once many Buddhist temples and monasteries in Buryatia, but after 1924 they had all been destroyed by the Soviets with one exception: a monastery about ten miles from Ulan Ude. It became a center for Buddhist learning, not only for Buryatia but throughout Russia. Whenever the latest whim of the central government allowed it, citizens would travel from Moscow and St. Petersburg to study under the monks who lived there.

Buryats talked of a history when things had been different. The tsars had been tolerant of Buddhists, for reasons that I have never understood. In 1740, Princess Elizabeth, Peter I's daughter, proclaimed that Russians were free to practice Lamaist Buddhism. Under Gorbachev, the thick ice of repression began to show cracks and eventually thaw. Two hundred and fifty years after Princess Elizabeth's edict, the Buryat monastery prepared for a visit by the Dalai Lama.

My aunt Dusya phoned our apartment and asked to speak with me. I'm working as a servant for the Dalai Lama's visit, she said. I thought you might like to be there. You can work as my assistant.

As I agreed a familiar sensation passed through my spirit. Something was changing inside me. It was like the movement of something great in the depths of a deep ocean; on the shore, I could only glimpse the surface.

You'll need to stay for a couple of days, Dusya added. You'll be paid. It will be a nice job for you.

Of course I would have worked for free. The city had filled with gossip for months about the Dalai Lama arriving in Siberia— would he come or not? It would be the first time a Dalai Lama had ever visited Buryatia or Russia. I had seen his photograph and memorized his kind eyes and soft smile full of deep wisdom.

I took the short bus trip to the monastery. As I walked from the village I allowed myself to experience the peace I had always felt when my father brought me there as a child. The *datsan* of Ivolginsk was painted in traditional colors of yellow and red. The metal bells by the entrance seemed ancient and otherworldly. Adjoining the *datsan* was the monks' residence, a plain building with spartan quarters. Nearby was a small hostel where the Dalai Lama and the monks who traveled with him would stay.

I found Dusya in the kitchen, where she was washing breakfast dishes. This will be your job, she said. Keep the kitchen clean and bring food and drink when the Dalai Lama asks for it.

I took a clean apron from her and tied it around my neck. Did you come through the back door like I told you? Dusya asked.

I said I had. Good, she replied. Now you'll understand why. I need you to take this tea tray out to the main hall. Give it to the Dalai Lama. It's his favorite.

I held the tray with shaking hands. It seemed strange that this simple little pot of tea and ceramic cup were meant for such a holy man. My heart kicked in my chest in anticipation of being in his presence.

Go on, get it over with, Dusya said. You're going to be spending plenty of time around him. Go ahead and get used to it.

I walked down the long hall, hearing the sound of voices growing louder as I approached the main meeting room. When I opened the door I gasped. There was barely room to walk, the floor was filled with people sitting and kneeling. There were monks in shaved heads and red robes. Behind them I saw people dressed in fashionable suits and shirts, looking as though they had traveled from Moscow and perhaps the West. A few heads turned toward me as I walked into the room, keeping my head bowed.

The long room seemed to explode with color. The pillars that supported the ceiling were painted in bright stripes of yellow, green, red. Some pillars depicted fantastical illustrations of fish and clouds. Ceremonial drums in green and red were supported by wooden stands adorned with cloth of deep blue with embroidered designs. At the end of the room was a great golden Buddha, looking into infinity with eternal grace and calm.

The teapot clattered on the tray with my body's shaking. I looked up and saw a flash of yellow monk's robes—a young monk sat close to the Dalai Lama, handsome, his eyes sparkling. He was about eighteen. He saw me and smiled.

I looked upon the face of the Dalai Lama. Gentleness, power, humor, understanding. He stopped speaking for a moment to allow me to place the tray next to him. He gave me a brief nod of thanks before resuming his discussion. I couldn't understand the language he spoke.

In the kitchen Dusya was chopping vegetables for lunch. A huge pot of rice boiled on the stove, sending steam into the air.

Look at your face, she said. You're practically giving off light. He has the same effect on everyone.

I didn't know what to do, I said. I just gave it to him.

That's fine, Dusya said. We're here to feed him and take care of him. Keep your head bowed, be polite. It's the monks who have to behave in a special way. They're not allowed to stand up in front of him and they have to speak in a ceremonial manner.

Can he speak Russian? I asked. Or Buryat?

Dusya shook her head. He speaks English a lot, she said. It's basically the international language. I don't understand a word of it.

Nor did I. Again the glacier in the depths of my soul shifted. Links were joining in an invisible chain. I would learn the languages, see the places that the Soviets had refused to allow me to dream about. The world would shrink for me.

I served the Dalai Lama and his monks their lunch and dinner. When my face grew familiar to him, His Holiness brightened to see me. I sensed him as a phenomenal spirit housed in an ordinary man's body. He gestured and spoke to me as I gave him his bowl of rice, but I had to shrug to indicate that I couldn't understand him.

I cleared away the plates when they were done eating. The young monk I had seen before watched me with a radiant smile. He pointed at himself and said, Lobsang.

Irina, I said softly, stacking the dishes.

Lobsang always sat close to the Dalai Lama, as though they had a special bond. I captured his face in my mind. He looked like a beautiful sculpture of a living Buddha with perfect features. His ears traced delicate curves, his cheeks sloped down to a gentle mouth. Our eyes met whenever I entered the room.

I think they need more tea, I said to Dusya in the kitchen. I stopped scrubbing the dishes and put water on to boil.

They just finished a pot, Dusya said. Why would they want another one so soon?

No, I'm sure they do, I said.

Dusya shrugged and left to make sure the monks' quarters were clean. I watched the water begin to simmer, wishing I could make it boil faster. Because as soon as it was ready I would get to see Lobsang again.

I leaned back against the wall. What was I thinking? He was a monk at the right hand of the Dalai Lama. He could never love me. But I recalled the look in his eyes when I brushed against him while filling his water glass. His eyes had been attentive upon me, curious.

I was in love with him. I imagined myself exploring the exquisite lines of his face with my fingertips, kissing his flawless forehead. I conjured the conversation we might have if we could find a common language.

The water was boiling. I poured it into the teapot and smelled the steeping leaves. My breath came shallow and fast. I couldn't control my feelings.

In the evening the sky was clear and dark; the stars emerged and blinked down upon the hills. I came inside and checked my work. The dishes had been dried and put away. The pots had been scoured and hung from their hooks. The trash had been bagged and set outside in steel cans. Dusya remained outside, smoking a cigarette and sipping a cup of tea.

I walked through the hostel to make sure all the dishes had been collected. I found two teacups in a side room and put them on my tray. The central meeting room was empty. I collected a few cups and saucers and straightened the tablecloth where the Dalai Lama usually dined.

A hand brushed my shoulder. I turned around, prepared to take an order for a late snack. It was Lobsang, holding a book in his hand.

I put down the tray. A second before I had felt placid and tired; now I was electric with eagerness and worry. I looked away, unable to meet his gaze. He began to speak in his clear, calm voice. I fought against my desire to touch him, to make him understand the power of my feeling for him.

He motioned for me to sit down at the table then joined me. We were alone in the room, and I suddenly feared that our being together was wrong. I worried that Lobsang would get into trouble, that I would be the cause of unpleasantness in his life. The thought was unbearable.

Lobsang held up his book so I could see the title. It was a Russian-English dictionary. He flipped through the pages, looking for something. His mouth pursed in concentration. I could smell the light aroma of his body as he shifted closer to me.

He motioned toward the dirty dishes on my tray. *Spasebo,* he said. I understood that he was thanking me for serving him and the Dalai Lama.

Preyatyel, he said, struggling with the word. Friend. He pointed at himself, then at me.

I laughed, clasping my shaking hands together. In his voice was a sweet innocence that I had thought only children possessed.

Lobsang searched through the book for words, chewing on

his lip. I couldn't understand the next word he said; he shook his head in frustration and tried to find another. Finally he put the book down and started speaking to me in English, as though if he tried hard enough we might have a conversation in that language.

I'm sorry, I said. I don't understand. Can you speak any Russian?

He kept talking, the words nonsense sounds to me. We laughed at each other and clasped hands. A current of life passed from him into me. I felt my head begin to drift as though it were floating.

Ya Irina, I said. I am Irina.

Dusya called out to me from the kitchen. Lobsang looked up at the sound of her voice and smiled.

I have to go, I said. I wish we could talk. I would like to tell you—

I stopped speaking and grasped his hand again. I'll see you later, Lobsang, I said.

At sunrise the Dalai Lama sipped tea and ate biscuits. No meetings were scheduled until later in the day, though he showed no signs of fatigue after speaking with hundreds of people the day before. He behaved as though the world amused him, and as though he loved the world very much. He listened attentively to his monks' deep voices, answering them with just a few words. His slight smile never left his face.

I brought a pitcher of water to the table. Lobsang grinned at me. I wondered what he had felt the night before. I had gone to sleep nearly crying with love for him.

The Dalai Lama stood up from his chair as I approached. I worried that I had offended him somehow. The monks bowed to him constantly, and the space around him was always perfectly arranged. I knew none of their ceremonies or rituals, so I easily could have upset him.

I put the pitcher in front of him and waited. I could tell he had some business with me, because his eyes met mine and he began to speak to me. I was relieved to see that he seemed relaxed and happy.

Is there something else you need? I asked him.

He beckoned me closer; when I stood next to him he reached up and put his hand on the top of my head. I felt warmth emanate from his fingertips. I was filled with a sensation of complete serenity and peace. Life will go on. Life will be good. The Dalai Lama removed his hand and looked into my eyes. They were twin pools receding into the infinity of existence.

That night I looked again into the stars. The Dalai Lama was leaving in the morning. Lobsang would go as well, and I would never see him again. I shivered, not from the cool air but from the nameless emotion that consumed me.

I had grown up understanding shamanism and Buddhism, incorporating each into the truth of my world. The atoms in my body resonated with knowledge. God was not an omnipotent being living in the clouds. God was the universe, everlasting and ever-present. The parts of which I was made also constituted the sun and the earth. I worshipped the air, the animals, beauty and mystery.

My knowledge was so limited. I wondered how many other lives I had led, how much I would learn in this one. I was at the beginning of the process, while the Dalai Lama had come so far. Still, he accepted me. He allowed me to feel his radiance. He laughed with me. Buddhism taught that it was acceptable to worship other gods, to join other religions. Each action was a step toward enlightenment. Each moment in the universe connected to the next, the infinity of reality always widening.

Dusya found me in the grass behind the kitchen. She sat down next to me.

What are you thinking about? she asked. Why are you sitting out here by yourself?

I was thinking about my life, I told her. I was wondering where it would take me.

Dusya was silent for a moment. You're a special girl, she said. I think you'll travel far someday.

I want to, I admitted.

It was a long day, she said. I'm tired. Come inside. His Holiness might never be here again. Let's see if he wants anything.

From one year to the next it felt as though our entire world was collapsing. In Moscow I had seen workers striking on television. Housing shortages were critical throughout the USSR. Prices in Ulan Ude were rising. We reused our tea bags until they lost all flavor because a new box cost far too much.

The summer heat had once brought life and energy. Now it seemed oppressive. Trips to the market turned tortuous. Could we afford a loaf of bread? Would we be able to afford anything a month from now?

I sat on the sofa in our apartment with a lunch of bread and berry jam that my grandmother had made in the village. My mother sat at the table sewing a pair of pants. My father was at the theater rehearsing his orchestra.

I turned on the television to a news program. I don't want to watch that, my mother said.

I don't think there's anything else on, I told her.

She looked up from her work. Wait, what's that? she asked me. Turn up the sound.

Mikhail Sergeivich remains in his *dacha,* the announcer said. It is not clear when he will return. The Communist Party has announced that he is ill and unable to continue his role as general secretary.

What does that mean? I asked. How can Gorbachev be sick? I saw him on TV last week and he looked fine.

My mother put down her sewing. I remembered when Brezhnev died. Our apartment had been filled with the sound of sobbing. People wept in the street, asking, What will happen to us now? What will we do?

This was different. Gorbachev had spoken of reforming the system, of admitting the mistakes of communism so that we could move onward to the glorious future we had been taught about in school. He had spoken to the people as though they were adults, leaving behind the paternal edicts of Brezhnev and his aged successors.

On television they showed tanks rolling into Moscow. My father came home from rehearsal early, shaking his head.

It's happening, he said, as though voicing a fear he hadn't dared speak about before.

Things won't change that much, my mother said.

The television's glow danced on the lenses of his glasses. That's exactly what I mean, he said. Nothing will ever change.

The tanks occupied the city. The young soldiers waited for their orders. Gorbachev, we would learn later, was held under armed guard at his *dacha*, unable to act. His wife, Raisa, became ill with fear.

The people filled the streets of Moscow, knowing well that they could be shot dead. They challenged the prevailing order in a fashion that they had only recently considered possible. Babushkas stuffed flowers into the barrels of soldiers' guns. Men and women crowded around the tanks. You cannot shoot us, they said. We are your brothers and sisters.

Boris Yeltsin had just been elected president of Russia. He leapt on top of one of the tanks, demanding that the soldiers inside come out and look into his eyes. I watched him and heard the cadences of his commoner's voice. My family and I huddled together, fearing what the autumn would bring.

The coup collapsed. Gorbachev returned to Moscow but seemed a diminished man. Yeltsin stood at his side, openly berating him for his mistakes. It was as though the world felt as I did. Something momentous was about to happen. Life outside my window went on as before, the season passing into autumn.

I visited the village and heard from old friends that Alexsandr was still living there. We had exchanged letters for months after we saw each other last—romantic declarations of love and passion—but the letters had stopped coming until recently we had almost completely lost contact. As soon as I reached the village I sent word that I would like to see him, unsure how he would react but still feeling a warm ember of love for him within me.

He sent word that he would like to see me. I walked along lanes that I had known my entire life, remembering all that I had ever been. When I saw him approaching I tensed for a moment until I saw his familiar smile. We clasped hands and said an awkward hello.

We walked together in the twilight along the road. We looked straight ahead as we walked, but I glanced at him out of the corner of my eye as I listened to our shoes scrape the rough surface at our feet. He looked older, less sure of himself somehow, but in the curve of his face I still saw the features of my first love. Soon we sat together in a small clearing near the place where we had first kissed.

It sounds like you're doing many exciting things, he said to me in a quiet voice. His eyes seemed captivated by the lengthening shadows of the evening.

I didn't say anything at first. I could feel him breathing next to me, his chest rising and falling.

I have to go into the army, he said, with his tone answering a question that I hadn't asked.

Something in his voice sent a little burst of pain exploding through my heart. He sounded frightened of the life that lay ahead of him.

It's only a couple of years, I said.

He turned and looked into my eyes. I remembered the first time we met, in the sunshine of summer. The last time I had seen him, in the chill of autumn.

I reached out and touched his hand.

You're right, he said. When I come back I'll live here. Just like now.

He leaned forward and lightly kissed my cheek. I circled his neck with my hand and pulled him closer, feeling his heart against mine.

I could hear the birds speaking to each other—their last words of the long day before they went to sleep—as we slipped down to the soft grass. His hand moved over me lightly and I felt his touch like electricity. Our lips met and I closed my eyes. We made love gently in the quiet of the night, sharing the passion of a first love that would never repeat itself. I felt my life change in a gentle passage from one stage to the next, held his hand and whispered into his ear. My first love, I thought in that moment. It had been beautiful.

I never saw Alexsandr again. When he returned from the army he married a village girl and had two children very quickly. My fate took me across the world while his kept him rooted to the place where he was born. Many times my thoughts return to him, to his soft voice and boyish features. He became a part of the cosmos of my past, unchanging like a star in the sky.

The Baltic nations declared their independence. News filtered into Siberia on television as the winter snows piled high on the sidewalks. I sensed the anxiety in everyone around me.

The future was uncertain for the first time. The Soviet State that had both dominated our lives and guaranteed our protection had begun to totter. Gorbachev resigned on Christmas. The Soviet Union no longer existed. Siberia was now simply part of Russia. Russia was part of *Sodruzhestvo Nezavisimykh Gosudarstv,* the Commonwealth of Independent States.

The weak winter sun rose the next morning. The shops opened. Citizens went to work. I listened to a clattering inside the wall; our building's pipes had frozen and the superintendent was trying to thaw them. The world was just as it had been the day before.

What does it mean? I asked my father. What is this commonwealth?

He shrugged. Who knows? he replied. Probably it means nothing. At least there has been no violence, no war.

The Soviet Union left the stage without a final soliloquy and without exacting revenge on those who had brought it down. It passed in the night without a whisper, so quietly that for a time no one noticed its passing.

The communists had taught us that the state and the people were locked together in an eternal mutual obligation. During the day many of us pretended to believe this, while under cover of night we dreamed of another life. Now it had come to pass, yet our powers of observation had atrophied so much that we barely recognized it. Soon we would learn that the old rules no longer applied. The State that had promised eternal vigilance over our lives would soon take away all guarantees.

I was too young to understand this, or even to care. The death of the Soviet State meant freedom—if not complete liberty, then at least some control over my life. I pictured the crowded boulevards of Moscow in the afternoon, the sound of music on the streets and sophisticated voices. I had to return.

At night I slept on Ilyana's sofa. We had worked together on the movie, and now we talked about the rumors. Gorky Studios was in financial trouble. The political chaos had left it in limbo. *The Adventures of Hadja Nasredin* might never be released.

During the day I walked through Moscow trying to absorb its energy. As the world changed around me I felt that transformation mirrored within myself. As I became a woman, I felt my soul expand, the borders of my reach extending beyond the known limits of the world.

I sat on the grass in the park watching people walking past. Men in business suits. Women in stylish jackets and skirts. They smoked, hurried, talked rapidly. I closed my eyes and turned my face toward the sun.

When I opened them I saw a woman sitting on a nearby bench smoking a long cigarette. She was beautiful, with flowing blond hair and regal features. She wore a very short leopard-skin skirt and boots that went nearly to her knees. Her clothes were definitely not Russian. Hoping she didn't notice, I watched her. She puffed on the cigarette and held it lightly between two fingers. She stuck her chin in the air as though defying anyone to speak to her.

She looked over at me. I glanced away, pretending to observe the ducks floating in the pond. When I looked back, she was still staring at me. She got up from the bench, dusted off the seat of her skirt, and began walking toward me.

I rose up and sat stiffly, prepared to apologize for staring at her. She walked fast and moved around people as though they weren't there. She both frightened and fascinated me.

She sat down on the grass next to me, arranging her skirt. I sat as well. Hello, she said in a haughty voice. I saw you looking at me.

I'm sorry, I replied. I didn't mean to stare.

She pulled out another cigarette and lit it, her fingers long and nearly translucent white. It was the longest cigarette I had ever seen, nothing like the hand-rolled ones my brothers smoked. She blew out a cloud of smoke and watched it dissipate in the air.

It's all right, I was looking at you, too, she said. I came over to tell you that you look okay.

I didn't know what she meant, so I said nothing. She flicked her head to shift her hair out of her eyes. I was instantly drawn to her because she was so different from anyone I'd ever known. I couldn't tell whether she loved me or hated me.

I'm a model, you know, she announced. So I always check people out. You have a different sort of look.

I'm from Siberia, I said. I modeled there before, in a fashion house where I worked.

A fashion house in Siberia? she asked with a smirk. What did you model, worker's trousers and fur hats?

No, real clothes, I said, feeling embarrassed, though I couldn't have said why.

She looked me up and down. You have a nice body, she said. But I don't know. You don't have any breasts.

I looked down, trying to see myself as she did.

My name is Nadia, she said. Now, you see my body? In fashion they like girls like me. You know, girls who are really built.

Nadia pulled back her shoulders. Her breasts strained against the thin cotton of her blouse. Men walking by on the park path slowed their pace to look at her as they passed.

Here, you want a cigarette? she asked. They're the real thing. From Europe. And tell me your name.

I introduced myself and took a cigarette from her. I didn't smoke, but she held out the pack to me as though I had no choice. She lit it for me and I began to cough. Nadia smiled and looked me over again, as though I were an object rather than a person.

I've done seven shows here in Moscow, she said. For four different designers. Evening wear, casual, swimsuits. It pays very well. I think soon I'll have enough money to go to Paris.

Paris? I repeated. She might as well have said she was buying a ticket on a rocket blasting into outer space.

Irina, put that out if you're not going to smoke it, she said, pointing at my cigarette. Those things aren't cheap.

I'm sorry, I said.

Stop apologizing all the time, Nadia said. Look, you're a pretty girl. I know a young designer who's always looking for models. I could introduce you to her if you like.

Nadia looked away, distracted. I touched her arm. Please, I said. I would like that very much.

She wrote down a phone number on a scrap from a magazine. Her name is Olga, Nadia said. Tell her I gave you the number.

Nadia stood up and fussed with her clothes. She took a deep breath as though she was suddenly bored and wanted to be somewhere else.

Thank you so much, I said, rising to take her hand.

Nadia shrugged. Don't mention it. If you came here all the way from Siberia, you need all the help you can get.

Olga's fashion house operated out of a theater. Backstage smelled of makeup and smoke, just like at home. I found her looking through fabric samples at a work bench.

You're Nadia's friend? she asked. She was only five years older than me. She wore a short skirt in green and blue stripes. The cloth was so exquisite I had to resist the urge to reach out and touch it. There were silks and shiny synthetics, cotton weaves in delicate color combinations. They were like nothing manufactured in Russia. I wished I had a camera so I could send a photograph to Larissa.

Where did you get all these fabrics? I asked.

My husband is a musician. He travels outside the country and buys them for me.

I looked around at some of Olga's designs on mannequins and hanging from racks. Her clothes were sophisticated, very Western to my eyes.

So you've modeled in Siberia? she said. I didn't know they have fashion houses there.

I told Olga about Larissa and her designs, and Olga seemed impressed that Larissa had trained in design in St. Petersburg.

It's different here, I'm sure, Olga said. We work here in the theater. We have a choreographer, and you're expected to dance. Have you ever performed before?

I explained that our shows in Siberia had also incorporated dance and theater. At every turn Olga expected my experience to be somehow lesser; I realized how much people in the great cities looked down on the provinces. I craved her acceptance as a person. I needed her approval as a professional. If I didn't find work, I would have to return to Ulan Ude. I had come this far and didn't want to stop.

Give me a chance, I said. I know I can do a good job for you.

She examined my features. You look different from anyone I've ever seen, she said. And you're tall—maybe this will work.

Olga took my measurements and fitted me for a dress. I walked around the workroom, watching the seamstresses stitching fabric. The atmosphere was very professional and efficient. I felt little of the warmth that Larissa had spread among her workers and models, but it didn't matter. When I returned to Ilyana's apartment that night she told me she was moving in two weeks. There wouldn't be room for me in her new place. I had to earn money, and quickly.

After rehearsing with Olga's models they took me to a cafe where they drank wine and told stories. Nadia arrived with a broad-chested boyfriend who played on a local soccer team. I met painters, actors, singers. Now that the government no longer pressed its firm hand down on personal expression, creative people were free to talk and laugh without fear of the KGB. I was quiet most of the time, intimidated by these older women and men and their experience, which seemed so much greater than mine.

I told Nadia that soon I would have no place to stay. She wrinkled her nose. Well, don't look at me, she said. My place is too small.

She and her boyfriend laughed. Hey, come on, I'm joking, she said. Let me ask around. Somebody must have a couch you can sleep on.

The next day she took me aside during a break in rehearsal. I found you someone to stay with, she said. But you have to be cool. They said it was all right as long as you stay out of the way.

That's fine, I said. I won't bother anyone.

I told her you were cool, so don't blow it. You're going to be staying with Marya Rostova.

The singer? I asked.

Nadia nodded slightly, as though afraid already that I didn't measure up to her standards of detachment. Marya Rostova was a singer known throughout Russia; I had seen her many times on television, both in Moscow and Ulan Ude. I could tell from Nadia's attitude that I wasn't supposed to get excited.

Treat her like you would anyone else, Nadia said. You're in Moscow now. You're going to meet a lot of different people. Don't make them think you're just a hick from Siberia.

I moved my things—a suitcase and a bag of clothes—into Marya Rostova's apartment. She was away on tour, I was told by a bearded man who answered the door. He led me into the living room, where a huge window looked out on the city. On the walls were posters of Paris and Madrid. The furniture was leather, the tables fine wood. The room was nearly as big as our entire apartment in Ulan Ude.

My name is Anatoly, the man said. There are usually a couple of people staying here, but we have room for you in the kitchen.

He flipped on the kitchen light. I saw a huge refrigerator and a modern-looking stove. The room was long, and there was a small cot set up behind a dining table and chairs.

I hope it's good enough, he said. We won't charge you any money to stay with us. If you're a friend of Nadia's, that's good enough for us.

You're a friend of Marya Rostova's? I asked.

He laughed. Not really, he said. But I'm her husband.

Oh, excuse me.

He laughed again. Don't worry about it, he said. Just stay out of Marya's way when she comes back from tour and everything will be fine. This can be a rough city, you know. You should be glad to have a safe place to stay.

That night I went to bed early. I found a small blanket and used my coat as a pillow. I turned off the lights and closed my eyes. In a few days I would receive my first payment from Olga, after my first show. It would be enough money to buy food and subway fare. I felt as though my life was balanced on a wire in a stiff wind. If I stopped struggling for an instant I would be overtaken.

I drifted close to sleep. Anatoly had left without telling me where he had gone. He had said he would wake me in the morning when it was time for his breakfast.

The front door opened and I heard several men's voices, talking loudly and laughing. They sounded drunk. I pulled the blanket over my ears. It didn't help. The lights came on in the kitchen, searing my eyes.

Oh, sorry, a tall man in blue jeans said. I didn't know there was anyone in here. Let me get something to drink and I'll leave.

Hey, Yasha, I forgot to tell you someone's staying in there, Anatoly yelled out from the living room.

I heard the television come on. Then someone put on a rock

record, so loud that I could feel the stereo's vibrations. Yasha rattled around in the kitchen cupboards until he found a glass, then turned off the light again.

I lay in the dark for hours, waiting for the party to end. The men's voices grew louder as they drank, and the music played until the middle of the night. I curled up into a ball with tissue paper in my ears and tried to sleep. In the morning my eyes in the mirror were red with fatigue. During breaks in rehearsal I lay down on the floor, asking the models to wake me when we were ready to start working again.

At the end of the week Anatoly told me there was going to be a party that night. I cringed. Every night there had been drinking and music, and people falling asleep in the living room at five in the morning. I wondered what a real party would be like for these people.

My friend Boris is leaving Russia on Saturday, Anatoly said. We're going to make sure he remembers us before he goes to Paris.

Again, Paris. How much does it cost to live there? I asked.

Plenty, Anatoly said. More than you can imagine.

He said this kindly, with a little smile and a pat on my shoulder. That day I had performed in my first Moscow fashion show, modeling Olga's designs for her fall collection. The fine fabrics had moved easily with my body, and I had surprised the other models with how quickly I had learned the choreographer's dance routines. I had little money, and only promises of more work in the future, but I felt as though the world would open to me if I pushed hard enough.

So why don't you stay up tonight? Anatoly said. It's going to be fun. Have a few drinks, let yourself relax.

Thanks, but no, I said. I just want to sleep.

I was exhausted and I didn't like to drink. I envisioned the place full of people and music and I knew I wouldn't be comfortable. I trusted Anatoly, but I wasn't sure about his friends. Some of them stared openly at my body, which made me uncomfortable.

Anatoly looked disappointed. Well, there are going to be people in the kitchen, he said. So you can't sleep there. Look, you can sleep in my bed with the door closed. That way the noise won't bother you so much. When everybody's gone I'll wake you up and you can move back to the kitchen.

I considered Anatoly my friend, even though I had known him a short time and he was much older than me. I agreed to his plan. It would be impossible to sleep in the kitchen that night, so I had no choice.

The bedroom was large, with high ceilings and modern furniture. I resisted the urge to look through the closet to see what kind of clothes Marya Rostova owned. Instead I pulled the covers over my head and went to sleep early. The last sounds I heard were of Anatoly greeting people at the door. Soon came the music, as loud as ever. But the closed door protected me, and I dropped into the deepest sleep I'd enjoyed since moving there.

I woke to the sound of screaming. So now I have to tell you exactly when I come and go? a woman yelled, her voice shrill and loud.

I didn't say that, you said that, Anatoly responded. His voice was deep, full of an anger that startled me.

And I suppose you can throw a party without telling me? the woman said. With girls and drinking? No wonder you look so disappointed to see me again. You probably have big plans for tonight.

All other conversation in the room stopped. Only the music played on, a song of happiness and passion that sounded out of place as a backdrop for these two bitter voices.

That's ridiculous, Anatoly said. Why don't you be quiet. You're embarrassing us in front of our friends.

You're the embarrassment, the woman said.

By now I knew who she was. Marya Rostova kicked open the bedroom door with such force that it smashed into the wall. I saw her silhouetted by light coming from the living room. She was tall and looked very strong. She was wearing big boots that laced up to her knees, with a tight skirt and blouse that accentuated the contours of her body. I sat up in bed and she noticed me for the first time. For a fleeting second I registered how beautiful she was.

What is this? she yelled at me.

I pushed myself against the headboard, feeling the pillows against my back. Nothing, I said. I'm just sleeping.

Anatoly appeared in the doorway. This is a friend of Olga's, he said. I'm letting her sleep here because she has nowhere else to go.

Marya took a step toward me. So she sleeps in my bed? she yelled.

I saw faces crowd around the open doorway. I pushed harder against the wall, frightened that she was going to hurt me.

I sleep in the kitchen, I said. I'm sleeping here for a few hours because of the noise. It's nothing more.

You little whore. You little bitch. How dare you come in here and seduce my husband?

Anatoly started to reach for his wife, but she wheeled around and thrust her finger in his face. Don't touch me, she warned.

I'll leave, I started to say.

Marya grabbed the blankets and threw them off the bed. Get out of here! she screamed. Get out of here before I kill you.

I walked through a gauntlet of strangers until I reached the kitchen, where my suitcase was wedged into the corner. I rubbed my eyes and tried to wake up. I was so tired that I saw wavy lines around the overhead light. I heard screaming and smashing from the bedroom, then glass breaking.

People in the kitchen started to talk, their voices slurred from drink. I can't believe it, one of them said. I've never seen them fight like this.

Anatoly burst into the kitchen, rubbing his beard and apologizing. I opened my suitcase and found a sweater and shoes.

Thank you very much for letting me stay here, I said. I tried to hold back my tears, but I felt my cheeks growing hot. There was nowhere for me to go, but I knew I had to leave.

She's temperamental, Anatoly said. She'll calm down, but for now I think you'd better go. It's not safe for you.

I found my roll of money and peeled off a few bills. Here, I said, handing them to Anatoly. This is for my rent.

He stuffed the money distractedly in the pocket of his jeans. I knew his mind was in the next room, with his wife who seemed to hate him.

This isn't right, I said, my voice breaking.

There were three men and two women in the room. They listened with little smiles on their faces as though we were an amusing soap opera. I could tell that, like her, they probably didn't believe me, either.

I'm going, I said, and pushed toward the door. I looked at the clock and saw that it was two in the morning. I wished someone would make me stop, but no one did, and nightmare images filled my mind. Under the Soviets Moscow had been quiet and mostly free of crime. Now that communism was dead the police had lost power. Murders were common. I didn't think I could survive a night on the streets.

I found a phone and called Olga. She answered the phone in a sleepy voice and listened to what had happened.

What can I do? she complained. I have no room for you.

I can't reach Nadia, I said. You're the only person I know to call. Tell me what to do. I'm afraid.

Olga sighed. You poor little girl, she said. Come over. You know where I live. We'll figure out what to do in the morning. I'll call some girls. Someone will have a room or a sofa for you.

I stood on the street and waited for a car to come. Taxis were not to be found. To get a ride I had to flag down a driver and strike a deal. I waved at a passing Lada, and the young man behind the wheel pulled over.

Where do you want to go? he asked. His hands were dirty with grease.

I told him Olga's address. He shook his head. That's a long way, he said. Two hundred rubles.

It was almost all my money, but I had no choice. We pulled out into the light late-night traffic. I kept my suitcase and bag of clothes clutched tight to my chest. Inside them was everything I owned.

I stepped into the morning light that seeped through the kitchen windows. The table was set for breakfast, with rolls and jam and tea. Because it was the weekend, I could take my time eating instead of rushing to rehearsals and fittings. I planned to spend the day in the park, reading and relaxing. I felt safety and warmth all around me.

Good morning, Irina, Katerina said.

Hello, Oleg said, looking up from his newspaper. Come, have something to eat.

I sat down at the cramped table. Husband and wife shifted

aside to make room for me. They had been married for twenty years, and their movements were synchronized and harmonious. I poured a cup of tea and let the steam warm my face.

Tatyana came into the kitchen rubbing her head. Why did you let me sleep so late? she complained. Irina, I told you I wanted to get up early.

You were sleeping so well, I said.

Don't listen to my daughter, Katerina said. If you'd have tried to wake her up, she probably would have boxed your ears.

Olga had called Tatyana the morning after I left Marya Rostova's apartment. Tatyana was a dancer and a model for Olga, and her parents owned an apartment with a small spare room. I had stayed with them more than four months, and without complaint they had taken me in as a daughter. They gave me food, old clothes, even small presents of sweets, never asking for money. I felt as though they had saved my life.

What are you doing today? Tatyana asked me, suddenly coming to life. She grabbed a biscuit and smeared it with jam.

I'm going to read outdoors. Maybe I'll do nothing, I said.

No, you're not. You're coming with me to the music center. There's a new band who wants to audition. I want your opinion.

I couldn't say no. Tatyana was slim and lithe, with red wavy hair and an oval face. She had accepted me completely from the moment we met, and in return I stayed up with her into the night, listening to her intrigues with boyfriends and other dancers. She had recruited me into her performance ensemble, which combined dancers with Moscow music groups. I had been in two performances with her, both of which had paid nearly as much as a fashion show.

All right, I said. I'll come with you.

My daughter has an interesting way of asking people to do things, Oleg commented. His smiled creased his mustache.

Irina doesn't mind, Tatyana said. She loves me.

I worked in three more fashion shows and performed with Tatyana when I could. A new dancer had joined the troupe, a girl closer to my age named Sveta. She and Tatyana started to spend time together, leaving me alone in the evenings. I burned with jealousy in my bed, wondering why this little betrayal felt so painful.

I lay in my small bed listening to the clock tick in the hallway. It was almost one in the morning, and I wondered whether Tatyana would return home before sunrise. Lately she had disappeared with Sveta one or two nights a week. When she returned, she seemed angry and didn't want to talk to anyone. I realized that I had been captivated by Tatyana, and I burned with unfamiliar jealousy.

There was a creak outside, perhaps the front door being opened quietly. I stared into the dark hall and listened. I feared Tatyana was lost to me, that we would never be as close as I would have liked. I feared what would happen to me if I had to leave.

Is that you, Tatyana? Katerina whispered in the night. I heard steps leading into the living room.

It's me, Tatyana said. Who the hell is it supposed to be?

Don't talk to me like that, Katerina said. I'm your mother. I was afraid it was a burglar, that's all.

Well, it is, Tatyana said with a bitter laugh. I'm going to steal everything and sell it on the black market.

Don't talk that way. I don't know what's wrong with you lately. Let me see your face. Have you been crying?

Leave me alone, please, Tatyana hissed. I just want to go to bed.

Her footsteps plodded slowly down the hall. Tatyana's door opened then closed again. I waited to make sure Katerina had gone to sleep before gently knocking on Tatyana's door.

Go away, she said, her voice muffled.

It's me, I said. It's Irina.

I waited. No response. A sliver of light illuminated the hall at my feet from the crack under the door. I pushed gently at the door and it opened. Tatyana lay in bed wound in a blanket. Her feet stuck out at the bottom; she was still wearing the low-cut leather boots she had bought after our last dance performance.

I thought I said to go away, she said, staring up at the ceiling.

That was very mean, the way you talked to your mother just now, I told her.

Tatyana didn't reply. I sensed the distance between us growing greater with every second that passed. I wanted to take her in my arms and kiss her face and hands. I wanted to bring her back to me.

I just want to sleep, Tatyana said. I don't feel well.

In the shadows of her desk lamp I saw her face. It was pale and sallow, and purple rings shaded her eyes. Her forehead looked damp with sweat.

What's wrong? I asked. Do you have a fever?

Just tired, she mumbled.

It wasn't the first time Tatyana had come home looking this way. I connected it back to Sveta, and again my chest burned with jealousy.

Where were you tonight?

So you're my mother now, too? Tatyana said bitterly.

I sat down on the bed next to her; she edged away. Her eyes darted away when I looked at her. I felt the bed vibrate with her shivering.

Tatyana, I feel I'm losing you as a friend, I said. I wanted to embrace her.

She pulled herself up on her elbows, seeming startled. Don't say that, we're good friends. You live in my home.

You're always angry, I continued. You keep secrets. You come home looking like this and you won't tell me why. I don't know what you're doing when you stay out all night.

I'm not doing anything bad, she said, staring at the floor. I promise you, Irina.

Tatyana, think about how you're acting. You've changed so much in the last few weeks.

You still love me, don't you? she asked. She met my eyes. Tears slid down her cheeks, and she reached out to touch my face. I took her hand in mine.

I don't understand my feelings for you, I told her. I've never felt this way toward a friend before. But of course I love you. That's why I can't stand to see what's happening.

She pressed her hand against her cheek. She felt as though a furnace raged inside her.

I took some drugs, she admitted. But nothing terrible. You have to believe me.

I had known this was the truth. Probably Katerina and Oleg did as well. It was been the unspoken secret among all of us since the first night Tatyana came home staggering slightly but not smelling of vodka.

Tatyana cried harder. You must think I'm a terrible person.

I don't, I replied. There's nothing terrible about trying new things. So now you know about drugs, and you don't have to take them anymore. Right? It's all over.

I guess so, she mumbled.

Go to sleep, I said, pushing her hair from her forehead. You'll feel better in the morning. Everything will start over then.

Stay with me, Tatyana said, grabbing my arm. Until I go to sleep. I can't stand to be alone right now.

I held her in my arms, feeling her shivers and sobs, until hours had passed. She continued to cry in her sleep, speaking in a voice I strained to understand but couldn't. I heard footsteps come down the hall and stop outside the door. After a few minutes they receded again and everything was quiet.

Tatyana lost interest in her dancing. I modeled Olga's designs and saved money. In the evenings Tatyana would come home and walk to her bedroom, speaking to no one. She would shower, eat, and leave again. Soon she was spending the majority of her nights away from her parents' house. I stopped asking her where she went. There was no use.

I called my father to tell him that I was working. In the background I heard the usual clatter and voices of dinnertime.

Irina, you should come home, my father said. Times are hard everywhere, but I hear how bad they are in Moscow. Drugs, the gangs. Your place is here.

I closed my eyes, relieved to hear the familiar sound of his voice. Soon, Father, I said. I promise I'll visit soon.

Visit? he asked. What do you mean? This is your home.

Of course, I said. I realized that now I considered Moscow my home. I hung up after listening to my father complain about the prices in Ulan Ude. It's all collapsing, he said.

I went to bed and pulled the blankets over my head. I had heard the fear and worry in my father's voice. He was concerned not just for me but for everyone, for our entire family. We had always been poor, but so had practically everyone we knew. Under communism everyone had bent the rules and done what was necessary to survive. Now it felt as though there were no longer any rules at all. The world spun in my mind like a dervish out of control.

I heard the door open, then Tatyana's voice. As usual she began arguing with her mother. Oleg's deep voice joined in, sounding angry. I put my hands over my ears, no longer able to bear it.

A few minutes later the door opened. Tatyana climbed into bed with me with a loud sigh.

Why can't they leave me alone? she said.

I didn't reply; from the sound of her voice I knew she wasn't herself. She had been a lifeline given to me by fate for just a short time. I understood that she would never be mine again.

Why are you crying? she asked.

I looked up into her face. Her cheeks were swollen and pale. Her eyes were lifeless and red. Her nose was running, and she hadn't even bothered to wipe it.

You look terrible.

Well, thank you very much. She laughed. It's cold outside. I'll warm up in a few minutes.

Did you have a good time tonight? I asked. I didn't want to condemn her for using drugs, but I could see that they held her like a fist. When I first knew her she had been full of lithe energy; now she looked dull and vacant.

It was fine, she said.

Were you with Sveta? I asked.

Yes, and a few friends, she said evasively. I have a new boyfriend, you know. His name is Mark.

Is he nice? I asked.

Sometimes, she replied, her voice suddenly far away. I don't think I'm going to see him anymore.

She leaned back against the wall and her coat opened. Underneath it she wore a shiny dress of an exquisite cut and buttons made of bone. Above her collar was a gold necklace. Her arm drooped down on the bed, and I saw her shining silver bracelet. She had never owned any of these things before. They were impossibly expensive, the sort of things we had once fantasized about owning when we talked late into the night.

Where did you get those? I whispered, keeping my voice low so her parents wouldn't hear.

Tatyana sat up, coming awake. She pulled her coat closed again, looking around as though seeking an excuse.

I bought them today, she admitted.

With what money? I demanded. We could dance for three years and never be able to afford a dress like that.

Don't look at me that way, she said. You don't understand. You work and you're good and you don't understand anything.

You're right, I said. I want to understand, but I don't.

You know how much we make from dancing, she said. It's nothing. And the same goes for your modeling. It's barely enough to survive. And what do you get from these Russian men? Nothing. They have nothing to give.

What are you saying? I asked.

Tatyana rolled over to face away from me. It's not what you think.

I believe you, I replied. I put my hand on her shoulder.

It's too hard to live, she said. I'm beautiful. I like men who admire me and treat me the way I should be treated. There's nothing wrong with it. I'm not a prostitute, I don't sell myself.

I waited before answering, trying to piece together what she had said. Foreign businessmen were coming to Moscow now, from America and Europe. I had seen girls gathered in the bars of expensive hotels, waiting to meet someone who could provide them with a better life. Some of them sold their bodies for sex, but not all. Others hoped they might meet a man who would provide for them, perhaps even take them out of Russia. It was the last hope for many women.

I rubbed the knots beneath Tatyana's neck. I understand, I said. I believe what you're saying. These things you bought are beautiful.

Tatyana turned over and pulled me to her. Her tears mixed with my own. She held me tighter until I shared the pain that wracked her.

There's nothing to work for anymore, she sobbed. Everything's foolish, there's no point. Nothing makes sense.

You just feel that way right now, I said. Things will change. Remember how much you love your dancing.

This made her cry harder. She clung to me so tightly that her fingers dug into my neck. I would have bruises in the morning.

You have to leave me, she said, almost out of breath. It's too late, nothing's going to change for me.

Stop it, I told her. Stop saying these things.

Leave me, I don't want you to suffer with me anymore, she said. I can't stand to see you hurting.

I won't leave you, I said. I love you.

Her eyes turned cold. Shut up and listen, she said in a cruel tone. You're leaving me, you're leaving this house. I can't have you around me.

Don't say that, I begged.

She got up from the bed. Her eyes were swollen from crying. I meant every word of it. I've made my decision. Tomorrow night you sleep somewhere else.

Tatyana closed the door quietly when she left. I lay alone in the darkness, wondering what would happen to me. The future that I had glimpsed through the years had disappeared again into darkness. Siberia, Moscow, all of Russia had turned into a place in which it was impossible to live. And now I had to face it on my own again.

I modeled at a private show for Olga; my payment would be in cash. A rock band was set up on stage, with a female singer with bright blond hair. The audience moved with the beat of the music and, as I stepped into the lights and crossed the stage, I felt the rhythm inside me.

The clients were the wives of men who had become wealthy since the USSR collapsed. The men drove expensive cars, bought their wives elegant clothes, and carried themselves as though they owned the world. They were the new mafia, gangsters who murdered and extorted.

The police were helpless. I had seen a police car trying to chase a criminal through the streets of Moscow. The police car had sputtered and groaned while the gangster's Mercedes sped away effortlessly. The mafia had better weapons, greater numbers, and no regard for decency. Their morals had decayed and rotted under the Soviet Union, and now that all controls had been lifted they did as they wished.

I had seen men chasing each other through the streets with guns; I had seen women robbed in the middle of the day while people watched helplessly. It was dangerous to be outside alone. The mafia had been known to stop women on the street and force them to have sex with them at gunpoint. Wherever I walked I stayed vigilant, watching everything around me. It created a pressure in my mind and heart that haunted me every day.

I crossed the Borodin Bridge over the Moskva River. I had gone back to Ulan Ude for a few months, bringing money to my family, then returned to Moscow. Life in Siberia was worse than in the capital. The ruble had collapsed. Life savings were worthless. Families sat out in the cold, selling their silverware and linen for enough money to buy bread.

I walked past the great stone arches of the bridge, severe in their beauty. After the fashion show I had eaten at a cafe with some of the other models and lost track of the time. Now the sun had set and streetlights lit my path. I was staying at a model's apartment near the edge of the city and I would have to flag down a car to take me there. I hated to do it, but as it grew later the streets would become wild.

A few cars passed; I waved at them, but they continued driving. I averted my eyes from two young men who walked past. They wore the sleek suits and walked with the swagger of the mafia. When they disappeared into the night without harassing me I exhaled loudly.

Another set of headlights appeared on the street. I squinted into the glare and waved. I swore at myself under my breath. I had stayed out too late, and people might be too frightened to stop for me at this hour.

The car's brakes emitted a grating metal sound as it slowed to the curb. I looked into the darkness inside and saw that face of a man. He had thin lips and a receding hairline. He wore a light sweater and smoked a cigarette. Perfectly normal. He opened the passenger door and I told him where I wanted to go.

I don't have a ton of money, but I can pay you enough, I told him.

All right, fine, he said. Get in.

He turned at the intersection and drove on. He steered us into a district with which I wasn't familiar. This didn't bother me; Moscow was huge, there were infinite ways to reach a specific destination.

I think maybe Gorky Street is the best route, I said.

He pursed his lips. I recognized a street of shops and realized we were headed away from my friend's apartment.

I know a better way, he said.

I watched his profile flicker with light and dark as we passed through the lights of the city. He held onto the wheel and stared straight ahead, acknowledging my presence only by blowing his cigarette smoke out the window rather than in my face. He signaled a turn and looked in the mirror to make sure the way was clear.

This is the outer ring road, I said. Are you sure this is the way?

He smiled. Of course, he said. Much faster. Don't worry, I've lived in Moscow all my life. I know all the best routes.

The highway ran along the edge of the city. Since my friend's apartment was far from the city center, it seemed possible that he was right. Since I didn't drive I couldn't be sure.

We drove into the night. Complete blackness filled the cloudy sky, and we passed fewer and fewer cars on the highway. I didn't own a watch, but I was certain we should have reached my destination by then. The road passed through a remote part of Moscow with a name I didn't recognize.

I gripped the seat beneath me. The driver still wouldn't look at me. I noticed that he was breathing heavily, the only sound in the charged air of the car. As he stared ahead he looked completely anonymous. Nothing about him was out of place, from his thinning hair to his worn canvas shoes.

He put his foot on the brake and slowed the car, looking into the mirror to see if anything was behind us. I remained motionless. The road ahead stretched into a void. There was no one around; to the side of the road were trees and fences.

The man turned to look at me. His expression was vacant save for a small sneer that curled his lips. He seemed to look past my face at a point somewhere behind me.

Now you're going to learn what pleasure is, he said. This will be something you remember for the rest of your life.

His voice changed from a calm, normal tone to a hard snarl. His breath came in short spurts. I turned around and grabbed the door handle, ready to run into the night. The cold metal lever turned uselessly in my hand, broken.

I turned to face him again. Waves of fear echoed through my head.

Tonight you will understand how much I hate you, he said. And how much I hate all women. You should thank me for teaching you. I will give you wisdom you could never get in any school.

He spoke slowly, almost melodically. He enunciated his words as though he was educated. Although his actions were insane, he seemed like a man in control of himself. I wondered whether this was the first time he had done this and guessed that it wasn't, for as he spoke it sounded as though he was reciting a script.

I felt a hot surge of panic, then willed it away. There was no way out of the car. He was stronger than me. If I screamed or fought, I knew he would kill me.

Maybe you're right, I said, sounding to my own ears as though nothing unusual was happening.

He blinked. Right about what? he asked.

Maybe you're right to hate women, I said. Maybe I hate them, too. Why do you feel this way?

He seemed shocked by the sound of my voice. Why do you ask me this? There isn't time to speak.

I'm curious, I said. I want to understand.

The road remained dark and silent. He had turned off the engine, and I could see his face only in deep shadow.

I've been married, he said. Have you?

No, I admitted.

He nodded, agreeing with himself in his own mind. I have a boy, he told me. He's ten years old, and he's the only person I love in this horrible, disgusting world. I want to kill everyone else, especially the stinking women.

As he spoke I felt that he had already deviated from his plan. His eyes saw me now as an individual.

I understand everything, I said. Women are always out to hurt you. They never do what's right. I agree with you—you can't trust them.

A tiny glimmer appeared in his expression. He looked at me with open eyes, as though I also knew the truth that burned in his soul. Perhaps he had finally met someone like himself.

I guessed he was about thirty-five years old. The armpits of his shirt were soaked through with sweat.

Why do you love your son so much? I asked.

Because he's pure, the man replied. Because he would never do anything to hurt me.

Those are good reasons to love him, I agreed. The night had turned cold, and our breath fogged the inside of the windshield.

My bitch of an ex-wife would kill me if she got the chance, he said. His voice was choked with emotion, as though he were confiding in a friend.

But your son is half hers, I said. And you love him. So she isn't completely evil.

He gestured weakly and turned away from me. I listened to his heavy, jagged breathing. I sensed his body stiffen. He was regaining his resolve.

What does your son look like? I asked.

He turned around and thrust his face into mine. Shut up! he screamed. Why the hell do you want to know? I don't want to talk about it, I don't want to remember it. I want to finish what I came here to do.

He sounded frustrated. I had nudged his mind off its track, and he fought with himself to regain his cold killer's aggression. I pressed against the car door with my back. The metal didn't yield.

What have you done to me? he yelled. I came here for my pleasure, and now you've ruined it.

His nostrils flared with anger. He slapped the steering wheel, then raised his hand to hit me. Instead he released a scream of pure rage and turned the key to start the engine.

I will never forgive you for this, he said, almost under his breath.

I didn't understand what he meant.

He pulled out onto the road and drove even faster than before. A truck came around a curve in the opposite direction, but it was gone before I could try to attract its driver's attention. I pressed on the broken door, wondering what would happen to me if I leapt from the car at this speed.

We drove another thirty minutes on the deserted highway. A freezing drizzle pelted the windows. I remained silent with my hands on my lap. When I glanced over at the driver, I saw him gripping the wheel and staring at the road. His lips moved silently. He was lost in the circles of his own thoughts, and I instinctively knew that if I spoke to him I might provoke another rage.

He drove on, expressionless. We were in the outskirts of Moscow, a place I had never seen before. I could stand no more. I had to say something.

You know, I like you, I said. You have a very original and unique personality, which is what I appreciate in people.

He said nothing.

You're a brave man with strong beliefs. I've never met anyone like you.

He slowed the car a little and his grip seemed to relax. He looked over at me, nodding his head slightly.

I think we should get to know each other better, I continued. But you can't come to my place, because my parents are home tonight.

I pictured my living room in Siberia, where my parents might be watching television and sipping tea. My father composing, my mother sewing.

So let's go to your place. But I need to call my mother and father to tell them I'm coming home later. They become very worried sometimes.

The driver's head rocked back and forth. I wasn't sure if he had even heard me. I was quiet again, unable to think of anything else to say.

All right, I thought I heard him say, though his voice was almost too quiet for me to hear.

He slowed the car by a row of warehouses; at the end of the block I saw buildings which were lit from inside.

Get out, he said. He stopped the car near a telephone box.

I could tell nothing from the tone of his voice. I didn't know whether he believed what I had said, or whether he simply wanted to be done with me. I had seen his mood change drastically from one second to the next, and I didn't want to provoke him. But the only way I could leave the car was if he opened my door from the outside.

Get out, he repeated, more insistent.

I tried to ask him to let me out, but my fear choked off the words in my throat. I grabbed the useless handle and turned it. I pressed against the door, hoping that he would see my struggles and understand what he needed to do.

He scowled as if disappointed, then opened his door and got out. In the mirror I saw his body pass around the back of the car. I looked at his empty seat and wondered whether there was time for me to take the wheel and escape. It was hopeless. I didn't know how to drive.

My door unlatched. He took a step back from the car and stared at me. His mouth hung open. He pressed his hands together.

I slowly got out of the car, careful not to brush against him. The rain had turned to hard pellets of snow; the air was humid and frigid. Our breath formed clouds that mixed between us.

I took a step toward the phone box and looked back. He was still watching me. I opened the door to the phone, stepped inside, and pretended to dial a local number. Through the booth's glass I could see his face inside the car, expressionless and observant.

I shook my head and pointed at the phone, as though the number I had dialed was busy. I pretended to dial again. There was no one for me to call, and I knew that the police would never arrive in time.

I could see the point of light from a cigarette inside his car. His face turned away from me, looking around to see if anyone was watching.

It was my only chance. I opened the booth and stepped out. A cold wind blew in my face; sleet struck my forehead and hung from my eyelashes.

I started to run in the direction of the lights I had seen. My feet slid on the street and I almost fell down. I thought I could hear his footsteps behind me coming closer, his hands ready to close around my neck.

But it had only been the echo of my own frantic running that I had heard. My breath burned hot and cold in my chest. I stopped. My legs were burning. Tears combined with snowy drizzle on my cheeks.

I turned around. His car was still there. He was inside it. I saw the pinpoint light of his cigarette as he started the engine and drove away. I shivered and coughed in the damp cold. I didn't understand why he had left me, what had stopped him from finishing what he started.

I was alive.

I continued to divide my time between Ulan Ude and Moscow.

In Moscow I modeled for Olga, as well as other designers, who were all trying to match the creativity and abandon of the West. Whatever money I made nearly disappeared when prices rose, and they always did. Whenever I came home I brought an envelope of money for my family. They were proud but took it. Underneath the crime and brutality of Moscow was at least some hope for the future. In Siberia, the disappearance of communism had left little in its place but poverty and despair.

You will always be a traveler, my grandmother's words rang in my mind.

But traveling where? I wondered. The Moscow of my dreams was something entirely different in reality. I walked the stage in beautiful designs, forging characters from color and suggestion. I had met artists and painters, people full of dreams and ideas. Communist dogma no longer insisted that we act and speak against the wishes of our souls.

Yet life seemed harder than ever for almost everyone. We could read any book we wanted, but they were so expensive they were passed from hand to hand until their binding disintegrated. The apartments were no longer apportioned by the Party, but rents were beyond the average worker's salary. The government promised a better future, but the people had learned to believe perhaps half of what they heard.

All my life I had waited for the future, relishing each moment in which I felt myself grow. I had friends, I was able to work. If life was hard, then I had to accept it. Each event unfolded for me with the perfection of fate's plan. The world changed, and I would change as well. It was all I could do.

I was contacted on the telephone by a woman representing a modeling competition called Photomodel. My grandmother was visiting my family from the village, and while I spoke on

the phone she looked through a few magazines I had brought
from Moscow.

We're bringing German photographers to Russia, the woman
told me. We'll have a demonstration of photographic German
techniques along with an exhibition. We also contacted a German modeling agency to help stage a beauty contest.

I understand, I said neutrally. Not all beauty contests were
legitimate. In some cases beauty was a currency like rubles to
the mafia. I also remembered my experience in China as proof
that the fashion industry was not always legitimate.

We'll pay in advance for your ticket here to Moscow and
back to Ulan Ude, she continued. And we'll provide hotel ac-
commodations for several days.

The contest sounded real, and my decision was made when
I heard that a European agency would be there. I had also
nearly run out of money in Ulan Ude, and I secretly feared
that it might be another year before I could afford a plane
ticket back to Moscow.

I hung up after writing down the specific dates. I would leave
within the week.

My grandmother looked up from a fashion magazine, open
to a page showing a beautiful blond woman posing on a rain-
spattered Moscow street.

You're leaving again, aren't you? she asked with a satisfied
smile. Always traveling. You have long legs; they will take you
far away. You have big eyes; you'll see many things.

I looked up at the clock hanging high over the crowd in the
Crimsky Val exhibition hall in Moscow. It was nearly time for
dinner, and I wondered if anyone would notice if I left the hall
a few minutes early. I had spent the day on makeshift sets
being photographed by German photographers. It had been tax-
ing to maintain the high concentration level I needed to communicate with them through the lens of their cameras. Other
models worked on all around me. Some of the photos would
later be used in fashion publications. Our payment would be
in experience rather than cash.

I had advanced as far as the finals in the modeling competition before I was eliminated. My stomach rumbled and my
eyes blurred from the constant intrusion of camera flashes.

After dinner I would sleep away the bustle and hard work. I could almost feel the sheets on the hard bed in the tiny room that had been provided for me.

Outside the main hall was a long dark corridor that led toward the exit. I stopped a moment to rub my aching feet. The photographers' instructions played in my mind like echoes from a dream: *Turn. Be angry. Face skyward. You are in love. You are a killer.*

My footsteps echoed in the silence. That day I had explored another realm of modeling. Working under the scrutinizing gaze of the camera required capturing an elusive moment. The possibilities were infinite. The camera, I had learned, saw more than the human eye. It turned fluid reality into an unchanging moment. It had the power to alter time.

Excuse me, a man's voice said from the darkness. I don't mean to bother you, but can I introduce myself?

I took a step back when he emerged from the shadows. His face was young, with kind, soulful eyes. His clothes were Western and stylish.

My name is Roland, he said. Would it be possible to get in touch with you? Can I get your phone number?

Men had called out to me before, asking my name, but I had never stopped to speak to them. This man seemed different; his manner put me at ease. I was in no danger. A sense of mournfulness seemed to lay at the edges of his spirit.

It's nice to meet you, I said, introducing myself. I'm sorry, but I don't have a phone number in Moscow.

I told him the truth; the room that Photomodel provided did not include a phone. Roland glanced away, seeming rebuffed.

I'm a photographer from America, he said, pointing at the leather bag he wore. I'm here working.

I thought they were all German, I said, gesturing back toward the hall.

I have a friend at the German agency organizing this, he said. They asked me to help, because Russians aren't great at organizing things these days.

We laughed. How do you know about Russia? I asked him. And where did you learn Russian? You speak like a native.

I was born in Latvia, Roland answered.

And now you live in America? I asked.

His face darkened. The communists made me leave, he said. This is my first time back in Russia since 1974.

Roland looked away as though seeing shadows from his past. His voice was soft, and I realized we spoke to one another as though we had been friends for years. I felt a warm rush of pleasure in his presence.

I wonder why I haven't seen you until just now, he said. The competition's taken three days.

They took us all over Moscow, I said. We were very busy.

Roland nodded. I wish I had seen you before, he said.

I looked toward the exit. Now my hot dinner and warm bed seemed less important. I knew that fate had again stepped into my life; somehow this man would be very important to me.

I can meet with you, I said. Tomorrow afternoon.

Very good, Roland said. A smile broadened his face.

I walked into the warm evening, replaying in my mind what had just happened. I envisioned a line from America to Moscow to Siberia, and pondered what hand had brought these places together for just a few days.

The next day I was late for our meeting. Rain pounded the stone sidewalks and ancient domes over St. Basil's. Clouds hung angry over the city, seeming low enough to touch. I ran the last half-mile to the exhibition hall. He might think I wasn't coming, that I didn't want to see him. I felt the collision of our fates slipping away from me.

He waited in an alcove wearing a long raincoat. At first he didn't see my approach and he gazed onto the street with quiet patience. I studied the lines of his forehead and nose. A serene yet intense intelligence radiated from him. He stepped into the rain, smiling when he saw me.

You made it, he said.

We stood close for a silent moment, each of us absorbing the other's presence. He was in love with me, and I with him. It had happened so easily that I had barely noticed it. And now both of us knew it was the truth.

I brought my camera, he said. Let's walk down the street. I want to photograph you.

We walked together through the gloom. Roland's camera clicked as he captured each moment separate from the one that had just passed. I looked into the lens and poured out my soul. He had stepped out of the darkness and brought light with him. I took his hand and we walked with our faces bare to the rain.

Roland had rented a one-room apartment on the outskirts of Moscow, about an hour by subway from the city center. From the subway we took a ten-minute bus ride to a complex of modern buildings. The yard outside was like a small park. We climbed the stairs to the fourth floor.

His room was barely larger than the sofa bed that it contained. He had a small wooden table and a stove with a few wooden utensils hanging above.

It's not much, he said, taking my jacket.

It's enough, I told him.

We kissed. The room was full with the sound of rain spattering against the roof. We held tight to each other and made love in the fading light of afternoon. In our caresses were all the fear and longing we had felt in our lives, and the untamed rush of hope that now passed between us.

We each told the stories of our lives, the other listening intently to every word. Roland was born and grew up in Latvia, which had been part of Russia in centuries past and had been made part of the Soviet Union just prior to World War II. It was a country that had been influenced in history by both Russia and Germany, but after the war it had been closed to the rest of the Soviet Union because the people there had strong memories of life in a democracy.

As Roland described Latvia to me I imagined it as a dark, Gothic place of rainy blackened streets and gargoyles looking down from tall stone buildings. It had always been different from the rest of the Soviet Union and from Russia, dating back to the influence of the crusading knights who had occupied the land centuries ago. I imagined fairy tales and dragons, and the dark forest goblins of myth.

Roland's father was originally from the Ukraine; he was a military captain who had been stationed in Latvia and had decided to stay there. His mother was from Moscow. They were part of the educated intelligentsia in Latvia; both his parents worked in Soviet industry, and they were a well-connected family. Roland's eyes shone as he spoke about summers spent on the Baltic Sea, walking over the sand dunes and swimming carefree in the waters.

When Roland was seventeen he gave a speech at school in which he criticized the Soviet system. His classmates had applauded him, but the director of his school immediately proclaimed him a counterrevolutionary. His father was interrogated by the KGB. This sort of trouble was not entirely new to Roland's family; one of his relatives had been repressed by Stalin in the thirties. Neither of his parents had been Party members, and in his house he had learned from an early age that some things could be said only in the privacy of the home.

The same week as his speech Roland was accused of trying to set the school on fire after someone smoking in the cloakroom burned a coat. The KGB interrogated him for seven hours and tried to make him implicate his parents. Luckily for him there was a summit meeting between Brezhnev and Richard Nixon the same year. Roland applied for an exit visa and, soon after, the two nations' leaders signed agreements that loosened some emigration laws. As a direct result of the summit, Roland was allowed to leave the Soviet Union for the United States.

That night we lay in the dark. Soft music bled through the wall from next door.

I only have two more days here, I said. I have to go home to Ulan Ude.

I know, Roland whispered.

We held each other tighter. We were like a raft floating peacefully while a storm raged all around.

In the morning we splashed to the bus stop, laughing like children. I had grown used to the feel of Roland's hand in mine. We rode the subway back to Moscow and went to a museum, then walked slowly through the market. I felt each moment's total clarity and infinite value. I pictured an hourglass measuring the hours until we would have to part.

The next morning Roland introduced me to Marina. She was an old friend of his who lived nearby and had arranged the room for him. She had been a teacher, but after *perestroika* she became a businesswoman. She was so successful she owned two cars.

We talked outside her apartment. After a few minutes she laughed. You're like two children in love, she said.

Roland kissed my cheek. I suppose we are, he said.

We walked through the grass knoll to a cracked parking lot. You two need some help getting around, Marina announced. You know I bought a new car. You can drive my old one for a day or so if you want.

The car was rusted and dented. Cracks lined the windshield. It was more than twenty-five years old and had been manufactured in Russia. I couldn't imagine it running for more than a mile.

Why not? Roland said. I haven't driven a car in such a long time.

He started the engine and steered us out of the park. I imagined that the car would fall apart at any second, with wheels and parts and metal flying everywhere. The engine sputtered and coughed, and a jet of black exhaust followed us down the road.

I don't think we should drive this too far. Roland laughed. I don't think I can put it back together after it falls apart.

The clouds passed over the city, leaving the sky blue and sunny. Roland steered through traffic to a Russian Orthodox monastery. We walked through the cemetery there, past the graves of Russian writers and generals from the Napoleonic wars. Just a few years before, worshippers who came to the monastery to pray had been photographed by the KGB. Even in its dying days the State had intimidated those who wanted to believe in faiths other than communism.

Inside the church we examined icons that had been crafted hundreds of years ago when the tsars had held absolute power over Russia. They seemed like golden windows into other worlds. Roland and I stood in silence, feeling the heavy presence of history. Our time together, already too short, felt like a blink in the great scope of reality. I felt tears come to my eyes and pulled at his arm for us to leave.

We stopped at a wood-shingled souvenir shop so I could buy postcards to take home. I want to buy some chicken to cook tonight, Roland said, and some good potatoes. I don't care how much it costs.

In front of us in line was an old man with a very young girl.

As Roland spoke he noticed them as well. I couldn't tell if the girl was the man's daughter or granddaughter because people in Russia aged so fast. But I could see he was a worker. He had dressed in his best clothes—a shabby black suit—to come to the monastery. His voice was thick and heavy, his movements clumsy. Though he might not have been drunk at the moment, his red eyes and veined nose were those of a heavy drinker. His back was bent from decades of labor, his face creased with lines.

But the girl shined like a beautiful doll, five or six years old and dressed in a spotless white ruffled dress. She was like a princess from a Russian folktale. I caught her eye and smiled.

The old man squeezed the girl's hand as we moved ahead in line. We're almost there, my treasure, he said.

He looked down at her with a bottomless love. She was obviously the brightest spot in his life. He smiled at her as though wishing to God that she would never know the suffering he had endured.

The line passed in front of a glass display of icons. They were new, manufactured in Russia again after years of prohibition by the Soviets.

The little girl pointed at a gold-and-red icon that shined from the case. It was perhaps a fourth as large as her entire body. It's so pretty, she said in a soft voice. I want that one.

I'll try to save some money, the old man said. Maybe in a couple of months we'll come back again and I'll buy you that icon.

I heard the pain in his voice—the little icon probably cost more than a month's worth of his salary or pension. But it was a piece of color and Russian heritage, and if she owned it, she would be able to pass on to her own children one day. But I knew he would never be able to afford it, not next month or next year. Buying clothes and food was hard enough for the common Russian; a luxury such as this icon was only for the wealthy.

I promise I'll try, the old man added softly.

Roland and I had to look away. Their turn in line came, and the old man counted out change from his pocket to buy the girl a little book of devotional prayers. After he bought it he pressed it into the girl's hands. We watched them leave, slowly walking up the path heading into the monastery.

Will this be all? the salesgirl asked, taking my postcards.

Roland and I looked at each other. Without saying anything, Roland pointed at the icon the girl had wanted from the display case. It was the most expensive thing there.

We want that, Roland said. And please hurry.

We found them inside the monastery; they had just entered and were walking between the rows of benches. We caught up with them and I touched the old man lightly on the arm. He looked up at me with a wary expression. Did I do something wrong? his eyes said to me. What could you people want with me?

Here, I said. This is for your little girl.

The icon was wrapped in paper from the store. The old man shook his head, confused, as he unwrapped it. When he revealed the icon he looked at Roland and me with bewilderment. He seemed completely thunderstruck, as though what had just happened was beyond his imagining.

See? he said to the girl. These nice people have come to give you this icon.

She looked at it for a moment, her eyes glowing, and then began to recite Scripture to us. *Blessed are the poor in spirit: for theirs is the kingdom of heaven. Blessed are they that mourn: for they shall be comforted. Blessed are the meek: for they shall inherit the earth.*

The old man stared at her as she recited, holding the icon in shaking hands. I wiped tears from my eyes at this vision of the past and future of Russia. The old man mouthed his thanks again, not wanting to speak over the girl.

She hadn't lived long enough to know the suffering he'd endured. She had been too innocent to know that things of beauty and transcendence were not to be hers. She didn't know the eternal hardship of Russian life. But as she recited the ancient words of Jesus, I thought again that there were many paths for understanding the sacred powers of the universe. And I allowed myself to hope that Russia was changing. Perhaps one day oppression would be only in Russia's history, and the spiritual strength of the young girl would be its future.

*   *   *

It was our last evening together, a fact that neither of us wanted to talk or think about. But that night I didn't fear that I would lose him; in my heart there was a certainty that somehow, no matter what happened in our lives, we would be together.

When evening fell the city seemed full of possibility and promise. Both of us were anxious; we wanted to escape the confinements of the apartment and the thought of parting. We needed to move.

Let's go for a drive, Roland said.

The car's engine strained and parts complained Roland spoke to it as though it was an old friend: *Please, just carry us for one more day before you stop running. Can't you see we're in love? Just do us this one favor.*

We drove to the outer ring road, where Moscow dwindled and began to blend into the countryside. I barely noticed the landmarks that passed by outside the window. Together we had created our own world out of imagination and love, a realm in which nothing would intrude.

The car puffed along as a grove of trees appeared near a dark stretch of road. Roland pulled off to the side. The brakes groaned. The car slowly came to a stop. We sat in silence and watched the few headlights on the road breaking the dark veil of night. The pavement was just a few yards away but might as well have been in another universe entirely.

Roland leaned across the seat and kissed my neck. I took his hand in mine and squeezed it tight to my chest. The joy between us was like a mist in the air that eclipsed everything. Our last night. And still I didn't think that we would lose each other. I didn't know why I thought this, or what I thought would happen, but in that moment I was certain.

We kissed and embraced, pulled each other tight. I could feel the strength of his love in his touch, in the soft words he whispered. The night air was cool on our skin but our love was like a spark that stoked into a roaring fire in an instant. We let our clothes fall to the floor of the car and allowed our bodies to seek each other. We made love in a way that I never imagined, fully in each other's presence, completely captured in a moment of union.

A car passed by, going fast. Its headlights illuminated the

interior of our lair for a second, then left us in the darkness again. We started to laugh.

This is perfect, I said. I can't think of anywhere else that I would rather be.

Roland let his hand slip across my cheek. We could get arrested here, he said, laughing even harder now. He pulled me closer.

A bus drove by slowly, almost pulling to the side of the road. As we were kissing we heard laughter and cries; it was the passengers on the bus seeing us for an instant through the windows. The bus sped up again and disappeared into the night. Then all was darkness.

Our souls were flying. We needed to move.

Roland started the car. It sputtered and made a weird noise. Come on, baby! he cried out to it, laughing as he turned the key. You have to start for us. We're going to the edge of the world tonight and we're not going to stop.

The car made a couple of grunting noises, as if it was not totally persuaded, but then it finally decided to join us. Roland turned on the headlights and pulled out onto the road.

I knew that my life had changed forever. What I shared with Roland was no infatuation between a boy and a girl. This was the love of my adult life, in which my spirit soared to the sky like a burst of light. Never before had I felt such freedom and elation.

We rolled down the car windows and let the night air flow through our hair. Soon we saw a little red light off the side of the road and, as we drew closer, it became a flame surrounded by people. In the dark we could see a motorized caravan.

Gypsies, Roland said.

Stop the car, I said. Let's go to them.

We walked through grass toward the fire, holding hands, fearless. The fire grew bigger and the scene more distinct as we drew closer. There were about fifteen of them, men and women with children running in circles, playing games. They saw us coming and, when we were close enough to see their faces, the Gypsies waved at us as though greeting friends.

One of the men stepped to the fore of the group. His hair was dark and wavy, his face enveloped in the shadows of the fire.

Your faces are full of joy, he said, his lips creasing into a smile. You are welcome to join us tonight. We're eating, singing. You should celebrate with us.

We walked into the center of the group, closer to the heat of the fire. Small children with dirty faces and no shoes were playing with a fabric ball sewn shut and filled with beads. A woman put her arm around my shoulder and offered me a piece of bread. Her eyes shone and flickered in the dark.

I sat next to Roland and we accepted vodka and food. It looked to me as though the flame that warmed us and cooked the meal also reached toward the blackness of the sky, wishing to fly. Before I could complete the thought, the sound of guitars and strings pierced through the murmur of conversation.

Eternal as night, the Gypsies' songs stretched from times lost to history into the present. They were full of sorrow, love, happiness, recollections of life. They enveloped us like a gentle mist.

The man playing the guitar stopped suddenly and addressed everyone around the fire. Tonight is our guests' wedding party; they are now man and wife. Let's celebrate.

The men and women broke into applause and laughter; a woman helped me to my feet and a man pulled Roland to his. When the music began we started to dance, looking deep into each other's eyes. I kissed his face and disappeared into an eternity where time stood still. We lost each other in the ecstasy of the dance, becoming one with the music. The Gypsies sang and whistled with affectionate encouragement.

We sang and danced for the rest of the night, stopping only to tell stories from our lives and join the Gypsies in consuming fiery vodka. The Gypsies' never-ending quest for freedom, passion, and love ignited a kinship between us—wandering lovers and these eternal travelers bound by history and blood—that went beyond words.

When the sun rose the silhouettes of Moscow's gray buildings were much closer to us that we had imagined. We were still outside the city, but not far off. We had been consumed in a moment of dreaming; we could no longer escape reality. Roland and I hugged and kissed the Gypsies and said good-bye. As we walked back to the car I could hear a soft melancholy song behind us.

Roland drove the car toward the city, into the dawning of

another day. The morning air was cool. We still hadn't talked about our parting. But now it was imminent.

The Aeroflot plane rose through the clouds high into the sky. I leaned against the window looking out. I wrapped my arms tight around myself and tried to control my sobs. Somewhere in the sky another airplane took Roland home to his life in New York. Our time together was over.

Coldness enveloped the plains of my soul. I was alone again. I realized how long I had waited and how much I had anticipated falling in love. Now Roland's absence created an emptiness inside that was nearly unbearable. I pressed myself deeper into the seat.

I remembered the love in his eyes when he looked at me. The gentle emotion in his voice when he spoke. His intelligent, kind-spirited humor. The sound of our laughter and the deep sensation when we had spoken of our pain. I felt his body against mine, his soul within my own. He was like a book without a first or last page, I could read forever and never become bored. I trusted him completely, and I knew he would never make me regret it.

This is life, I whispered to myself. Things happen for a reason. Accept it. It's another story you will tell yourself when you're an old woman.

With each mile that passed I imagined the earth spinning beneath me. New York, I said softly. I wished that I could will the plane to freeze in the air. The earth would twirl around, and when New York was under us I would allow the pilot to descend to the earth.

In Ulan Ude I received a letter in the mail from Roland. It was an official invitation to visit him in the United States. My hands quaked as I read it. I was supposed to present it to the immigration office in order to get an American visa. I turned it over and saw the outline of its official stamp.

I showed it to my parents, to my brothers, to Larissa and the models at the fashion house. No one had ever seen anything like it. It was from the West, from the American embassy. Walking home to my family's apartment, I tried and failed to picture America. How would they walk and talk? What would I do there?

In the morning I took the document to the exit-visa department at the local representative of the Ministry of Internal Affairs. A stocky man in a frayed uniform took the invitation from my hand.

What is this? he asked. Where did you get this?

My friend sent it to me, I said. He lives in New York and he wants me to come visit him.

Are you sure this is a genuine invitation? he asked, holding it up to the light. Are you sure this is real?

You should know better than me, I said.

The clerk called for his supervisor and they looked over the document together. It was clear that they had never seen such a form before. The supervisor asked me the same questions the clerk had a minute before.

I don't know about this, the supervisor said.

It's very unusual, the clerk agreed.

The only way to prove this is real is to send it to Moscow, the supervisor said. If they approve it, perhaps something can be arranged.

I came back to the office a week later, then a week after that. Finally the supervisor grew tired of me.

This isn't an invitation, he said, as though issuing a decree. This is just a piece of paper. We won't grant you an exit visa.

He ripped the document into little pieces and let them fall to the floor.

That night my life seemed flat and strange. Roland had disappeared. His letter had been rejected. I had lost my love, and I didn't know how to find him again.

When my grandfather died, he and my grandmother had been married for almost sixty years. They had lived through the rural collectivization of Stalin's policies, and had survived the Soviets' attempts to eliminate village life and Buryat culture. He had fought in and survived the war against Germany. They had made unity out of their parts, he of the sky and she of the earth.

He was gone, and I realized how many questions I had failed to ask him. Probably he would have remained silent. To him, answers were self-evident.

I walked along the frosty street in the city, voicing questions in my mind. Where will my soul go when I die? Into a bird? A tree? Grandfather had always answered this question after a villager died, but now he would never be able to do the same for me. His death had been a surprise; though he was old, it was routine in his family for men to live a decade longer than he did.

I had to stay in the city when the time for his funeral arrived. I lay down in bed and closed my eyes, my sadness making my body tired and weak.

In my dream I saw lights, heard voices. I didn't know where I was. Then I saw my grandfather coming toward me with his hand extended.

What is it? I asked him. You've just died.

He said nothing. He looked at me with his usual mysterious expression, part smile, part appraising stare.

I woke up shivering. The sheets were soaked with my sweat. My heart beat hard. I was afraid.

After that, my grandfather came to me often in the night. He started to tell me things that I only half remembered in the morning. In my dreams I wished for a tape recorder to preserve his words. Then I could talk to my family about what was happening, then I would have proof.

Grandmother became ill. She came to the city to visit doctors, who said they could find nothing wrong with her. She became weak and tired, and every day she seemed to lose her hold on life. My mother took care of her in our apartment and my aunt Masha came to help. We walked through the place with light steps, as though afraid that a sudden burst of motion might kill her.

In the night my grandfather came again.

What do you want? I asked him. You're scaring me. What do you want from me?

What you're thinking is right, he said.

I don't understand. Why do you keep coming to me? You're dead and I'm alive. I'm tired. You won't let me sleep.

What you're thinking is right, he said again. Our family believes my wife is going to die. This belief will make it come true. You must all change your minds. It's up to all of you if she will live or die.

I awoke clutching tight to my pillow. My forehead burned hot. I felt frightened and angry. Each time my grandfather visited me it felt as though he had taken something away from me.

I thought about what he had told me, and realization bloomed in my mind. Of course he was right. He had understood what I had only dared to think about in wordless notions.

I took my mother aside in the kitchen. What is it? she asked me. You look strange.

We're killing her, I whispered, motioning toward the living room. All of us. We're killing her.

Mother blocked the doorway with her body. What do you think you're saying? she whispered. How are we killing her?

With our feelings, our beliefs, I said. Don't ask me how I know, but I do. We have to believe she will live. We must feel in our hearts that she will survive.

My mother leaned against the doorframe and exhaled. I could see her struggle with what I had said. She loved her mother very much.

Masha came into the kitchen. I repeated to her what I had told my mother. Masha gave me a look full of poison.

How can you say this to us? she asked. You must not care for anyone. What a terrible thing.

My mother watched us silently. I tried to read what passed behind her eyes as she walked slowly from the room.

Grandfather came to me again. In my dream I shouted at him. I told him no one believed me. I told him that his visits were hurting me, that I couldn't take it any more.

My wife is still alive, he said in his familiar voice.

I know she is, I replied. In my dream I cried.

This is the important time, he continued. If she doesn't die before the new year, then she will live for a long time. Listen to her. Trust my wife and yourself.

You know more than I do, I told him. But why do you tell me these things? What can I do?

An hour later it was time to take my grandmother to the hospital. She cried out and lay down on the floor.

Don't take me there, she said. It's killing me. Let me stay.

Please, Mother, my aunt said. The doctors will help you.

My grandmother reached out for my hand. Irina, you're the only one who understands, she said.

I felt her familiar rough skin. What did I understand? Then I remembered my dream.

She shouldn't go, I said. She will get better if we all believe.

My grandmother got up and hid behind me. We faced my aunt and my mother. I could see that they both believed Grandmother had gone mad.

We have to stop it, I said. She will live a long time if we all think that she will. Haven't I tried to explain?

You're not normal, Masha said. The things you say make no sense.

Mother, don't you believe me? I asked.

She shook her head and looked away. But they didn't force my grandmother to go to the hospital. She lay back in bed and slept deep, a contented expression on her face.

In October it was time to collect the harvest. In Siberia this was every adult's job, even office workers. My Uncle Volodya left his job and went into the potato fields to work.

I lay in bed early that morning dreaming. I saw a scene and, even though I couldn't see my grandfather, I knew this was a picture that he had brought to my mind.

Volodya held a heavy bag full of potatoes, ready to load it into a truck. He dragged it closer to the open bed of the vehicle and paused. He heard a noise. The truck moved backwards and crashed into his leg. He fell to the ground, yelling in pain.

I went to the kitchen and asked if Volodya had gone to work that day.

No, he didn't, she said. He went to pick potatoes for the harvest.

There was no way to call the fields. I waited until early afternoon when the phone rang. Volodya was in the hospital. He had been injured in the same way as I had witnessed in my dream.

The next night I asked my family to sit down and listen to me. Masha, Volodya, my mother and father were there.

I don't know what you will think about this, I said, but I have something to tell you.

What is it? my father asked.

I've seen Grandfather in dreams. He told me about Grandmother. That's why I fought so hard for her. Yesterday morning he showed me Volodya's accident. I don't know what any of it means.

My father folded his arms and nodded slightly, as though encouraging me to continue.

I had to speak about it, I said. It's been too hard to keep it inside.

My grandmother slept in the next room. She lived through the new year. Soon she was completely healthy again.

The Ulan Ude newspaper printed a story about Pierre Cardin. The famous French designer planned to stage a fashion show in Red Square to celebrate his fortieth anniversary in the fashion business. Women who wanted to model in the show could send their photographs to Moscow. The best applicants would be invited to Moscow for a competition and the winners would actually model in the show.

I pictured the hundreds of girls from Moscow and St. Petersburg with their long cigarettes and short skirts, big breasts and blond hair. They would all hear about the contest, they would all apply. I wondered if I had a chance. The very idea of a great European designer coming to Russia was revolutionary in itself.

A month later I received an envelope from the committee organizing the competition. I was invited to Moscow. It would be a big competition, I was warned, so I shouldn't fly all the way from Siberia expecting to win.

I read the letter in the yellow light of afternoon then put it down on the floor of our balcony. The wan sun made little shadows on our wooden barrels, which we would need again in just a few months.

I had just enough money saved for a plane ticket to Moscow. I had a few friends there, so I could go from sofa to sofa, a day at a time. My life there was always harder and more dangerous. It didn't matter. I understood that my destiny pulled me into the world as though with a physical hand. I would return to Moscow and, this time, maybe travel beyond.

*   *   *

I arrived at the auditorium minutes before the competition was due to begin. There were at least a thousand girls and boys there, maybe two thousand. We were pressed together, breathing each other's air, our body heat rising. Nearly all of them were from the big cities. They smoked and looked as though they were beneath competing with anyone. They looked as though they had come there for a laugh. I knew that, inside, they desperately sought something to change their lives in the same way that I did.

There were a few girls from smaller towns who had come in by train or bus. They carried their little bundles of clothes and stood off to the side looking overwhelmed and intimidated. The din of voices rose in the high ceiling and echoed back at us. I wondered whether everyone sensed the tinge of desperation in the air.

I remembered the instructions I had been given: this would be a big competition, and choices would be made quickly, so none of us should be shy about showing our bodies. There would be very few winners.

I watched the Moscow girls gathered in small groups examining each other with sly glances. They smoked a brand of cigarette called *More.* They wore tight shirts to accentuate their breasts, and hair lightened to show streaks of blonde. There was a hardness in their eyes that frightened me no matter how many times I saw it. I waited near the back of the crowd, trying to see how the situation would develop, holding on to my bag and trying to find fresh air.

A girl in a tight skirt and short brown hair came up to me. She looked at my clothes, my body, as though assigning a value to my entire being.

Where are you from? she asked.

I thought that perhaps I had found a friend. Ulan Ude, I replied. In Siberia.

She sneered at me. Siberia? she repeated in a mocking tone. That's shit. You shouldn't even be here.

A man holding a clipboard emerged from the main hall. His eyes widened when he saw how many women were waiting. It took him several minutes of yelling and waving his arms to quiet everyone.

We have one hour to complete this contest, he shouted. Show

off your body, let us see how you look. And remember there will be very few winners.

There was a moment of stunned silence. There was no chance for me.

The silence shattered in an instant. Heels clattered against the ground. A few cries at first, then a cacophony of raised voices. The girls began pushing and elbowing each other to secure a place in line. Everyone there knew that the judges couldn't possibly see all of us in an hour. Those who were in the back of the line would probably never be seen.

Get out of my way, bitch, one girl said, shoving another in the face.

Get your hands off me, you shit, the second girl said, shoving back. I had seen them together five minutes before. They had been discussing where they had bought their skirts and shoes like the best of friends. Their snobbishness had transformed into utter vulgarity.

A single line formed in front of the entrance into the auditorium. I heard cries of pain, cursing, yells of protest. Bodies bumped and feet rustled on the floor like the sound of a stampede. Some of us hung back from the brawl, afraid and mortified.

Oh, God, I said aloud to no one. What am I doing here?

Beautiful women with faces like angels had transformed into devils. The noise grew deafening. A young woman grabbed my arm and pulled me toward the mass of girls.

Why are you just standing here? she asked. Let's go, let's push our way in. This is our chance.

You go, I said, I'm fine right here.

I felt ashamed of my own people. I considered Pierre Cardin and his assistants, and what they would think of Russians after this. We were all hungry, we were all desperate. But we should have kept our dignity.

From the very front of the line came a male voice. By the time it reached my place, near the back, it was barely louder than a whisper.

Walk quickly down the runway, he said. Turn left, then right, then move on. Take ten seconds at the most.

The line moved forward slowly. After twenty minutes I stepped through the door and saw the stage enveloped in spotlights. A small group of men and women sat in the audience below, talking to each other and jotting notes.

My turn came. I stepped out onto the stage, my gaze focused on the back of the hall. I walked quickly, turning, imagining myself a deer pausing in the forest.

I glanced down at the group huddled in the audience. The lights were so bright that I could only make out indistinct figures.

Yes, a man's voice said.

I realized this was the first cut. The decision was made on the spot, even before the model had a chance to leave the stage and retake her place in line. It took me almost a minute to register that I would be permitted to move to the next round.

I waited backstage with the other models. Though our numbers had been thinned out, my place was still far in back of the line. I heard nervous chatter all around.

Do you believe it? a girl said. Nadia Petrova didn't make it.

Good, someone else said. I can't stand her.

Little arguments. Petty bickering. I felt myself apart from it all, shamed and embarrassed. This was how they expressed their worry and fear.

A woman dressed in a tight black dress moved down the line from girl to girl. When she grew close I saw that she was handing out swimsuits and shoes. The next stage would be a swimsuit competition. There was no clock on the wall, and I wondered how much of the hour had already passed. Thirty minutes, at least, probably more.

The woman reached my place in line. She looked me up and down, asked my size, and gave me a suit to change into. Her expression was blank, as though she saw us as physiques rather than individuals.

This next stage is the last, she said as she moved on. This is the final competition.

The line moved forward slower than before. I couldn't see the stage, but I guessed that the judges were taking their time. They needed to be careful with their final choices. They would have specific needs for certain body types and looks to match the clothes they planned to show at Red Square.

I moved ahead a few steps. I hadn't allowed myself to imagine what might happen to me if I were chosen, but now there was time to think. The winners would be paid in cash. They would model in front of the international media, with a world-famous designer. They might even be invited to leave the country. I fantasized about Europe, about earning money to send to my parents so they could fall asleep at night without worrying.

I was closer to the stage, though I still couldn't see it. I heard voices outside and the scattered applause of perhaps a dozen hands. I would make it, I decided. Time would not run out on me. Perhaps I would be the last model to reach the stage, but I would show them that they should hire me. I would turn my body into a fantasy of sun, snow, the wind, a sophisticated glance.

There were six or seven young women in front of me, a few more behind me. I had begun to rock back and forth on my heels with nervousness.

That's it, a voice called out. Our hour's up. We're finished.

I replayed the words over and over in my mind. It wasn't possible. I had come all the way from Siberia. All I had wanted was an opportunity.

No! one of the girls ahead of me screamed. You can't do this! This isn't fair! You have to look at me!

She was tall, with a beautiful figure and long blond hair. Because her place in line was close to mine I had heard her speaking earlier. They will choose me, she had said. Because I have the look everyone wants. I want to be famous. Pierre Cardin will make me famous.

Part of me had resented her boasting, but I had understood that she had been trying to convince herself of the truth of her own words. She ran out onto the stage screaming and crying. The rest of us who were left behind gathered around the stage entrance. We watched her find Pierre Cardin, who stood quietly with a little notebook. She grabbed at him and started to beg.

This is a disaster, I said. I looked around the edges of the room where we had left our things. I would find someplace to stay and something else to do. I could see that this fashion show wasn't part of my fate.

How many girls are left? I heard someone say. I looked out. It was Pierre Cardin who had spoken.

An assistant came backstage. He counted us off, ten in all, then left. The girls who had gone before were still standing onstage in their bathing suits. I understood then that the final decisions hadn't been made.

Pierre Cardin walked through the crowd of young women on stage. Out, out, in, out, out, out, he said. As though he were picking fabrics by hand.

He stepped through the door leading backstage. Pain and regret animated his features. It had been like a shameful cinema. The crying, the fighting. He had come from France to work, to create something beautiful, and this spectacle had been his reward. All our lives we had been taught to be proud of Russia and our culture. Now I had seen the harvest of the previous years' strain on our people.

Pierre Cardin looked around at those of us remaining. His eyes met mine, and he walked to me and took my hand. Yes, he said, motioning toward me.

No! shouted a brown-haired girl who had been in front of me. Why her? We were in front of her. This isn't fair.

The other girls turned and looked at me with genuine hatred. I was frightened—they were desperate and so angry. They had been through an incredible fight only to be turned down. For a moment I worried about what they might do to me when this was over.

You have to take me, another girl said. Are you stupid? Look at me! Are you blind?

I shouldn't even have to enter this idiotic competition, another girl said. This is an insult. You must have shit for brains.

Pierre Cardin turned to leave the room. I winced at the words that were shouted after him as he walked away. His assistant called out for me to come to the stage. The other models shot horrible looks at me as I passed between them.

About twenty girls and a few boys had been chosen. A photographer arranged us on stage and snapped pictures. I smiled into the flash again and again. It would be hours before I entirely understood what had happened.

It was night, the air warm with the breezes of late spring. Red Square was illuminated all around. The Red Star of the Kremlin shone from atop its spire. Lenin's tomb seemed like a mute witness to everything that was about to transpire.

A huge stage hugged tight the great Kremlin wall. From it I

could see the Moskva River. Above the haze of light I could see the stars lighting the inky black sky. I peeked through the curtain at the crowd. They thronged the wide cobblestone expanse of the square, people standing shoulder to shoulder. Television cameras were set up around the stage; bursts of light from flashbulbs glittered through the crowd like earthbound stars.

I felt as though I might rise into the air and merge with the wind and stars. I sat motionless while the makeup artists did their work, and the hairdressers pulled my long hair back into a ponytail which they wrapped around my head. I stared into the mirror entranced at the person who was appearing there.

The crowd grew more noisy. Here, here, a voice said behind me. Watch me move. This is what you're going to do.

Her name was Ving. She was a Chinese model who had grown up in France. She was tall and elegant; her limbs moved in willowy curves. She had worked with Pierre Cardin for years, and she was the only model from the West whom he had brought with him for the show.

When you reach the front, you turn like this, she said, her chin rotating to the left. Walk like you're tough. Let them know how beautiful you think you are. Convince them of your beauty.

There had been no rehearsals, only fittings for the clothes and simple instructions about what to do on stage. This would be my first Western-style fashion show, with music but no dance. I would have to communicate my stories in my steps.

Ving's hair was long and black like mine, and she had been given the same wrapped ponytail as me. I caught her eye and she smiled at me. I felt as though I could have studied her forever, every line of her elegant features and graceful body.

The show passed like a blur of pure energy. With each outfit I tried to convey my strength as I walked the runway. I felt the passion of the crowd that now extended to the edge of my sight. It was a moment of freedom and expression, of embracing beauty after drab hopelessness.

Toward the end of the show Ving and I modeled identical outfits, with identical hairstyles and makeup. I walked by her side feeling the confidence and joy that surrounded her. At the sight of us the audience roared and I felt both their power and mine. We were there, we had triumphed. We would have a future that had once seemed impossible.

The show ended and all the models gathered backstage. We were surrounded by video cameras and reporters. I heard languages that I didn't recognize. I had brought an English dictionary with me, and I took Pierre Cardin's hand when he had a free moment.

Thank you very much, I said to him. I love your work as a designer. This has been a beautiful event.

He squeezed my hand and took Ving's arm. With us on either side he walked back onto the stage with the other models following. We stood in the night air together, the Kremlin looking like a thing of beauty. The air began to fill with bright fireworks. The crowd roared with approval.

I stood in this swirl of color and sound and beauty. Tears streamed down Ving's face, and when I turned I saw that the other models were crying as well. I felt the multitude's intensity upon us, the joy and release of what we had made happen. Oppression did not always have to win—creativity and passion could conquer. It was possible.

Oksana had worked on *The Adventures of Hadja Nasredin* as a makeup artist. She was tall and thin, with sandy hair and a broad face. She shared a little apartment in Moscow with three other women. Once or twice a week she allowed me to stay with her while I was in the capital.

I sat at her table in her cramped kitchen. At one side was an apartment-scale refrigerator that hummed and hissed. At my other elbow was a low basin that was used for washing dishes and clothes.

I have a friend I want you to meet, Oksana said, sipping tea. He's your kind of person. Full of dreams and ideas. In love with beauty.

What kind of work does he do? I asked.

He's a painter and illustrator, Oksana said. An artist.

I agreed to meet him. I was still awed by the sorts of men and women I encountered in Moscow. They seemed to be filled with imagination, always aware of the possibilities of every moment in life. I imagined them hiding under rocks and tree branches during the time of the Soviets, tentatively coming out from under cover when Yeltsin dissolved the Soviet Union.

Yuri lived in a small flat in Moscow. When I first visited him he prepared sweet tea and led me to the room where he worked. We ate *baranki*—a life-saver-shaped dried cookie, the size of a doughnut, crunchy like a pretzel but not salty. When he showed me his paintings and illustrations I heard the pride in his voice. My gaze wandered along the confident lines his hand had drawn, the bold colors with which he filled the emptiness of the canvas.

What is this painting? I asked him.

The dove of peace, he said, gesturing with his thin-fingered hand along an expanse of delicate lines and shades. His hair curled around his pale ears, his dark eyes shone. Later that afternoon we walked together through the hazy grayness of Moscow streets through people and traffic; nothing bothered us, it was a wonderous meeting of the minds.

Yuri asked me about Siberia, made me describe the colors and shapes of Lake Baikal. He closed his eyes and tried to create pictures in his mind from my words. I felt that our minds connected.

We reached the museum just before it closed; inside Yuri explained to me works from the Russian Constructivist period—sculptures by Lisitsky, Malevich, Tatlin, that were made of wood, glass, and plastic, and hung from the walls and ceilings.

These works were intended to represent the new age, Yuri said.

The Age of Communism, I said, watching his eyes dart around the work of artists of previous generations.

Communism, he repeated. Industrialism. The new and bright world of man and machine. The hope of a great and wonderful future for mankind.

We walked together into the night, holding hands, talking about the films of Eisenstein and Tarkovsky. I could feel the history of Russia surrounding my spirit and lifting us both into the sky with our great enthusiasm for the future, for the new free life full of beauty and promise.

In the coming weeks I watched Yuri at work in his apartment. His forehead creased with concentration as his hand moved over canvas or paper. He would stop for a moment, rubbing his face, and ask me what color he should use next, or whether the composition required a stronger line or something more delicate. I was thrilled to be at his side, sharing my thoughts with him. Never before was I part of such an artistic collaborative process.

When he was finished we sat together on cushions talking about art and beauty. We had no idea how young we were, how naive others might have thought us. Our only concern was the deep bond that had grown between us almost from the moment we had met.

Yuri opened the window and we sat in silence, listening to the traffic from the street below. From somewhere in the next block a man's deep voice yelled out a name we couldn't understand.

It's just beginning, he said, lying back and closing his eyes.

What's that? I asked.

He didn't need to explain anything more. History was taking hold and events were unfolding on their own. No one could stop the changes now, they ran too deep.

It's as though we're living in the middle of a history book, I said.

Yuri opened his eyes a sliver; he was starting to fall asleep.

An illustrated book, he added, with all new colors, all new ways of looking at things.

I want the side of good to win, I said, not thinking of the words before they sprang from me.

In late September I awoke in the morning and looked out the window. The sky was bright, the air warm. In the living room my friend Oksana was watching Channel Two on television.

What's the matter with you? I asked her. You look so frightened.

She pointed at the TV screen, where a Moscow politician jabbed the air with his finger and spoke in an angry voice.

It's falling apart, Oksana said. The renegades have barricaded themselves inside the Russian White House. Yeltsin says they have no right. It's going to be a war, I can feel it.

I looked at the screen. The White House, symbol of the Russian Parliament and the new democracy, was under siege. Already it was being described as a *putsch*, the renegades from the Parliament against the authority of Yeltsin. Democracy had to attack in order to preserve itself.

I felt a shiver run up my spine, sensing this new democracy about to shatter all around me.

Women were crying in the streets. Men were gathered on the street corners, drinking, yelling, fighting. Political opinions opened the sores of old grudges until each word carried decades of meaning. I walked quickly to Yuri's apartment, trying not to let myself become swept up in the chaos that lay under the surface of the day.

Yuri was watching a small black-and-white television and waiting for me to arrive.

We should go out, he said. We should try to understand this, try to help if we can. To defend our right to be.

Yuri put on his jacket, shaking his head. We had to help the pro-Yeltsin forces; only they could ensure that the democratic changes would endure.

We walked together to the White House. A crowd had begun to gather; people pointed up at windows inside of which we could see the forms of people moving about. No one was allowed in or out of the building. Soldiers carrying guns milled in small groups, waiting for orders.

Let Yeltsin die! a man screamed. What has he done to us? He wants to be the new czar. Because of him we are starving. His reforms and advisers serve American interests.

A loud roar of disapproval came from the people around him.

Go inside the White House with your reactionary friends! a woman yelled.

These renegades from the Parliament are breaking the law, a man shouted.

We need a man like Stalin now, with a firm hand!

Yuri and I walked carefully through the crowd, avoiding the loudest, most angry people. Everyone wanted freedom, though each person seemed to have a slightly different interpretation of what this meant.

But I thought I understood what was happening. A faction

was trying to take over the government, just as when the military had tried to oust Gorbachev several years before. Whatever the word freedom might have meant to us, we knew that we had to raise our voices or it would be lost to us forever.

I saw the images of faces around me like images in a kaleidoscope. An elderly woman, her features knotted with weariness. A young man, his skin red with anger. A young woman, her mouth twisted as she yelled above the noise. A small child holding onto his father's hand with eyes wide with something that looked like wonder.

Yuri had disappeared for a moment because he had seen an old school friend; when he returned he was breathing fast with excitement.

There's going to be an assault on the Ostankino television station, he said to me.

We both understood what this meant. The antidemocratic forces wished to take over the people's means of communication. Since the fall of the Soviet Union, television had become both a symbol of new freedoms and the source of information that would have been suppressed in years past.

That can't happen, I said. We have to go there.

Yuri looked around us at the growing crowd; I watched him open his senses and absorb the danger all around.

You're right, he said.

This is like everything we talked about, I told him. Freedom, peace. We can't let it get away from us.

By then other people had heard the same news about the Ostankino station. Angry voices raised in protest. It felt as though the world was falling apart, and that only the will of the people could possibly save us.

When Yuri and I arrived at the television station it had started to grow dark. There was a square in front of the station, and by then it was filled with people. Voices shouted, thousands of bodies milled about as though waiting for something to happen.

Yuri grabbed a man by the shoulder and asked him what was happening. The man had a shaggy beard and his eyes were distorted by thick glasses.

There are troops inside, protecting the place, the man told

us. A military general had just been in front of the complex with a bullhorn, giving orders.

The windows were lit inside the sprawling compound of studios and offices. Yuri and I moved around the edges of the crowd, listening to the voices and looking at the faces. Arguments erupted, men shoved each other in the chest.

Yuri! I called out. He was no longer by my side.

I stood up on my toes and looked all around, trying to find him. He had been pulled away from me by the current of thousands of people moving and pulling each other in every direction. In front of the station itself something was happening: it looked like a sort of tug-of-war.

A voice shouted something that I couldn't understand above the din. I called out for Yuri again, but I couldn't see him anywhere. I heard a man singing and playing guitar: it was an old Soviet victory song.

There was the sound of a gun being fired, then screams. The crowd seemed to erupt in the instant that followed, screaming with a single terrified voice. Bodies pushed against me, feet trampled mine.

Yuri! I yelled out again, but by then I could not hear the sound of my own voice.

The sounds of gunfire were like twigs breaking under my feet in the forest. A woman screamed, so loud that her voice was distinct above all others. An explosion erupted from somewhere close to the building, perhaps inside it. I heard shattering glass and the noise of wreckage falling to the ground.

The people around me were transformed in an instant into a turbulent sea; I was pushed through its waves and currents. The more I fought, the less control I had. I lost my balance and almost fell to the ground; I grabbed onto a woman's shoulders to stay on my feet. If I had fallen, I surely would have been crushed. I stopped calling out for Yuri and allowed myself to be pushed away from the television station. My feet lifted off the ground and I floated amid the men and women, staggering when I again came to earth.

There were more shots, explosions. I put my hands over my ears to try to drive away the sound. When I was free from the crowd I reached a small hillside, an oasis of quiet from which I looked back at the television station.

The mass of people looked like an undulating body of water. The sun had gone down, and flashlights and search beams moved across the tops of thousands of heads. The commotion of noise was incomprehensible, save for instants when a single voice would rise above the others, calling someone's name or shouting in anger.

The army, police, and ambulances started to arrive from the main road; the crowds parted to let them pass. I moved through the throng calling for Yuri. I was sure he was somewhere close to me, that I only had to open my eyes and I would see him.

I heard the sound of sirens pierce the night. Some people ran away from Ostankino, their faces white with fear. Closer to the TV station I could see the lights of the building still burning.

Get away from here, a woman said who was running away from the station. There's going to be more shooting.

I can't find my friend, I told her. But by then she was gone.

A sense of menace still lingered in the air. I needed to find Yuri, I wanted to be with him.

I walked toward the ambulances, which were parked close together and surrounded by people. It was then that I realized that people really had been hurt, that the shots and explosions had been real and not the product of my imagination.

The ambulance lights were harsh and bright; as I moved closer I kept one hand in front of my face to ward off the glare. I didn't know what I was looking for, what I thought I would find. But still my feet moved, one in front of the other.

There was a woman covered in blood, her dress torn around her shoulders. She wept quietly in the grass as a medic tried to find the source of her wound. I saw an old man lying inside an ambulance, motionless, his fingers curled into claws and resting on his chest.

I pushed lightly through a group of people who had gathered to gape at the wounded. As they parted to let me pass I saw a stretcher being carried toward the ambulances. The person on the stretcher was a thin man; although his hair hung over his face, I recognized the familiar curve of Yuri's mouth.

I called out Yuri's name and ran toward him. He was loaded into an ambulance; the doors shut before I could see whether Yuri had heard my voice. I pressed my face against the glass ambulance window and shouted his name again until my throat burned with pain.

Get away from there, a medic said to me. That boy is seriously wounded. We have to get him to a hospital.

Wait, I pleaded. Let me come with him. I'm his friend. Let me—

There's no room, the medic said, climbing into the ambulance. We're taking him to the Sklifasovsky Institute. You'll be able to find him there.

I watched the ambulance vanish down the road; moments later it was joined by others, their sirens blaring in the night. I walked slowly away from Ostankino, my hands pressed together to keep them from trembling. From behind me I heard voices yelling again, angry and insistent, dragging the chaos deep into the night.

It took me hours to reach the hospital. The wounded lined the halls—some seriously hurt, others not as critical. Those who were conscious looked shocked and hollow, as though they were unable to understand why they were injured or even who had hurt them. The light inside seemed too bright, too harsh.

I found a desk where a harried nurse was talking on the phone while passing out charts and papers to a constant stream of doctors and nurses who approached her. When she hung up the phone I told her Yuri's name.

We are good friends, I said. I know it would help him to see me.

The nurse opened a chart. Can't you see what's happening here? she asked in a cold voice. A lot of people were hurt at the station. You're just going to have to wait.

I understood from her voice that she felt the same as everyone else in Moscow—frightened, confused, in dread of the future.

I found a doctor in the hall and told him Yuri's name. I had to jog to keep up with him as he moved quickly down the hall.

I don't know who that is, the doctor said, pushing his white hair form his forehead. I don't know the name of everyone I treated tonight.

Please help me, I said. I have to—

But by then the doctor turned the corner and was gone. He didn't look back at me as I called for him.

I walked past several rooms, where inside patients were lying on cots and beds. I heard crying, moaning, angry cursing. But I couldn't find Yuri.

I returned to the nurse. You have to help me, I said. Please. Please look in your papers and tell me where my friend is.

The phone rang and she picked it up. We need more blood down here, she said. How should I know where you're going to get it? I have enough to worry about.

When she hung up the phone she looked at me as though seeing me for the first time. Who do you want? she barked at me.

I told her Yuri's name again. In my mind was a picture of him on the stretcher.

The nurse looked through her papers, shaking her head. She looked into my eyes and asked me, Are you a relative?

I said, No, just a friend.

Her eyes became warmer, but with a steely voice she said, I'm sorry, we could not do anything. Your friend died on arrival.

In a daze I walked through the streets all the next day, not listening to what I was told, not speaking to those who approached me. I was almost run over by a car while crossing the street.

I remembered Yuri speaking to me, his voice husky from cigarettes, his eyes cast up to the ceiling, a smile appearing on his lips. Our talk of freedom and beauty had led us through the city to Ostankino. Our love of life and each other had given us the strength to make our presence known to those who wanted to take it away. Yuri died in a whirlpool of history. Did it matter that his death changed anything? I'd like to think he and others like him protected fragile freedom with their hearts.

He had been the friend I had always wanted to have, someone with whom I could speak as though we shared a single voice. I had loved him, and I would see his shadow, hear his voice, know the shadows of his thoughts, everywhere that I went.

I stayed up late into the night composing a poem, searching for words that would always rekindle his memory:

Don't go; stay in my memory forever.
Don't go; we need no blare of speeches.
Let us stay a moment for a moment longer.
And everything we dreamt will come together.

For days I walked the streets of Moscow. I barely slept. When my eyes were closed I saw Yuri's face, then the bright flashes in Red Square during the Pierre Cardin fashion show. I thought I knew now what I wanted. I had wandered as far as I could within Russia. I needed to find another place to explore.

I had no plan, no idea how to go anyplace. The embassies were packed with citizens trying to obtain travel visas. I didn't know how much international plane tickets cost. I didn't know whether I could find work anywhere, modeling or making clothes or working in stage productions. But I understood that my soul had opened, and that it would change the contours of my destiny.

I had to go to Paris.

My friend Kristina was from St. Petersburg. She dressed and moved like a girl from the big city, but she was sweet and warm beneath her urban swagger. We met in the afternoon at a cafe on Arbat Street in Moscow. The air was warm, and I could hear the sound of an old man playing his violin on the street for kopecks.

There's not enough work here, she said, stirring her coffee. And when there is work, it doesn't pay enough. And when it pays enough, I have to deal with these mafia guys thinking they own me.

She said aloud what both of us felt. Kristina was tall and beautiful, and had been modeling in Moscow longer than I had. She had listened transfixed to my experience at the Pierre Cardin fashion show.

You see? she said. The French know how to do it. Better fashions, professional modeling agencies. And Paris.

You sound like you've already made your decision, I said.

I have, she replied. I'm going to Paris.

Do you think we can find modeling jobs there? I asked.

We? she said. What do you mean?

You'll need someone to keep you out of trouble, I said.

Kristina beamed and took my hand. Everything happens for

a reason. I had decided that fate wished me to be in Paris, and then Kristina had appeared with her own plans. I didn't worry about what might happen in the West. The only way I could have failed would have been to ignore the forces that compelled me there.

Kristina knew a company in St. Petersburg that sold tickets to Paris much cheaper than the outlets in Moscow. We counted our every ruble, knowing how thin our money would become after we converted it to francs. We stood in interminable lines at the embassy full of crying children and men in expensive suits who a few years before had worked in drab offices and lived in common apartment blocks. At night we went out with friends, who offered us moral support. After returning five days in a row we were finally granted tourist visas for France.

When the plane was in the air I watched the fields of Russia recede beneath me. Kristina and I had laughed like little girls while we waited in line to board the craft, but now that we were in the air we became completely silent. The plane banked into a turn, and for a second I feared that we were returning to the airport. But we flew on, heading west, into the clouds.

No one from my family had ever been to the West. We hadn't been allowed even to dream of such a voyage. Now I recalled the evenings I spent as a girl lying awake wondering about the world. Living even in Moscow had seemed impossible then, but history had changed everything.

We're going to do it, Kristina said nervously. We'll become big models and live in Paris for years and years.

I listened to the engine's gentle whine as we ascended. I wished for just one fashion show, a single chance. Then I would be happy. I could return to Ulan Ude and tell my friends what Western fashion was like. I would remember Paris when I was an old woman in Buryatia. This would be the greatest voyage of my life.

Paris unveiled itself to me like a magic realm that had previously existed behind a closed curtain, shut off from my view. Wide boulevards, narrow winding streets. The smells of bread and coffee, limitless fruits, vegetables, meats. The statuary of a culture that linked the past and the present in a free exchange of ideas and energy. I was stunned speechless with each new sight.

Kristina and I found the community of Russian émigrés. Most of them had left Russia a long time ago, before the fall of the Soviets, and they all wanted to know what Russia was like now. Were the stories of crime really as bad as they had heard? Could you find an apartment? Were the Communists really gone?

I met a painter named Robert who had emigrated from St. Petersburg more than twenty years before. He was very intelligent and warm, and he had a beautiful wife. He said it was his duty to show us Paris, and he escorted Kristina and me to the Louvre and the Champs Élysées. We walked together along the banks of the Seine, and Robert pointed out objects and revealed their names in French. His manner was easy and free, and I observed him in order to see how to behave.

It's time for us to look for work, I told Kristina on our second day in Paris.

I know, she replied, I have a map. We'll get a list of all the agencies and fashion houses and start tomorrow.

Do you have photographs? I asked. I had a few pictures from my family album in Ulan Ude.

Some, Kristina said. She showed me her handful of snapshots.

Neither of us knew how the fashion business worked in the West. We didn't understand that models carried thick books full of glossy pictures, and that they made appointments and worked with agents. We knew only what we had learned in Russia: if you want something, go to where it is and be prepared to wait. Life in the Soviet Union had taught us never to give up, and to ignore anything that blocked our way.

I walked through the smoked-glass doors of a modeling agency. Pictures of beautiful women lined the walls, their faces staring out from framed covers of *Vogue, Harper's Bazaar, Marie Claire, Glamour*. The reception desk was separated from the rest of the agency by a locked door. I walked up to the desk slowly, hearing my footsteps echo in the quiet room.

Quesque tu fais ici? the receptionist asked. She was dressed in a severe black suit and glasses with brown oval frames. She didn't look at my face as she spoke to me, instead staring down at her appointment book.

I spoke almost no French, just fragments of English.

I . . . I model. Show. Photo, I said. I pantomimed taking a picture, walking along a runway.

She looked up at me, peering over her glasses with her eyebrows raised. *Vas y, vas y,* she said, her voice snapping the air like a whip. Come on, come on.

I handed her three pictures of myself that I had brought from Ulan Ude.

The receptionist glanced at the photos and rolled her eyes. She shook her head and said, So, you don't have a book?

A book? I repeated. I nodded, unsure precisely what she meant. *A book.* Maybe this was like a university. Perhaps I was supposed to have read something before I came in for an appointment.

With your clippings, she said, more impatient now. Your print work. Do you have a portfolio of pictures taken by a professional photographer?

I took a minute to answer, trying to piece together what she had asked me. I nodded still, wanting her to think that I agreed with everything she said. Finally I had to admit that I had none of the things she wanted.

She sighed. I don't think we can help you, she said. She looked down at her appointment book and resumed her work. As far as she was concerned, I had already left.

I . . . I Paris model, I said in a halting voice, straining to find words. Photo. Good. Yes. Thank you. I try. Russia. Paris.

The receptionist's pencil rolled onto the floor. *Merde,* she cursed, bending over and picking it up. When she sat upright again she looked at me as though I were an annoying child.

You worked in Russia? she asked. *Merde.*

She picked up her phone, dialed a couple of numbers, and spoke in rapid French. Sit there, she said, motioning toward an empty chair. Someone will come see you.

A half-hour later a man dressed in an expensive suit came through the locked door. He talked to the receptionist for a moment; she motioned toward me and said something in an exasperated voice.

Vas y, Vas y, he said, waving his hand for me to come to him.

He held out his hand for my photographs and glanced at them only for an instant. He looked at my face and asked me to turn to the side.

You have an interesting face, he said. Where are you from?

Where. From. I knew these words.

Sibir, I said. I shivered as though I were cold. I lifted my arms in the air and growled like a bear, thinking that Parisians would imagine Siberia to be a land of icy cold and bears walking the streets.

How interesting, he replied.

I model. Moscow, I said. I work Pierre Cardin.

Here, he interrupted, handing me the photos. Thank you for coming. *Merci.* We cannot use you.

He glanced at the receptionist and they both shook their heads as though they thought I was insane.

I stepped out to a crowded street. It was afternoon, growing hot. This had been my fourth visit to an agency that day. The shoes I had worn from Russia hurt my feet after a long day of walking. The result of all my attempts had been precisely the same. Nobody would take me.

I became friends with Robert and his wife. He observed everything around him with total intensity, including her. When she stepped into the room, his eyes remained fixed on her with complete infatuation. He would take her in his arms and say, I hope you are ready, because now I am going to kiss you a thousand times.

They hired me to babysit their child when they went out together. They paid me enough money to buy food and Metro tickets to the design houses and modeling agencies. Kristina had been fortunate and had already been taken on by an agency.

Let's celebrate, Robert said. I'll take you to a real French club tonight. There will be lots of fashion types. Music, interesting people.

I don't know, I said. I was tired and disappointed that I couldn't find work. Every minute exhausted me as though an hour had passed. The Metro, the vending machines, the traffic—

they were all new to me, ferociously appealing but intricately complicated.

We'll go and have fun, Robert said. And don't expect to come home early.

Robert, I don't know, Kristina said.

I won't take no for an answer, Robert declared. This isn't like anything in Moscow or Russia. You have to expand your minds and see new things. Don't worry, you'll be with me. You'll be safe. Just have fun.

That night I searched through the clothes I had brought from Moscow. I was a girl from the country of Russia, and this was a Paris nightclub. I wanted to look like the people on the streets, dressed in tasteful, perfect outfits.

Robert arrived in cowboy boots and jeans, with a cowboy hat and the pipe that was always in his mouth or hand. I could tell from his smile that he was excited. The pleasure he took in sharing the West with us was so strong that it was contagious.

What's wrong? he asked. He looked over the clothes I had stacked on my bed.

It's no good, I said, feeling a swell of embarrassment. I don't have anything to wear. I can't go.

Take it easy, Robert said. It's not important. Just wear something casual. You're beautiful. Just put on some makeup and something simple and sexy.

His words calmed me. I knew then that twenty years before he had felt like me: unsophisticated, unknowing, the product of a society that emphasized obedience and conformity. I went into the bathroom and started to put on makeup in the same style that we had employed for Larissa's fashion shows.

When I came out, Robert's face dropped. Oh my God, he said, where do you think you're going?

Did I put on too much?

He nodded. It's all right, he said, don't worry. Look, just try to copy this.

He opened a copy of the French *Glamour* magazine and handed it to me.

Kristina had watched us from the doorway. You lived in Moscow longer than me, I said to her. You know about these things. Help me.

Yes! Robert said. Help her!

Kristina took me into the bathroom and, with one eye on the magazine and the other on my face, created my look. When she was done I began to dress.

Why do you have so many pantyhose? Robert asked.

In Russia today you wear pantyhose with everything, I said. No matter where you go. They keep you warm.

Robert stroked his chin as he considered this. It's not the same in Paris as Siberia, he said. But tonight it's a little chilly. I think they'll be appropriate.

I selected an outfit that Larissa had designed. It was an embroidered miniskirt and jacket in gold and brown made of thin wool, with sable around the cuffs and collar. It was edged in delicate embroidery, and I considered it the first truly nice outfit that I had ever owned. Robert looked at it with a skeptical eye.

This skirt is very beautiful, he said. But I don't think it's what you want to wear tonight. Let's find something more fashionable for Paris.

He looked in my suitcase and found a pair of lycra pants with bell bottoms. These are great, he said. They'll show off your long, thin legs.

People in Russia wear those for exercise, I told him. They're not considered fashionable at all.

Black is fashionable now, he said. And so are bell bottoms.

Bell bottoms are out in Russia, I said.

Well, now you understand, Robert said. Russia is so behind the times that by the time something is unfashionable there, it's coming back into style in the West.

He looked through my clothes and found a black blouse cut high above the waist. I dressed in the next room and returned in my outfit, wearing my hair down on my shoulders.

Look at you, Robert said with approval. You look like Barbarella.

Who is that? I asked. Does that mean I look bad?

No, no, it's great, Robert replied. You look like something out of a movie. You're ready for adventure.

Kristina went through her clothes and mine, trying to select something that would impress the fashionable people of Paris. Robert watched with an indulgent smile.

You'll both be great, he said. We'll see photographers and

painters and playboys. You might even meet a French movie star.

Robert opened the door to escort us out. I'll make Parisians out of you or I'll die trying, he said as we stepped out of the building and into the cool night air.

You'll never forget living under the communists, he added. But you'll learn to stop living the way they taught you to live.

The taxi stopped near Place Opéra, near the club. The entrance was black. The people waiting to be let in were all dressed in black. Men stood outside dressed in black suits and ties. I saw people being turned away and thought we would never be let inside. Everyone looked so glamorous, their clothes so rich, their faces and hair so beautiful. Surely they would know that I was not one of them.

Robert led Kristina and me across the street to the club. At the entrance the doormen bowed to us and waved us inside.

Just like that, I whispered to Kristina.

We walked through a dark, barely lit corridor. Loud, throbbing disco music hit my ears. The rhythm filled me and I wanted to dance right away. But I felt all eyes in the club turn to look at me. I became stiff, almost afraid to take another step. I felt as though the people there were appraising my value and finding me wanting.

Robert wrapped his arms around Kristina and me and led us slowly to the bar. Men and women sitting at tables all around us looked up and smiled. They said hello to Robert and nodded greetings to me.

Look at you, Robert! a man said from a table. You're out tonight with *two* beautiful women!

Of course! Robert said, laughing. What do you expect?

Robert twirled his pipe in his mouth and bought us glasses of champagne. I took a sip of mine and allowed my hungry senses to take in nourishment. The music pounded on, driving, witty, humorous. Glass and metal reflected shards of light around the room. Men and women talked and smoked, leaning back with ease and comfort.

A man waved at Robert and crossed the edge of the dance floor with confident strides. He kissed Robert's cheek and whispered something in his ear.

This is Jean, Robert said. He's the owner of the club.

I shook his hand, feeling myself growing more comfortable. Robert leaned close to Jean and explained who Kristina and I were. Jean nodded quickly, his eyes widening.

Jean turned to me. Do you like this place? he asked in English.

I barely knew French, and only a few words of English. Yes, I said.

Jean smiled and, after speaking with Robert, left us. Robert led us to a table from which we could watch the room.

This is what they meant in school when they talked about the decadence of the West, Robert said to me. It's not so bad, is it?

I sat down and absorbed everyone's appearance, from their hairstyles to their shoes. Robert noticed that I was transfixed by a pair of stunning women two tables apart from ours. They were very tall, with exquisite bodies and perfectly made-up faces.

Do you see them? Robert pointed. They are transvestites.

What does that mean? I asked. They only eat vegetables?

A little smile played at the corner of his lips. Irina, he said, you're thinking of vegetarians. Transvestites are men who dress to look like women.

Really? I said, not sure what he meant.

Robert read my eyes and knew I didn't comprehend what he had said. Those are men, he said.

Where? I asked.

Right there! Robert said. Those women you are looking at. They aren't women, they are really men.

I was stunned. They look better than most of the women, I said.

I know who those two are. Patricia and Alex, said Robert. They're nice, fun people.

I don't believe you, I said.

Robert laughed loudly. Come on, let me introduce you to them.

We went to their table. I was shy at first. Part of me believed that Robert was playing a joke.

These girls are my friends, he said to them. They just came here from Russia.

Patricia and Alex smiled and said, Oh, honey, you two look so cute.

I took their hands and told them that they were beautiful. I stared into their faces, trying to find the truth of what Robert had told me. I barely believed they were alive and real, that they were able to transform themselves so completely.

Patricia rose from the table and pulled me onto the dance floor. She wore a tight dress and fishnet stockings. Her long hair was piled on her head in an exotic style, her body lean and beautiful. I had to remind myself that she was a man.

I felt embarrassed and alone on the floor with Patricia, thinking that everyone in the club knew more than I did about what to think and how to act. I tried to lose myself in dance and began to move wildly to shed my nervousness. I looked around and saw that people on the floor were allowing us more space in which to move. The music was so loud that I couldn't hear my own voice. Patricia grabbed my waist and twirled me around.

From the edge of the floor Robert's face beamed with happiness. *Davay, davay!* he shouted to me. Do it! Do it!

Another song began. I lost myself in my movements and the music. I was afraid to stop dancing, because I would then again have to face uncertain reality. A fever came over me, and I allowed my body to release all of my insecurity. The frustrations of my life met the sense of freedom and abandon that engulfed me. Finally I collapsed into Patricia's arms. She dragged me back to my table, where there were fresh bottles of vodka and champagne.

A few strangers had joined Robert to watch me. *Rus, Rus,* they said. Very nice. Very nice dancing.

Patricia kissed my cheek. Thank you, darling, she said.

Robert poured a glass of cold champagne and put it in my hand. Here, he said. Quench your thirst. You worked hard out there.

People continued to stop at our table to say hello to Robert. It seemed he knew everyone there. They smiled at me and clinked glasses, offering toasts I couldn't understand. Robert laughed, enjoying it all, playing ringmaster.

Jean came to our table. His straight hair was long on top and short at the sides, and he brushed a lock from his forehead as he whispered to Robert. He pointed to the other side of the room, where I saw a black door that was barely visible in the dim light.

Robert got up. Come on, he said. We're going to the VIP room. It will be very interesting for you.

Why? Have I done something wrong? I wondered. I had no idea what VIP meant, but I knew it had to be important. In Russia everything secret and vital was given an acronym: KGB, USSR.

Robert knocked on the black door and a little slot opened at eye level. I saw a shadowed face. Robert announced his name and the door opened. I went in with Robert and Kristina, followed by Jean. We climbed a black staircase in near-darkness; I held onto the hand rail, my balance affected by the exertion of dancing and the champagne.

We reached a room that looked like a long, comfortable parlor. Soft light revealed plush sofas and a few chairs scattered around the room's periphery. It seemed private and quiet, as though we had traveled from the hectic club into the serenity of someone's apartment. Men and women looked up and greeted us with friendly gestures as though we had known them our entire lives.

A woman waved at me and said something in English. Glittering bracelets ringed her slender arms.

Yes, I said, repeating my only English. Good, I added.

I sat with Kristina and Robert in a space that was cleared on the largest sofa. Isn't that nice, Kristina said to me. People gave up their seats for us. That would never happen in Moscow.

Robert carried on conversations with several people at once, speaking both English and French. I was impressed at how easily he could switch back and forth.

A young man and his girlfriend joined Kristina and me. They began to speak in English. I shook my head.

You are from Russia? he said in French.

Oui, Kristina and I said in unison.

The couple smiled blissfully. *Trés bien,* he said.

I felt warmth and friendliness throughout the room. I was overcome by the realization that I had traveled thousands of miles to this little chamber, where I was treated like a friend who had returned from a long voyage. Conversation flowed, punctuated by laughter. Kristina knew some English, and she spoke to a woman who took the chair next to us.

Across the room a man sat with his legs crossed in front of a little table. His body obscured his movements, but I saw his hand moving, then his head bow down close to the table. I heard him sniffing loudly, then he sat upright and rubbed his face.

What is that? I asked Robert. What is he doing?

You're like Alice in Wonderland, Robert said. So many questions. Don't worry, he's just enjoying himself.

Kristina was no longer next to me. I looked around and saw her sitting with a few other girls on another sofa. They were seated close together, smoking cigarettes and giggling.

Hey, Irina, Irina, Kristina said, almost singing. Come over here and try this. It's wonderful.

I joined her. A small pile of white powder lay on the table. *Chto eto takoye?* I asked. What is this stuff?

It takes your pain away, she said. If you have a headache it will make it go away. It makes you feel happy and alive.

Nyet spasebo, No thank you, I said to her in Russian. I don't have a headache.

This made her laugh. She leaned back on the sofa and took a drag on her cigarette.

Seeing her happiness, for a moment I was tempted to join her. But everything was new and unknown to me. I felt as though fate had allowed me a lucky evening and that I shouldn't press for more. It was a comfortable, accepting atmosphere, but my uncertainty kept me from the table.

I joined Robert and waited until he was finished speaking with an older man with a gray-flecked beard and thick glasses. Robert turned and put his arm around my shoulder protectively.

So, are you glad you came here? he asked.

Very much, I said. Your friends are very nice.

You feel comfortable? he said.

I leaned close to him so other wouldn't hear what I said. What is that white powder? I asked. It's drugs, right?

Robert looked at me as though he hadn't understood how inexperienced I really was. That's right, he said. It's cocaine.

My pulse beat fast with sudden fear. I had been taught about cocaine in school. It was an awful drug. If you tried it once you became an addict. Everything good in your life ended and soon you would die. You wouldn't eat or drink, you would only want more drugs. I thought of Tatyana, who had taken heroin rather than cocaine. I barely knew the difference between the two, but I had seen how quickly that drug had changed my friend. I didn't want to die; I knew that I was at the beginning of my journey, that there were many things left for me to see.

Don't be scared, Robert said. No one is going to force you to do anything. If you don't want to take it, that's great for you. I'm not taking it. But if other people want to try it, that's their business.

I watched a young girl bend close to the table and sniff the white powder. I shivered involuntarily. I felt as though I would become a drug addict just from watching her, that I would fall into one of the sophisticated Western traps that my teachers had warned me about.

Everyone here likes you, Robert whispered into my ear. So relax. I don't want to tell you that drugs are either good or bad. It depends on the person. Some people are going to take drugs. You can't let it worry you.

I understand, I told Robert. But I'm not going to take anything.

Robert laughed at my seriousness. Great, he said. You're a very smart girl. You know how to look out for yourself.

When we left the club light streaked the eastern sky and Paris had begun to wake up. The streets were busy with traffic and people rushing to work. We walked the pavement together, exhausted. My mind was filled with images of faces, the sounds of voices. It felt as though a lifetime had passed while I was inside.

I walked the streets every day with my map of Paris and list of design houses and modeling agencies. Everywhere I went people looked at me strangely. They asked me where I was from, how I had arrived in France. I learned a new word that sounded strange and amusing to me: *go-see*, which was what an important appointment in the fashion business was called. But no one hired me and none of the agencies wanted to represent me. I thought that someone had to open an agency for Eskimos.

I learned that the current favorite style was called *grunge*. It meant wearing tattoos, short, severe hairstyles, dirty clothes with holes. I knew that I couldn't fit in with this style, that my look was too unusual.

You're very interesting, I heard over and over. But we don't know what we could do with you. Perhaps you could come back later.

I waited with other young women on the floor in corridors outside photographers' studios, waiting for a chance to have our photographs taken. I talked with girls who had done work for French magazines. They told me about the sets they had worked on, the difficult schedules and long hours. I yearned for one chance to show someone how hard I could work and how much creativity I would bring to a show or photo session.

You know what your problem is? a Russian model said to me outside a design house. We were waiting together in the sun for an assistant to return from his lunch.

What's that? I asked.

Your face, she said. You're too Oriental. Too weird. Your face is flat like a dinner plate. I don't think you should waste your time.

I didn't become upset that she spoke to me like this, but instead I contemplated what, to me, was a new idea. She pointed out that once there had been only white models in the magazines and runways, blondes with blue eyes. Then black women had started to appear. Only once or twice there had been a successful Asian model—such as Pierre Cardin's Ving— but Asian women were rare in fashion. I hadn't thought that my looks would be considered too risky for the business.

Don't be mad, the model said. I'm just telling you the truth.

The agencies told me I was too elegant, too glamorous, too feminine for grunge. I wanted to tell them about my summers spent baling hay in my grandparents' village, or cold autumn evenings shredding carrots on the floor until my hands bled. But I didn't have the words.

I went to the movies to learn English. I would watch anything in English with French subtitles. *Basic Instinct, Batman, Funny Face, The Terminator, 101 Dalmatians, Doctor Zhivago,*

Myra Breckenridge. I saved my babysitting money to buy tickets and sat close to the screen. I lost myself in fantasy, but when the movie ended I had learned a few more words.

There was still time on my tourist visa. I would work at least the one fashion show I had promised myself. I would knock on every door in the city. I would walk every square inch of pavement. It was impossible that I could have traveled so far for my dreams to dissolve.

A few days later I came into Robert's house and called out his name. I'm back here working, he yelled from his studio.

I put down my bag. The smell of the fine tobacco he smoked in his pipe filled the air. Dramatic cloth curtains covered all four walls in the room, like a theater set. He had painted them himself; when they were pulled together, they depicted an afternoon in St. Petersburg.

Robert was in the back room talking with a man dressed in a brown suit. Robert leaned back in a chair, relaxed, while the man stood.

The painting you wish to buy has already been sold, Robert said in a quiet voice. He waved to me in greeting and motioned to an empty chair.

I don't mean any insult, the man said quickly. I understood that he was an art dealer. Robert often conducted business in his home.

Either way, it's true, Robert said. He lit a match and stoked the tobacco in his pipe. He was dressed in jeans and boots. He looked like a wise old Gypsy who had finally decided to stop roaming.

I'm sure we could go higher with our price, the man said.

You're asking me to break a previous agreement. I can't do it, Robert said calmly.

The dealer wrung his hands. Your paintings are all very attractive to us, he said. If you break your current agreement we will surely have more business for you in the future.

That's fine, said Robert. But I simply can't go back on my word.

The man looked down at the floor. I had thought we could reach an accord. Perhaps I was wrong, the man said.

Robert stood up. Then our business is finished, he said. It's been very nice talking with you. Please call on me another day.

Wait, wait, the dealer said. Let me go back to the gallery and talk to the owner. I'll call you later this afternoon, maybe we'll wish to buy another piece.

Robert shrugged. If you like.

Robert escorted the dealer to the door. I started to clean the living room—Robert and his wife now paid me for cleaning as well as babysitting. I was able to pay for the shared room I rented and my own food, again making my own way.

I wanted you to watch that for a reason, Robert said when he returned. You have to understand that the creative life means a lot of hard work and a lot of negotiating. Just like your modeling. Be smart and stand up for yourself.

I recognized Robert's tone of voice; he wanted to talk. He was also a good listener. We had spent hours talking about Buryatia, with Robert firing a new question as quickly as I had answered the last one.

That's also why I introduce you to so many Russian emigrants, he added. They're good people, but there's more to it. These people who left Russia a long time ago as enemies of the state have a lot to teach you about survival and endurance. The world's a hard place, Irina, but you're smart and you're strong. I don't like to see you getting discouraged.

I just came from an appointment, I said.

Robert tapped his pipe in an ashtray. What kind of appointment? he asked.

With a modeling agency, I said. They took me as a client.

Robert smacked the table with his fist. Excellent, he exclaimed. This is your start. I knew it would happen.

It's a small agency, I said. But they seem nice.

Robert folded his arms. Just remember what I told you. The artistic life is full of traps. Stay smart and aware, and you'll only fall into half of them.

At the end of the week I dressed quickly in my room. I had just paid the week's rent in the 100-franc notes that Robert and his wife paid me. With some of the money I had bought a loaf of fresh bread and a piece of cheese, which I snacked on from the small dressing table next to my bed. My new agency had sent me to a couple of castings, and said they were trying to find me work with one of the French magazines. That night they had invited me to a dinner. My booker, the person who arranged work for me, said the owner of the agency and some clients would be there. I hadn't asked for more information. I had little money left over after paying my rent, and a free meal would make my savings stretch a few more days.

I waited outside my building. The booker had said a car would be sent for me. This made me feel important. Surely they thought highly of me if they sent a car and driver. They must have thought I had great potential. The car arrived and I rode through the streets with other models from the agency. Their clothes were nicer than mine and they all seemed to know each other.

The restaurant was packed with people eating a late dinner. Soft classical music played from hidden speakers. The men wore fine suits, the women fashionable dresses. I heard the low hum of polite conversation.

This is the nicest restaurant I've ever been in, I said to the model next to me. I could never afford a place like this.

Me either, she said. Now I know I picked the right agency.

Our table was one of the largest in the room. The owner of the agency, a slim man in a tie and silk shirt, sat with a group of men I didn't recognize. They were all in their forties and fifties, and they had wine and ashtrays arranged before them. They stood up when we came to the table; everyone introduced themselves and sat down again.

What are we going to order? one of the models asked.

Something expensive, the girl next to me whispered. We all laughed.

The older men talked with the bookers and staff from the agency while the models sat together learning about each other. One girl was from Germany, another was English. They were all surprised and curious to learn where I was from.

Did you live on a glacier? one of them asked.

Were there prison camps nearby? said another.

I explained that I had grown up in a city, that Siberia was not all wastelands and labor camps. The food arrived and we talked about how difficult it was to find modeling work in Paris.

It seems like every beautiful girl in the world is in this city, said the young German woman. Too much competition.

I think we have a good agency, I said. They'll find something for us.

Giselle, a representative from the agency, got up from her seat and came around to our side of the table. She was slim and well dressed, with short hair that was always perfectly in place. She leaned close to the models and spoke in a very quiet voice.

You girls are being somewhat rude, she said. You're only talking among yourselves. Pay some attention to the men at the table. They're important for our business.

She spoke to us as though we were children who had forgotten our manners. I felt embarrassed. The people from the agency were serious and worldly. I would do anything they asked of me.

We talked with the older men about where we were from. They were all French and seemed curious about our lives. They were all old enough to be our fathers. I didn't ask what sort of work they did; I was afraid that Giselle would again criticize my manners.

After dinner our group left together in the cool night. We walked to Place Vendome, staring up at the lights and buildings lining the streets. My dinner had been the biggest meal I'd eaten in days, and I felt happy and content. I was also tired, and I had to be at Robert's house early the next morning to babysit his son.

I found Giselle and took her aside. This was a very nice evening, I said. But I have to be up early. When is the car leaving to take us back home?

A cool breeze blew a little pile of leaves along the street. The car? she asked, as though she didn't know what I was talking about.

How else am I going to get back? I asked. I didn't have the money for a taxi, though I didn't want to admit it.

Oh, don't be in such a hurry, Giselle said. Let's ask our friends. Maybe one of them can drop you off.

Giselle went to the one of the men in the group and whispered in his ear. He had seemed to be the most important man there. Whenever he had spoken, the others had stopped to listen.

This is Martin, Giselle said.

I'm very pleased to meet you, Martin said, kissing my hand. He had a deep voice and dignified way of speaking.

I looked at Giselle, unable to understand what was happening.

You were very interesting at dinner tonight, Martin said. His gray hair receded from his temples. His eyes were bright and intelligent.

Merci, I said.

Giselle tells me that it might be possible for us to know each other better, he added. I would like that very much.

I looked into his eyes, trying to interpret what he meant. Oh, Irina is so shy sometimes. Giselle laughed.

Vous êtes trés belle. You're very beautiful, Martin said. Perhaps we could speak alone, where it is quiet and we can hear each other.

I looked at Giselle. Her eyes turned cold and she sighed with frustration.

Now I understood. This is a mistake, I said to her, suddenly feeling angry.

Irina, don't be rude, Giselle said. Martin took a step back and looked away, pretending not to hear.

I'm sorry I can't make this evening turn out the way everybody thought, I blurted out. But I didn't know what was expected of me. I can't do this.

Don't be stupid, Giselle hissed.

She didn't have to say anything else for me to understand what she meant. I had been invited to an expensive dinner with wealthy older men. Why did I think they had paid for my food, my wine, my driver?

I didn't know, I said to her. You have to pick the right people before you try this kind of thing. Somebody else might enjoy it, that's fine, but I'm not interested.

Please don't be upset, Martin said. I certainly didn't mean for any misunderstandings to occur.

I believe you, I said, but this is wrong.

By now the other models were all watching me, along with the bookers and the agency owner. This is unfortunate, Giselle said to Martin. But what a wonderful evening it's been.

She took his arm and led him away. Before she was gone she looked over her shoulder and glared at me. Her look nearly struck me down where I stood.

I found another agency. The fall collections would soon begin and designers were holding castings every day. I was given assignment slips with exotic names on them: Chanel, LaCroix, Givenchy. They were words from a fairy tale, mystical sounds. I pronounced them like incantations, as though speaking them would open a gate in the sky.

I walked through expensive and glamorous districts to my appointments, thinking each time that I would be hired and my life would change. I stopped in front of windows full of elegant dresses and examined their every detail. I had hoped my experience with Pierre Cardin in Moscow would help me in Paris, but it didn't seem to matter. It had been a fleeting moment, perfect but ephemeral.

My agency made an appointment for me at the house of Givenchy. I wore my best outfit, a black jacket and short skirt that Larissa had made. On the jacket's lapels was rich ornamentation, evocative of China or Tibet. On the back was an embroidered design intended to evoke the roof of a tent—Ghengis Khan's shelter during his travels. The ends of the sleeves were made with pieces of sable. They were clothes that filled me with strength and confidence.

I stepped through the glass doors and gave my appointment slip to the receptionist. A tall model with short black hair walked past me and out the door, her expression revealing nothing.

I was led into a large, stark room. A crystal chandelier sparkled from the ceiling. The floors shined so brightly that I saw my own face at my feet. Men and women waited for me, their arms folded. They were dressed in white robes that made me wonder if this were a hospital rather than a fashion house.

Walk from there to there, a man said, pointing. Let us see how you move.

He had soft eyes beneath thin hair; I sensed he was in charge. This was the first time I had been seriously considered for a show. To me there was no procedure, no tradition. I knew only of the shows in Ulan Ude. If they wanted me to move, I would need music.

Would you mind playing music? I asked.

They paused for a moment but agreed. A young man turned on a portable stereo and inserted a cassette. Rock music began to play.

I started to move, a swan opening my wings. My arms floated around me, tracing invisible wavy lines in the air. I heard Lena's voice ordering me to become the music, to move with its flow. I walked from one end of the room to the other, interpreting the melody I heard.

When I finished there was only stillness. The song ended and the design staff stared at me.

Where do you come from? a woman finally asked.

From Russia, I said. I just arrived here.

She got up from her chair and led me to a door. They'll give you a dress in there, she said. And when you return, just walk. No more dancing. This collection will be very modern, and we want you to move in a more simple way.

In the short hallway outside the dressing room I saw framed photographs from decades past displaying Givenchy creations. I sensed the history of the house, the tradition of creativity and style. I recognized a photo of a woman dressed all in blue from a book I had seen while still a girl in Russia.

I pulled the dress onto my body, replaying what I had been told. No dancing, just walking. They hadn't liked what I had done. I wondered if they were talking about me in the next room. But the woman had been diplomatic and friendly. Perhaps there was nothing wrong. I was lost for a moment in confusion, wondering what to say and how to behave. I hadn't learned yet that there was no dancing on the runways of Paris.

Would you like your music again? a man asked me when I came back into the room.

Please, I said, my voice quiet. I willed myself to resist the melody and simply walked from one end of the room to the other.

That's great, said the woman who had told me only to walk.

Very nice, another man said. You're lovely. You've done a great job.

I shook hands with everyone in the room, my eyes full of their white robes. They liked me. I knew that this time I would be hired. I would walk the runway in exquisite clothes, full of creativity and spirit.

That afternoon I returned to the agency. My booker was a woman in her forties with bright green eyes named Marie. She waved a phone message in the air between us.

Givenchy didn't hire you, she said.

But they were so nice, I replied. They liked me.

I'm sure they did, Marie said. But that doesn't mean anything.

I sat down and put my face in my hands. I was used to fighting, I knew about being denied. But this time I had been so close.

Your problem is that you're too exotic, Marie said. Look at how you dress. You're like a hippie. The designers don't know what to do with you.

I can do the jobs, I said. I'm a hard worker.

At least try to dress better, she said. That jacket you're wearing—it's too ethnic. You should buy some expensive shoes— Prada or Chanel—and shorter dresses to show off your long legs. Try to be more sexy. And you also need an expensive, glamorous handbag. That's how you create a look.

The agency paid me 500 francs a week—about $100—for my room, my food, and my transportation. If I hadn't worked for Robert and his wife I would have starved.

I'll try, I said, knowing I could never do what she advised.

Good, Marie said. Remember, this is your one chance. Thousands of beautiful girls come to Paris every year looking for modeling work. You're not the first, and you won't be the last.

I lay in bed listening to the cars in the street below. That afternoon I had sent a small amount of money to my family. In my imagination I flew high in the sky, almost in space, looking down on the earth's curve extending from Paris to Siberia. Little lights dotted the planet, and I saw the great darkness of the lake.

There was a knock on my door. I had a telephone call from my agency.

I have an appointment for you with a famous designer, my booker said. You have to go there right now.

I looked at the clock. But it's almost eleven o'clock, I said.

I hung up. There was no way I could refuse such a call. This was one of the few designers I had known by name in Russia. I dressed quickly and ran to the Metro.

I found the street of the designer's offices. The moon was high in the sky and I walked past women standing on street corners looking into cars as they passed. They were dressed in tight, revealing clothes, and they regarded me with blank hostile stares.

The designer's offices were unlocked. A young receptionist sat behind a desk leafing through a phone registry. I said hello, but she didn't look up. It was as though I didn't exist.

I told her my name. Still she ignored me. I told her I had an appointment. She looked up as though I had offended her. Fine, she said. Why don't you sit down and wait. Someone will come for you.

I sat on a small sofa where I could see the steps that led upstairs. Soon it was close to midnight. I had asked the secretary several times what was happening. Just a few more minutes, she said. They're coming for you. Don't get excited.

An hour later they came for me. The designer descended the steps as part of a procession. First came a little dog wearing a white collar, looking around like a human, with a snobbish expression. Then a very slim woman in a dark suit and a shawl over her shoulders and a smoking cigarette. Next were a pair of young men, their eyes locked on the floor.

I couldn't believe all of these people were working at such a late hour. I stood up. Three more men came down the steps, and I finally recognized one of them as the designer. They walked past me as though I wasn't there—everyone moving as though in a stylish trance—and went into a side room and closed the door.

I considered for a moment, then went to the door and turned the knob. The secretary leapt from her chair. You can't go in there, she shouted. It's not allowed.

But it was too late. I opened the door and saw a series of surprised faces. The designer sat at the head of a long wooden table. Behind him were his entourage, arranged as if posing for a portrait.

Thank you for contacting my agency, I said to the designer.

I handed him my collection of photographs, which I had arranged into a proper book.

His hands shook as he reached for the book. His eyes were shielded by dark sunglasses. When he opened the first page he examined the picture for a very long time, as though unsure precisely what he was looking at.

The assistants behind him watched me with pasted-on smiles. They tried very hard to appear relaxed, as though everything was fine.

The designer turned to the next page and slumped back in his chair. His gaze drifted over my picture slowly. His head tilted to the side. He asked for a cigarette in a husky voice, and accepted it with trembling fingers. I could see that he was more than ill; his look was one that I had seen in Moscow. He was so high that he could barely sit up.

I didn't get home until two in the morning. I hadn't been hired for the collection. The designer had gotten up from the table and left the room with unsteady steps, apparently forgetting that he was in the middle of speaking with me.

I cried in the dark. I thought of Roland in New York for the first time in weeks, and remembered the days we had spent together. The world had seemed very cold since then. All that kept me in Paris was the certainty that my life would be worse when I went home to Siberia.

I sat at a glass-topped table at an outdoor cafe. I opened my notebook and jotted down the names of the agencies and fashion houses which I intended to visit that day. The list looked stark on the page; part of me feared another day with no results, no success. I looked around at the other tables, where friends and lovers talked in French, exchanging smiles and touching hands. I felt as though no one saw me, no one would ever notice me.

I ordered a cup of tea and, while it cooled, began to write a letter home to my parents. I didn't want them to worry, so I wrote that everything was going well. It was, like an old Russian expression from a Gogol story, a "saintly lie." In my letter I described the cafe, the fresh air, the traffic on the avenue.

When I looked up a waiter was standing in front of me. I reached for my purse, thinking he wanted me to pay for my tea. Instead he put his hand over mine to indicate that I didn't need to give him any money.

I can pay, I said.

He handed me a piece of paper and pointed to a table under the shade of a large umbrella where an older woman sat alone. She stared at me openly, her eyes fixed on mine.

I opened the paper. It contained a name and a telephone number. I looked up from it and saw that the woman was still watching me.

I thought I must have looked like someone she knew. Or perhaps I had run into her at one of the agencies and she remembered me. I waved at her to say thanks and returned to writing my letter.

Somehow I knew she was approaching before I looked up; when I did, she stood next to me, blocking the sun. She wore a deep-blue dress open at the neck to reveal a gold necklace. Her hair was pulled into a tight bun that revealed her slender neck; her skin was pale and flawless, her nose symmetrical and fine. Her eyes stared into mine.

Hello, I said. Thank you for the tea.

It is nothing, she said. Her expression was serene yet intense; I felt the power of her personality in her shining eyes.

Do I know you? I asked.

I would like to know you, she said. What is your name?

Irina, I said.

She smiled and repeated my name, then motioned to the paper that the waiter had brought me.

I hope that you will call me, she said. When you have time.

She walked away, her lithe body disappearing around the corner as though she had never been there. I put the piece of paper in my notebook, not sure what I would do with it. I remembered the intensity that had burned in her eyes, the sense that she could have whatever in the world she wanted. I went to my appointments and, for the moment, cast the image out of my mind.

Early the next week I went through my notebook trying to find my letter to my parents so that I could mail it. My days had begun to feel like a long lonely march from one modeling agency to the next; discouragement had begun to weigh at my heart. It seemed no one was interested. I wondered what to do next, whether I should stop trying to model. My thoughts moved to returning to Russia, an idea that hovered like a dark cloud. I thought again, as I often did, of Roland and whether I would ever see him again.

I absentmindedly flipped from one page of my notebook to the next until I saw the folded piece of paper that the older woman had given me at the cafe. I opened it up and read the name and number again.

I could see the soft lines of her face, the subtle point of her chin, her eyes that met mine with fearful intensity. I remembered the way she had looked at me and wondered what would happen if I called her.

She had seemed so much more sophisticated than me, with her stylish dress and jewelry. I wondered how someone like her lived, what her house would look like. She had seemed so interested in me; perhaps I could speak to her about my loneliness and frustration. She seemed like someone who had experienced the world; perhaps she would understand me and help me find the strength to go on. She might even become my friend.

I called the number. A man answered and I asked to speak with her. Her voice brightened when she realized who I was.

I'm so glad you called, she said. Would you like to come see me today?

I hesitated. Yes, I would.

She gave me an address near the Champs-Elysées. When I hung up I felt my heart quicken. I wasn't sure why I had reached out to this stranger in the way I had. But I knew that I would keep my appointment with her.

Her house was in an aged stone apartment building ringed by trees and flowers in a very old part of the city. A stiff, formal doorman in a uniform called her on a telephone; he seemed almost surprised that I was expected upstairs. He led me to an elevator, where another man ceremoniously held the door and let me off at the correct floor.

A young man opened the thick wooden door for me; he was well-dressed and polite. He called out her name and, when she came into the room, he looked at her with downcast eyes. I didn't know who he might have been, a servant or a lover. She told him to leave and he was gone without a word.

She was dressed in a long ethereal dress. She wore bright nail polish and high heels. Her face was set with friendly expectation as she took my purse and placed it on an antique sideboard.

We stood facing each other. I smelled her perfume, something delicate.

Welcome, she said. I'm glad you came.

I couldn't look into her eyes. I felt like turning away, hiding my face. The room in which we stood was a sort of parlor; antiques in wood and marble lined the walls, punctuated by high windows shaded against the afternoon sun. Candles burned in brass holders, and after I took a deep breath to relax myself I could hear soft music playing from somewhere I couldn't see.

Let's go sit and talk, she said with a little laugh.

Her house was like nothing I had ever seen before. I watched the way she walked, the way she held her hands, trying to imitate her as we sat down together on a sofa in a little room at the end of the hall.

Would you like tea? Something to eat?

No, thank you, I replied

She put one arm on the back of the sofa and smiled at me again. I dared a look into her eyes. They were like fire, burning with confidence and power. I kept her gaze for only a few seconds more before I turned away.

Please tell me about yourself, she said.

In a halting voice I explained where I was from and how I had come to Paris. I felt embarrassed about my poor French, I felt clumsy. The more nervous I became, the more I talked. I explained that I was frustrated with trying to find modeling work, that I wasn't sure how much longer I could persevere. She nodded sympathetically, not saying a word.

When I was done talking she shifted closer to me. I remained where I was. I felt a force emanate from within her then a sensation as though I was under a spell. I felt small and weak before the force of her will.

I want to tell you why I gave you my number, she said to me.

I looked into her eyes. I could feel the warmth of her body as she moved still closer.

I watched you for a long time at the cafe, but you didn't see me, she said. She put her hand on my neck and let it rest there.

I didn't move as her hand pressed against a knot of muscle. She released the pressure on my neck and began to caress me as though she were petting a cat.

You appeared to me like a vision, she said, like a pure angel.

I felt myself shift closer to her. I lost myself in her shining eyes, swallowed into the deep ocean of her personality. I felt no danger from her. I knew she would not hurt me if I stayed.

She took my hand and I closed my eyes. I felt the warmth of her lips against mine, the soft touch of her fingers on my breasts.

I had lost hope that I would ever love, she whispered to me. But now that I have seen you I have hope again.

She unbuttoned my blouse and moved her hand in slow circles over my skin. I breathed in sharply, allowed my hand to graze her cheek.

I don't want to frighten you, she said.

I'm not frightened.

I felt the soft press of her skin against mine, our chests beating with a single heartbeat. I allowed myself to become lost in the fullness of everything she represented to me, and all that she said I meant to her. She held on to me. I was drowned in passion; the dark clouds in my mind began to dissipate. She understood loneliness, desperation. Through her desire she filled me with new energy, recharging me with love. I saw her only once more, casually, on Champs-Elysées a month later. We stopped, smiled at each other and, like old friends, chatted for only a brief moment. It would be the last time I would ever see her.

I asked my booker if any Japanese designers in Paris might be interested in me. Forget it, she said. They want to hire Asian girls even less than the Europeans. It's a dead end.

The collections began, with daily fashion shows throughout Paris. I felt as though a great game had begun and I hadn't been asked to participate. But I received a call in the morning from a Japanese agent. She had seen some of my pictures and wanted to meet with me.

It's no wonder you can't find work in Paris, she said when we met. You're all wrong for this season. You look like you came from a fairy tale, and all the designers want girls who look like they live on the streets. If you come to Japan, though, I can find work for you.

She offered me a one-month contract with Chanel for a trip to Japan. I would travel to twenty-two cities in one month, doing four shows a day. It would pay enough for me to keep my room in Paris and send money home to Siberia.

I'll do it, I said. But why did you choose me?

You're different, she said. You look Asian, but your energy and behavior are partly Western. You're completely different, and once people understand this they'll find it very appealing.

I thought about what she had said and began to comprehend it. A generation before, I never would have been allowed to leave Siberia. My people were almost unknown to the world outside Russia. My country had endured pain in this decade, but our world was opening its eyes to a new morning. I didn't feel that I was anything extraordinary. But I lived in the crossing currents of history, in a reality that would be crafted by the imaginative and the tenacious.

Many people in Japan assumed I was Japanese, and taxi drivers didn't want to take me when I tried to speak English to them. Their car doors opened and closed automatically, without being touched. Neon lights twirled in strange hieroglyphs. There were no addresses, only directions, and I was constantly lost. I felt that I was in a sea of vending machines and electronics, a world of busy abundance for which Paris had done little to prepare me.

My agency arranged a room for me with a middle-aged Japanese couple, where I would stay until the tour began in two days. I was left after quick introductions to Eiko and her husband, who were deferential and polite. And I met their cat, a huge white animal who stared at me with the knowledge that the apartment was his and that humans lived there as his guest.

The apartment was only three very small rooms, more cramped than my parents' home in Ulan Ude. I put my suitcase in my room and, when I returned to the kitchen, began speaking to them in English I had learned from the movies. They shrugged, shook their heads, and talked in Japanese.

We sat down together at the dining table and tried to find words we both knew. There were none. Their big white cat stalked into the room looking offended and vengeful.

Eiko pulled a family album from a shelf and sat down next to me. She spoke Japanese in a high, musical voice, pointing at her relatives. In all the pictures the men and women were smiling. Amid the pictures of people were photos of the cat in all stages of its life. With his fine features he almost looked Japanese to me, as though he had taken on the characteristics of his parents. I began to understand that the cat truly was like a child to this couple, that he influenced them and controlled the way things were done in the house.

I found my packet of photos in my suitcase and brought them to the kitchen. I showed Eiko my parents, my grandparents, my aunts and uncles. I spoke English and Russian and she listened intently, repeating my words back to me. It began to feel as though we understood each other.

Eiko pointed at a pot boiling on the stove, then at an empty plate. She opened the pot and talked in a questioning tone. I got up. Inside the pot was fresh rice. The pot was actually a device that boiled rice all day.

I pointed at the pot, then at the picture of my parents. This rice maker is incredible, I said. As soon as I make enough money in this country, I'm buying one of these to send to my parents.

It was like a Buryat fairy tale my grandmother had told me about a pot of food that was always full, no matter how much the people ate from it. There was never any need to put food into it, for abundance would magically appear. Reality in Russia was as far from this story as possible.

Eiko led me into my bedroom and pointed at the mat on the floor where I would sleep. She held up her finger for me to wait for a moment, then she and her husband returned with a pot of tea, cups, and a colored cloth that she spread on the floor. She poured tea for me, then for her and her husband. I understood that this was a ceremony to welcome me into their home.

Before they left me for the night Eiko put her hand on my arm. She didn't speak but looked deep into my eyes. I understood somehow that she cared for me, that I was safe. I thanked her, knowing she would understand my tone if not my words. The cat watched us from the doorway, brooding and jealous.

Water was rationed in this household. Every time I needed to take a shower or wash my hands I had to go to a board of buttons that controlled the water flow. Eiko had explained it to me the night before, pointing to each button then walking me to the water source to which it was connected. By the time I awoke in the morning Eiko and her husband had already left for work. I pushed what turned out to be the correct button and squeezed myself into the cramped shower. Whoever designed Japanese bathrooms didn't intend for them to be used by someone who is 5'10".

I ate rice and vegetables in the kitchen and opened the letter that Chanel had sent to the apartment before I arrived. I had an appointment that afternoon with the tour's organizer, and we'd leave the next morning. I unfolded the itinerary and saw the long list of cities we would visit; I had never heard of most of them. At the end of the letter was the time and date of my airplane trip back to Paris.

I looked up from the letter, sensing eyes watching me. It was the cat. He stood in the hallway, his eyes fixed, his body unmoving.

Good morning, *koshka,* I said. My name is Irina.

The cat was still like a statue. He took a deep breath as though preparing to strike. I understood that this was his house, and that I was an intruder. His white fur contrasted against the dark carpet. His eyes gleamed.

I like your parents very much, I said. They are the same age as my parents. They have similar faces.

The cat stood straighter. He seemed more human than animal.

I know this is your apartment, I said. But the agency put me here, so what can I do? You're keeping me from my bedroom and the bathroom. Could you please step aside?

He seemed so intelligent that I hoped he might understand. But instead of moving he bared his teeth. A deep guttural noise came from his husky body, like the call of a wildcat. He arched his back and his hair stood up in spikes from his back. I let out a scream of surprise, which I instantly regretted—he seemed to recognize my fear, and it made him look even more threatening.

I edged into the living room, trying not to scare him. I sat on the sofa and tried to think of what to do. I turned on the television, hoping the sound would make him calm.

The phone rang. When I picked it up I saw that the cat was now watching me from the doorway.

Irina? a woman's voice asked. Would it be possible for you to come to your appointment at Chanel one hour earlier than previously arranged?

Yes, I can do that, I replied.

I hung up the phone. The cat had moved inside the doorway and crept slowly along the wall of the room.

You'll have to let me leave, I told him. Then you'll be happy. I'll be gone, you'll have your kingdom all to yourself.

He opened his mouth and hissed, then let out a terrible wail. I ran past him into the hall, imagining him chasing me all the way to my room. I dressed and looked out again. I couldn't see him. I caught a glimpse of white fur when I ran toward the front door and let myself out, but I escaped without a scratch.

I left Eiko's apartment building with no definite idea where I was going. The subway station was just a few minutes away, and when I found it I unfolded my map. The writing was in Japanese, impossible for me to read.

Excuse me, I said to a woman walking past. Do you speak English? Or French?

She glanced at me and walked away without answering. The terminal was full of little stores and people walking fast, their eyes straight ahead as though they had been programmed to reach their destinations without any deviation. Incomprehensible words echoed from unseen speakers. I tried to stop a man in a business suit, but he walked past me.

I realized that I would never be able to ride the subway without help. I asked an old woman if she spoke English, then another businessman. I called out to every person who walked past until a young man carrying a backpack stopped for me.

What can I help you with? he asked in impeccably pronounced English.

I showed him my map, my money, Chanel's address. He patiently explained the subway route I needed to take and how much it would cost.

Inside the train I felt as though I had stepped into a dream. I had to push through the crowd to find an open place to stand. I looked down the row of seats and saw the same image, repeated again and again: men in white shirts and black ties, holding suitcases, reading newspapers. They wore their black hair in the same short haircut. Their lips were pressed together and their eyes averted in identical expressions.

A few people slept standing up, relying on the press of bodies to keep them from falling. When their station was announced their eyes opened, they straightened, and they left the train. I watched the tunnel lights passing outside the window and listened hard for my destination.

A television set was installed above our heads. Some passengers watched it, others ignored it. I watched a colorful advertisement for beer, then a man and woman talking and sharing a piece of candy. I was so entranced that it took me several minutes to realize that I had missed my stop.

We have to give you a Japanese name, the agency representative said. From now on you will be called Baikal-Iriko.

It was important for me to speak Japanese to the clients; they might become offended otherwise. I was taught simple words and phrases. If someone asked my name, I said, *Watashi wa Baikal no Iriko-des.* My name is Irina from Baikal.

The other foreign models and I were kept separate from the Japanese models. How we acted and what we said, we were taught, would be as important as how we worked. Every aspect of our time was to be strictly regimented and organized.

I arrived twenty minutes late for one of the first rehearsals. The show was much later in the day, but we were told to arrive a minimum of six hours before. I had trouble with my directions, and when I came into the hall no one commented on my tardiness.

When I received my first paycheck I saw that an hour had been deducted from it. I called my agency and told them I had been only twenty minutes late. Why had they penalized me for an entire hour?

This is an important lesson for you, I was told. In Japan you must never be late for your job. The fashion business is like any other. Be happy you only paid an hour's salary for this education.

I would work six weeks for Chanel. Only eight girls had been chosen for the tour, four Japanese and four foreigners. I was given a contract to sign that was written in Japanese. My agency sat me down and translated it for me.

You are to be paid the rate for Japanese models, the agent read aloud.

But why? I asked. They know I'm not Japanese.

You are Asian, she said. For these purposes, it's the same thing.

Since I had arrived, I felt that everyone I met had silently pointed out to me that I was a foreigner. Now I was considered Japanese. I couldn't understand.

What's the difference? I asked. Why does this contract have to say what country I'm from?

Japanese models are paid less than foreigners, she said bluntly. Almost half as much.

I looked at the numbers she wrote down for me, specifying how much I would be paid. This wasn't the time to fight. If they paid me less than they could, I had to accept it. The money I earned would allow me to stay in Paris a little longer.

That night I telephoned my parents and told them about my job. My father congratulated me.

I'll be able to send you some more money, I said.

That's very kind, he replied. Make sure you take care of yourself. Get enough to eat.

Governmental subsidies for the arts had been cut in Russia. Every theater faced an impossible economic crisis. There was almost no money to pay anyone, and actors and administrators at times worked for nothing. The few francs and yen I sent my family were as valuable as gold.

The Chanel tour began. Every morning we arose early for our train, plane, bus, or car, always moving from one place to the next. In the trains we moved so fast that I felt as though

I was flying. The Japanese had created a wonderland in which to live—telephones and televisions were everywhere, and I sensed the nation embracing technology like a second body. Wires and circuits became as vital as hands and feet.

At night we were booked into the best hotels in whatever city we were staying. I had lived in a rundown apartment in Paris and slept in living rooms in Moscow. I closed and locked the Japanese hotel room behind me, allowing my five senses to absorb the greatest luxury I had ever experienced.

The bathtubs were deep, the water hot. I stayed in the water for an hour at a time. There was free shampoo, soap, lotions—all would have been too expensive for me in Russia, if I had been able to find them.

I was able to order food to my room, no matter the cost. I ordered several items from the menu. Chicken, fish, beef, steamed vegetables. I had never tasted such variety. The meat was tender and succulent, nothing like the stringy cuts I had eaten in Russia. I ordered fruit with exotic names, and slices of cake. I wished I could send some to my parents, though of course the food would have spoiled by the time it reached Siberia.

How many people are staying in your room? the concierge asked.

Just me, I replied. I have a very healthy appetite.

I walked across the carpet and felt its softness between my toes. I parted the curtains and looked out on the lights and wealth of Japan. It was all mine. I didn't have to count every penny. For the moment I no longer felt that disaster was waiting to claim me the moment I was no longer vigilant.

I had to be ready to leave the hotel at six every morning. Each show was the same, with the same collection of clothes, identical music, the same order of appearances on the runway. We had rehearsals at every location, then performed four shows a day. The collection was lustrous and beautiful. I was taught to walk quickly and efficiently on stage. Soon I felt the steady rhythm of the days pass like a comforting hand touching my soul.

The other models and I talked and laughed during the few minutes that were our own. There was an American and a

Brazilian. We told stories of our homes and families, and after a few weeks the luxury of my hotel rooms thrilled me less. I lay on my huge bed and remembered my little bed in Ulan Ude, the sounds and smells of my household.

In Osaka we finished our fourth show of the day. The applause from the audience was polite and restrained. Backstage we changed out of the expensive designs into our own clothes. Behind the hall, vans waited with their engines running to take us to the hotel.

You did very well today, the organizer said. Tomorrow we will begin again. Remember how much responsibility you have assumed. The good name of Chanel relies on your diligence and bearing.

In my room I ran water in the bathtub and ordered food. It seemed that I would never have enough sleep. Now that I was alone I allowed myself to feel the tension that knotted my back and shoulders.

Be good, they told us every morning. Be nice today, smile. Have a good word for everyone.

I had only lately realized how tired and isolated I felt. I turned on the television and leaned back on a cushion as the evening news began. The announcer spoke with great seriousness as he began the first story.

I turned up the volume. I couldn't understand everything he said, but the video images made it clear. A hurricane had hit Tokyo, one of the worst of the century. The streets ran with water like rivers. Winds had torn roofs from homes. The Shinagawa subway station, just a few minutes from Eiko's house, was flooded from nonstop rain. Some people had died, and it looked as though the hand of nature had risen up in anger.

A reporter stopped a woman on the street who was bailing water from her ground-floor apartment and had stepped outside to rest for a moment. When the interview began I saw her face change. Her fatigued expression shifted into a smile full of propriety.

There's no need to worry, she said. With Japan's technology everything will soon be straightened out. Things will return to normal. Life will be better than ever.

I struggled to understand how she could say this. No one I had met in Japan had ever complained about their circumstances. In the most difficult moments they would smile and speak in pleasant voices. The Chanel models could make mistakes in the program and receive little comment, but harsh words would always come when someone moaned or complained about the day's travel schedule or grueling rehearsal itinerary.

It was a country of greater wealth than seemed possible. It bustled and worked as though there was no other way to live. With each new city at which I arrived I marveled that there could be more buildings, more people, more things. I felt as though the tour would go on forever, with infinite new cities and endless money from buyers and clients.

I watched a policeman helping old people walk through knee-deep water out of their apartment building.

The waters will go away in time, he said to the camera. We will still be here. Hurricanes, earthquakes—we can withstand them all.

The next day we returned to Tokyo for a short break before another round of shows. In the train I had felt tears in my eyes. I was so tired I could barely gather my thoughts, and now I would have to face a city in the middle of a terrible disaster. But when I arrived I saw that everything was the same as before. Within a single day the deep waters had been conquered.

I had a day to myself. I found a Buddhist temple and monastery near Eiko's apartment late in the day. There was a park with little bridges and trees where I walked in a light evening mist. Beyond the walls were the cars and congestion. Inside there was silence and serenity. I saw monks trimming grass and carrying buckets from one building to the next. They focused their eyes straight ahead and left me to my own thoughts.

Inside the temple I smelled the incense and allowed my eyes to wander over the ornate carvings. I knelt and silently prayed. Somewhere inside me was a peaceful center that I needed to find again. I was the girl, then the woman, who had fought back fear and worry and tried to make her life wherever the world had taken her. I stayed absolutely still and searched within for my strength, for my conviction that the changing world was a beautiful challenge that I relished facing.

I sat down on the grass outside and looked up at the full moon and stars. I didn't have a watch, I had no idea how long I had been there. Still the monks left me alone, allowing me to simply exist amid the tranquil beauty.

The monastery made me think of Lobsang; I pictured the serenity and kindness in his eyes. Then I saw Roland, his lips curled into a gentle smile. I wondered if I would ever see him again.

I had seen Lake Baikal in winter and Moscow in the heat of summer. I had walked streets in Paris that had seemed infused with centuries of sophistication and style. I had shot across the crowded land of Japan like a bullet in a train filled with machines that linked each person to every spot on the globe.

But in the sky all was the same as it always had been. Moonshine, sunrise, the wind, the stars, remained constant no matter the place, the language, the politics. The human voice was the same exquisite instrument no matter what words it formed. The universe luxuriated in its timeless eternity, not caring whether we ever found a pause in which to cease our motions and reflect on its power.

I felt a light touch at my shoulder and opened my eyes. Insects buzzed softly in the trees. A monk stood over me, smiling. I had fallen asleep in the warm night air.

All you all right? he asked. I saw concern in his eyes.

I'm fine, I said. Thank you.

He returned to the monastery. I yawned, feeling as though eternity had claimed me for a short hour. I would return, one day, to its embrace.

Eiko and her husband treated me like their child, speaking affectionately and asking me to call them when I was traveling. They sat me down with the cat and explained that I was part of the family. In time it let me live in the apartment in a state of fragile truce. The only condition was that I talk to it in the same manner as his parents did: pleading, flattering, loving.

One evening Eiko came home from work with a bundle wrapped in paper. She gave it to me and told me to open it. Inside was a beautiful doll in a fine dress, with perfect hand-painted features.

This is for you, she said.

Very nice, her husband said. Lovely, like our Irina.

Eiko put her hand on my cheek. Why are you crying? she asked. Don't you like it?

I hadn't possessed beautiful things as a child. Some of my classmates' parents came home from trips to Moscow bearing dolls and toys. My mother and father would have loved to do the same, but there was never enough money from their theater wages. So I had learned never to ask for such things. A doll such as this was very expensive, in Tokyo as well as Moscow, and I had kept a secret wish through my life that someday I would have one.

Of course I like it, I said to Eiko. I love it. I'll keep it forever.

By the time I returned to Paris, I was an experienced model. My agency scheduled two photo sessions for *Dépêche Mode,* a magazine popular with younger girls. I felt the camera on me like an objective eye. I tried to imagine myself as it saw me, pleasing it, evoking a mood that it would capture in an essential moment.

I added the magazine pages into my book of photographs. Now when I went to a design house the casting agents took me seriously. It was as though I had crossed an invisible line. It had meant nothing to them when I said I was capable of doing the job. They wanted concrete evidence that they could hold in their hands.

I waited in line in the afternoon heat, hoping for an assignment in a show for the spring collections. Sometimes it took hours for my turn to come, but of course that didn't matter to me. Behind me was a model named Brandy.

Where are you going after this appointment? I asked her.

I have an appointment with Chanel, she said.

I wondered why I didn't have an appointment as well. Though the Chanel organization in Tokyo was separate from Paris, my experience in Japan could have helped me. An hour later I telephoned my agency.

Chanel is having casting appointments for their shows, I said. Do you have anything arranged for me?

We're going to try, they said. Chanel made a request for some models, but we're not sure if we're sending you.

I hung up the phone. I didn't understand the fashion business, why an agency would send one woman and not another. I saw Brandy walking out of the design house where we just auditioned. She was checking her watch.

I called out her name. I'll go with you, I said. I have an appointment today also, but I lost the address.

I had no idea what I would do when I arrived at Chanel, but I understood that nothing would happen unless I acted on my own. I was working more often than before I went to Japan, but already my money had begun to run out. Life in Russia had taught me to continue knocking on doors even if they seemed to be locked and bolted.

At Chanel the receptionist sat behind security glass with a list of that day's appointments. Brandy gave her name, along with an identification number. The receptionist passed her a sticker and waved her through the door.

Oui? Bonjour? the receptionist asked when I stepped up to her desk.

I have an appointment for today, I said.

She looked through her list, shaking her head. I'm afraid I don't have your name here, she said.

There must be some mistake, I told her.

She checked the list again, though I could see she didn't believe it was possible that she was in error.

I realized that I would have to play a character: a successful, very busy, arrogant fashion model. I put my hand on my hip, shrugged, and shook my head.

Well, I'm sure it doesn't matter, I said. Maybe the appointment was made for another day. Anyway, I'm here now. I really don't have time to discuss it. I have other appointments.

She tapped her pen on the desk. I watched her weigh what I had said. Finally she shrugged. She pressed a button and I heard the door unlock.

Inside were exquisite textured walls and plush sofas and chairs. A young woman greeted me and told me that I could sit down while I waited. Soon a woman with a thin face and her hair pulled back into a bun joined me and asked to see my book of photographs. I watched her slowly leaf through them. Her forehead wrinkled with concentration.

Très bien, she said, handing me the book. Come with me.

She led me into another room and told me to wait. I sat

down in a metallic chair that looked like a piece of abstract art. A man in a suit and tie came into the room and held out his hand for my book. He looked through it quickly, nodding his head as though agreeing with someone who wasn't there.

Bien, he said. Follow me.

He led me into another empty room and told me to sit. I could hear voices in the next room—men and women talking about the fit of a piece of clothing. I held my photo book close to my chest. I was certain that soon someone would run into the room shouting that I didn't really have an appointment. I imagined myself being led out to the street, the door closing behind me forever.

Irina? a man's voice called out.

He led me into a huge white room full of Chanel products. Clothes, accessories, all beautiful and glamorous. Women sat arranged in chairs wearing sophisticated glasses on their impassive faces, smoking cigarettes from tortoise-colored holders. I tried to make no noise with my steps. I was led to a table where a man sat watching me cross the room.

I'm Jean-Paul, he said. Let me see your book. He took off his glasses and looked at me. I noticed that his short hair was graying at the temples.

I want you to try something on, he said.

He found a short sleeveless black dress that would fit me. I put it on behind a screen, and when I came out he clapped his hands.

This is an incredible girl, he announced to the room. Look at her face! Where has she been? Where did she come from?

No one spoke. I wished I could hold the moment in time and live it again and again. I had tried for months to be in such a room full of beauty and glamour. I had waited my entire life to hear those encouraging words.

I from Siberia, I told him, still struggling with French. I be fashion model. I like to find work. I want one show with a great house. Chanel.

Jean-Paul smiled. Maybe I'll have to learn some Siberian so we can talk, he said. He took my hand and said, Come with me.

He led me through hallways, stopping to knock on office doors. He introduced me to men and women sitting at desks and drafting tables. Some of them asked me to turn left or right, to step into the light or away from it.

Mr. Lagerfeld is here today, Jean-Paul said. I think he'll want to see you right away.

I made a small noise, like a little gasp. I had thought someone would look at my book and send me away. Perhaps they might take my number and call me in a week. Now I stepped through a high door into a spacious office. There was a bustle of activity centered around a man sitting at a table. When I came into the room the people parted and I saw Karl Lagerfeld. His big dark glasses obscured his face. He sat with his hands folded.

This is Irina, Jean-Paul said. She just came in today.

The people in the room moved closer to me. When they spoke, it was like a chorus of voices.

Oh, she's great, a woman said. Look at her long legs.

She's so skinny and tall, said a man in a silk shirt. Look at how that dress fits her.

Her cheekbones, someone else added. Just look at them.

Karl Lagerfeld got up with a smile on his face. He spoke very quickly, as though he had so many ideas that his words were forced to pour forth in a torrent.

You have such an interesting look, he said. He traced my face and hair in the air with his hands.

I knew you would like her, Jean-Paul said.

Very interesting, very unique, Lagerfeld said. Can we try something else on her?

Hands touched me, helping me sit, guiding me into another room. I started to take off my shoes and a woman told me to stop.

Don't do that, she said. We have dressers to help you with that.

Let us take care of you, a young man said. Which would you like: tea or coffee?

Tea, I said. No. Wait. Coffee.

I'll bring you both! he replied enthusiastically.

I tried on pants, dresses, gowns, and suits for Karl Lagerfeld and his assistants. With each outfit I was given compliments, and I wasn't even permitted to tie my own shoes, button my own buttons. As a girl I had dreamed of being a princess, and now I felt like I had become one.

I was asked where I was from and how I had made it to Paris. You will be free for our shows? a woman with a calendar said.

I began laughing. Are you kidding? I asked. That's why I am here.

When I left afternoon had turned into evening. I walked slowly through the streets, smelling the fresh air. It had rained while I was inside. I decided that I would use a little of my saved money to buy dinner for Robert and his wife.

I had done it. I would work my one fashion show with a great designer. If I were never asked to model again I would still be happy. I imagined myself rowing a little boat on Lake Baikal when I was old. I would tell my grandchildren about Paris and the house of Chanel.

My experience modeling in Japan had prepared me for the Western shows. There was to be no dancing, no theater. I walked to the end of the runway in an elegant cream-colored suit and paused. Flash bulbs exploded all around me, filling my eyes with light. I smiled and looked toward the far horizon. I tried to communicate joy and excitement in my face and posture.

My phone began to ring more often. Other houses requested me for their shows. I cashed my checks and sent money to my parents through some Russians I had met who were going home. Each morning I sprang from my bed with energy.

I sat backstage at a Chanel show looking into the mirror. My long hair was pulled away from my face. The makeup artists had accented my cheeks and eyes. They had again created a vision from my features, a picture of someone else. I stared at her, wondering what she thought and what were the textures of her dreams. Photographers and video crews wandered the edges of the room, and journalists interviewed the designers and models. I sipped a glass of juice, careful not to damage my makeup.

I wondered: Is this a dream? Is this real?

Two women dressed in Chanel clothes approached me slowly as though silently debating who should speak first. I looked up and recognized them as the heads of the Chanel Japanese tours.

Irina, it's so nice to see you here, the older woman said. She wore a leather bag hanging on a strap from her shoulder.

What are you doing here? the second woman asked.

I'm working for Chanel again, I said. But here in Paris rather than Japan.

They exchanged glances. We would love to have you on the next Japanese tour, the first woman said.

My agency had contacted me the month before, saying that they had booked me for another tour in Japan. I had wanted the work, because it paid well and because my opportunities in Paris had seemed more limited. But at the last minute the organizers had cancelled the offer.

That's very nice of you, I said. I'll have to think about it.

We'll pay you a better rate this time, the younger woman said. She paused. She seemed to have wished she hadn't mentioned money.

I shook their hands. It was nearly time for the show to begin. Before I stepped into the lights I pondered what had just happened. I no longer had to beg for work. Perhaps my single fashion show would turn into more. I remembered Japan, the punishing schedule and long hours. Perhaps I would do it again. Perhaps not. For the first time in my memory, I had a choice.

After the show I went to a cafe near the Arc de Triomphe with a group of models. Outside the glass windows the cars streamed like fish in a river. Conversation buzzed all around us.

I've already booked a flight for New York, a model named Gabrielle said. My agency says they can get me work for the American collections. It's going to be a great season.

I listened in silence. New York. I pictured tall buildings and streets full of unique, energetic people. I had seen images in movies and books. For a second I wondered whether Roland still lived there. He still lived in my heart, but I knew that I would never see him again.

What is it like, New York? I asked quietly.

Several voices talked at once. It's the best. There's no place like it in the world. I feel like I'm flying every time I go there. The collections there are always so much fun.

They're interested in foreign models? I asked.

Gabrielle took my hand. Of course they are, don't be silly. She laughed. If you're really serious about your career, you have to work the New York collections.

The conversation drifted to the current Paris shows. After a while I stopped listening. My imagination was full of skyscrapers and canyons made of concrete. It didn't matter whether I modeled in New York or not. I merely wanted to stand on its streets. America was a land of movies and fantasies. Only obtaining a visa and the great cold ocean stood between me and its shores. I knew that I had legs long enough to step across the world in a single stride.

The next morning I took my Russian passport and French visa to the American embassy. A security stopped me at the door and asked for my purse. He looked inside, then made me step through a device that checked my body for metal. I was cleared to go in.

The line wound around itself and filled the huge room. I stood up on my toes and saw that only two windows were open. I heard the sound of babies crying and people moaning with fatigue. I stood still and folded my arms. After a half hour the line had barely moved.

An hour became two, then three. The line inched forward. Still only two windows were open. I occupied myself by observing how people were dressed, what they said to each other. I felt an old stillness reborn inside me. Another line. I could have waited for days if I had to.

I moved close enough to hear the conversations at the windows. Perhaps twenty people remained in front of me. As I waited I heard a woman's voice speaking from the window on the left.

That won't do, I heard her say. Take that home and fill it out and come back tomorrow. Yes, you'll have to wait in line again.

A few minutes later I heard her voice again. You're not listening to me, she said in an angry tone. If you don't listen you'll never get what you want. I don't care. It's all the same to me.

God, I pray I don't get her, said the man in front of me. He wore a green jacket and a matching cap.

I held tight to my papers and hoped I wouldn't either. I waited and watched as a man moved through the line checking documents. When he reached me he looked at my passport and shook his head.

You can't come here with a Russian passport, he said. He wore an official uniform with epaulets on his shoulders.

Why not? I asked.

You simply can't, he replied. He took my arm lightly to lead me out of the line.

Since I've already waited so long, just let me get to the window, I said. I'll ask my questions and then I'll leave.

He pulled me out of the line. Immediately the person behind me moved forward to take my place. There are other papers you will have to fill out before you come here, he said.

I understand you have your procedures, I told him. But I'm so close to the window. I can learn everything I need to know there.

He scratched his chin. I'm not supposed to let you, he said.

I had spent my life bargaining and making deals with government officials. I knew that if I kept pushing he would allow me back in line.

I won't make any trouble, I said.

He waved me back toward the line with a defeated expression. I found the man in the green cap and started to take my place behind him again.

A woman tapped my shoulder. She had long brown hair and a stern expression. You can't do that, she said. You left the line. Too bad for you. Go to the back.

You have to be kidding, I said.

She's right, said a short man behind her. I don't recognize you. I've been waiting here for hours. I won't let you cheat us.

You're crazy! I shouted. I've been here with all of you for hours. We've waited here together.

Tough shit, yelled the woman. You're not getting back in line.

The official who had taken me aside heard our voices and joined us. Let her back in. It's only fair, he said in a steady voice. From his manner I saw that he had seen such arguments countless times.

I waited another half hour, not once looking at the people behind me who had tried to have me removed. I felt my legs shaking. I never knew of such things happening in Russian lines. People saved places for each other, they helped make sure no one was cheated. In Russia we had all been in the same predicament; we had tried to be fair to each other.

My turn was near. I saw the woman with the cruel voice behind a window. She had gray hair and a frown that never left her face. The man in front of me reached the front just as the other window opened. He sighed with relief.

Next, said the gray-haired woman.

Good afternoon, I said to her, trying to sound like a businessperson. I gave her my papers and passport. I gave her a slip of paper my agency had provided, with a man's name and address. He was my contact in New York, which I knew I needed in order to qualify for a visa.

She glanced at the papers. No, no, it's not possible, she said. Next.

Wait, I said, almost choking. I'm trying to get a visa to go to the United States.

What for? she said.

Because I've never been there, I said, feeling instantly as though I was begging. Because I think it's a great country to visit.

It's not possible, she said. I don't have time for this.

Why? I asked. Because I have a Russian passport?

She grimaced as though I had offended her. That's right, she said. If you want to go to the United States, then fly back to Moscow and apply for your visa there.

But I'm in Paris, I said. Why should I go all the way back to Moscow just to apply for a visa?

It's what you have to do, she said.

I started to put together all the English I had learned. I want to go to Washington, I said. To the White House. I want to go to the Yankee Stadium.

I don't care, she said over me. I don't care what you want.

We began to speak at the same time, our voices rising higher and higher. We stared into each other's eyes, and I understood

the sort of game we were playing. If I stopped fighting she
would eat me like a tiger.

I want to go to New York, I yelled. I want America. I want.
I want.

You can't, the woman said, her voice blending into mine. I
won't allow it. It will not happen. Will you please stop talking?

She took a deep breath and rubbed her forehead as if it
ached. She sighed and looked at my papers again.

Who is this person you're going to visit? she asked. Is it
your boyfriend?

No, I replied. Just a friend.

Who is he? she asked. What color is his hair? His eyes?

I had never met my contact, so I improvised. Black, brown,
I said. He's an artist. I'm a model.

I see, she said, leaning back. You want to go to America
and work.

No, I just want to go there, I said, which was true. Business
is business. I don't know if I will find work. I just want to see
New York one time in my life.

Do you have a boyfriend here in France? she asked.

I knew she thought I wanted to immigrate illegally to
America. Yes, I do, I told her.

What does he do? she asked. What kind of relationship do
you have? Do you live together? Do you sleep together? When
was the first time you made love?

I made up answers as quickly as she could ask questions. I
pressed my hands to the counter to keep them from shaking.
I felt as though I had done something terrible and that I was
being interrogated by the police.

She shook her head. See what kind of person you are, she
said with a dark smile. You have a boyfriend here in Paris, and
now you want to go meet another man in New York.

I said nothing. She was enjoying this, it was putting her in
a good mood.

Does your boyfriend in Paris know your American boyfriend? she asked with a smirk.

Yes, he does, I said bitterly. They're the best of friends.

What's going on up there? someone shouted from the line.

Get her out of here! We're waiting! a woman screamed.

I looked at the clock on the wall. The embassy was closing

in less than an hour. Once it did, everyone in line would have to return the next day and wait again. Unlike in Russia, saving places in line from one day to the next was not allowed. I felt sympathy for the people behind me, but I had arrived before them. This might be my only chance.

Again the woman and I started to speak at the same time. You must leave. Why? You have to go. I want to go to America. It won't be allowed. Just give me my visa.

The woman's face turned bright red. She took a few deep breaths that made her shoulders shake. If you don't leave this instant, she said, then I will call the police and have you arrested.

A familiar feeling came over me. It was just the same as in the Soviet Union. I was doing nothing wrong, I was asking for nothing unreasonable. But I was being denied simply because the person on the other side of the counter represented total power. Nothing I did or said could change the fact that I was nothing, that I had no way to decide my own fate.

I stamped my foot on the floor. No, I won't move, I said.

You're too much, she replied, folding her arms. Leave right now while you have the chance.

Nobody has the right to remove me from this place, I said in a loud voice. I'll leave when I want to—after you give me my visa.

Go back to Russia, you stupid girl, someone shouted from behind me.

You don't even know what you're saying, yelled another.

What are you going to do? I asked the woman. Have a big policeman come and beat me up?

No one's going to beat you up, she replied. Just leave.

What have I done wrong? I have papers, I'm not a criminal. Why should I be denied the right to travel to America simply because you've decided that you don't like me?

Arrest her! a voice shouted from the line.

I turned and stared down the people behind me. It felt as though I had lived all my life in situations such as this. I had learned to be strong and to fight back. I knew that nothing in my life would ever happen unless I forced it to come into being.

The policeman who had taken me from the line earlier came

to the window. What's the matter? he asked the woman behind the glass. Is this girl causing trouble?

I haven't done anything wrong, I said. I'm simply not moving until this woman is fair to me.

I started to say something else, but the woman held up her hand for silence. She threw my passport and application across the counter at me.

I'm tired of it, she said. Come back tomorrow and pick up your visa.

I will, I said excitedly. And after that, I promise that you will never see me again. It will be my gift to you.

For a second a little smile flickered across her tight mouth. I felt like grabbing her hands and praying to her as though she were a goddess. I was afraid to say a word more, anything that might upset her and make her change her mind.

That night I went to Robert's house and showed him the little stamp the woman had put on my papers. He stared at it for a long time with an amazed expression.

You have to be kidding me, he said. How did you get this?

I fought back, I said. I refused to leave until they gave it to me.

He turned the stamp this way and that in the light, admiring it.

I've lived here for twenty years, he said. I've never heard of a Russian citizen getting a United States visa in France. It's against all the rules.

That's what they said at first, I replied.

Robert gave me a long approving look. You're a fighter, he said. That's good. You deserve your trip to America.

I gathered together all the cash I had saved from the collections after paying my expenses and sending money home to Siberia. I barely had enough to buy the ticket, which was about $500. I left most of my things at a friend's house and packed a single bag for the trip.

The plane left Paris in the early afternoon. I saw the sprawling city disappear beneath me, then there were only clouds. I felt the line of my life moving farther and farther west, as though I had gained the power to make the globe spin backwards.

A young woman with glasses sat in my aisle; our eyes met and we said hello. When the plane was in the air we asked the man between us if we could switch seats.

My name is Crystelle, she said.

I introduced myself. You look like a model, I said. Her hair was cut into a flowing wave of color, her features perfectly balanced.

I am, she said. I'm going to New York for the fashion shows.

I am, too, I said.

Crystelle looked excited. Now I have a friend there, she said.

Have you ever been to New York before? I asked her.

No, have you?

Never, I said. I never even dreamed of it until a few months ago.

Crystelle took my hand in hers. She closed her eyes. We're going to do well there, she said. I know it.

*I*n my dreams I heard the stewardess's voice: We are beginning our descent into JFK Airport in New York City. The weather is warm and clear. There are a variety of buses and taxis available to take you into the city.

I shook my head and tried to wake up. My heart began to beat fast in my chest. I looked down at the land unfurling itself for what seemed like hundreds of miles. A light haze hovered between us and the ground. I saw buildings extending into infinity.

We're here, I said, waking up Crystelle.

She blinked, still groggy with sleep. We made it? she asked.

I squeezed her hand. She had also begun to shake with excitement.

We came down from the skies like visitors from another universe. Crystelle and I waited together for our baggage, then we walked together toward customs.

Why have you come to the United States? a man in uniform asked me.

Because I've never been here before, I told him. Because almost everyone in the world wants to visit here.

Crystelle passed through the line after a few minutes. The officer examined my Russian passport and said that I would be detained for a while.

I'll wait for you! Crystelle called out to me.

They escorted me to a back room that I guessed was reserved for exceptional cases. They took my Russian passport and visa and examined them carefully. A uniformed man left the room, announcing that he had to make some calls to check the validity of my papers.

I sat back in my chair, not caring. I could have spent the entire day in customs and it wouldn't have mattered. I had arrived in New York.

The man returned and switched on a computer in the corner of the room. The screen came to life with rows of colored names and other information. His hands worked quickly on the keyboard and he took notes on a little pad of paper.

I felt a pang of worry. I had never met the man whose name I had used as a contact. What if he turned out to be some sort of criminal? I gripped the arms of my chair and prepared myself for anything. Part of me expected the officer to rise and say, No, this isn't going to work. You can't come to America. You can't even go back to France. There's a plane leaving for Russia in a couple of hours, and we're putting you on it.

Finally the man got up from his chair and sat across from me. You've come to America as a tourist? he asked.

I have, I replied. I've worked as a model, but mainly I just want to see the country. I came here because I've always dreamed of it. I grew up in Russia. If there's work for me, there's work for me. But mainly I want to walk down the street and smell the air. I want to tell my children someday about my trip to America.

The officer looked over his shoulder to a man sitting in the corner. They seemed as though they didn't trust me.

What if I say I don't believe you? he asked.

He gave me the same stare as my teacher had, as my school director had, as my neighbors had, as the embassy officials had. I looked back into his eyes, trying to make him understand my strength.

He went back to his computer and worked some more. Finally he stacked all of my papers and handed them to me.

Have a nice time in the United States, he said.

Yes! Thank you! I cried out. I kissed his cheek. He backed away, stunned.

Crystelle was still waiting for me outside. We embraced and screamed with happiness. We waved for a taxi and got in. I gave the driver an address I had been given for an agency in Soho. I had been told they might provide me with a place to live. If no one wanted to hire me to model, I would at least have a place to sleep until I had to return to Paris.

I stared out the window as the driver hurled us through traffic. The highways blended then spliced off into side roads. I fought off fatigue from the long flight when we entered Manhattan. We crossed a great bridge and my breath caught in my chest. Everywhere I saw people, buildings, stores, roads. The buildings seemed to rise into the sky and press close to each other for comfort. I marveled that such a great city had been compressed like this. Everywhere I saw such a wealth of detail that I could have stared for hours.

Here we are, the driver said, stopping on a busy street. Crystelle and I paid him from our small cache of American dollars.

We went into the old-looking building and took the elevator to the second floor. We carried our suitcases into the agency's lobby. It was a big loft with high ceilings and windows looking out onto the street. A huge round table sat heavily near the front door, covered with hundreds of photographs and ringing phones. My ears were filled with bells and voices. I saw young women and men moving fast between desks, shouting, waving paper.

I thought it was a vision of craziness. For some reason I had imagined New York would be an island of placid calm after Japan and Russia. That fantasy disappeared after an instant.

I gave the receptionist the name of my contact. She disappeared and returned with him a few minutes later. He wore a beard and glasses. He took our modeling books and looked through them slowly.

The shows are starting in just a few days, he said.

I came as soon as I could, I replied.

He thought for a moment. All right, you can stay in the models' apartment. I'll give you the address. There are some other girls from the agency staying there. They're all very nice.

I'm glad to hear it, Crystelle said, her voice heavy with tiredness.

Everyone here will be good to you, he added. Make yourself

at home. Your working permits just arrived. Tomorrow morning we'll begin making appointments for you with all the designers.

I tried to believe what he said, but it was difficult. After all, we were just two more models in New York City. We had come late, no one knew who we were. He would simply give us a list of addresses and hope for the best. I vowed to myself that I would enjoy every second in the city. Soon I would have to go home again. Soon this new life would be like a fantasy, a dream half remembered.

The apartment was on Houston Street and Sixth Avenue. It was a two-level place in the building's basement. A representative from the agency came with us. He unlocked the door and told us to bring our bags inside.

From the entryway we could look into the kitchen. There was a girl cooking on the stove. She had black hair and wore a tight T-shirt. She came out of the kitchen with an angry expression.

Two more? she yelled at the agency representative. Are you people insane?

Crystelle and I looked down at the floor. This wasn't our place, this was a foreign country. We knew nothing. We simply wanted to sleep and eat.

Yes, these girls are moving in, the representative said in a calm voice. We're going to bring in an extra bed and put it in the living room. Don't worry, it'll be fine.

Oh, it will be fine, the girl said sarcastically, waving a big wooden spoon.

Look, they are nice girls, he said. You are nice girls. You will all be friends. I'm sure of it.

He said good-bye to all of us and left. The door closed behind us. Crystelle and I stood in the entryway with our suitcases at our feet.

I could tell this girl had lived in the apartment for a long time. She shook our hands very quickly as though she hoped we would leave afterwards.

I'll show you the place, she said. Down that hall is my bedroom. When I want to sleep, nobody can make any noise. No music. No yelling. I don't like to be disturbed. And I don't want either of you using my bathroom.

That night I slept on a little mattress in the corner of the living room. The other models came home throughout the evening. There were eight of us, including Crystelle and me. There were only three bedrooms. I quickly discovered that the living room was common space. I curled up and failed to drift away amid a cloud of cigarette smoke and the constant commotion of conversation.

But I didn't care. Unable to sleep, I went up to the roof of the building. I saw the great concrete mountains lit up and piercing the darkness of night. I saw the streets straining with traffic. I heard voices calling out for one another. I had done it. I had again turned into a giant. Again the world was resting in the palm of my hand.

I woke up early the next morning. I still hadn't adjusted to the time switch from Europe. Crystelle and I bought a map and looked at our list of appointments, trying to figure out how to reach the great fashion houses. The streets were sunny, and we were energized by the life all around us. I felt incredible energy and power coursing through me.

If anyone needs a sofa or table moved, just let me know, I told the other models at breakfast. I tapped my toes on the floor, my body aching for motion.

Most of my appointments were on Seventh Avenue between thirty-eighth and forty-second streets. I learned that most of the major designers' houses were very near to each other. At my first appointment of the day I was given a cup of coffee.

Where are you two from? the casting agent asked. She wore a casual skirt and sandals.

From Siberia, I said. Crystelle is from France.

You came all the way here for the collections? she said, seeming impressed.

Of course, I said. This is the place to be.

The woman laughed and wrote down our names in her book. She asked us how old we were, where our families lived. I felt as though I were speaking with a friend. It was the exact opposite of my early days in Paris.

Nearly every appointment was the same. Americans were open and talkative. They wanted to know who I was, how I had come to their country. They were eager to help me when

I stumbled speaking their language. When I walked for them they encouraged me and told me I was doing a nice job.

I brought my book to every appointment. The casting directors looked through it, complimenting me on my work.

Everyone is so nice and easy here, I said to a director at one of my final appointments of the day.

You think so? she asked.

I do, I replied. I come for my appointments and everyone wants to talk. Everyone is very positive.

You know, she said, people in New York have a reputation for being rude.

That's impossible, I said.

That night I fell into a deep sleep on my mattress. The voices and smoke and the sound of the television didn't keep me awake. My bones sank into the thin mattress as though they were made of stone.

It had seemed too easy. Surely no one would hire me. Perhaps I could work a single show, maybe two if I were lucky. Then I would see the Statue of Liberty and Central Park before I went home. I had achieved so many of my dreams. To dream further would be to tempt fate.

The next morning the agency called our apartment at nine o'clock in the morning. I was still asleep in the living room when I heard one of my roommates' voice. It sounded as though she was angry.

What is this? she said. Someone is sending a limousine? For who?

Crystelle shook me awake. You have to get up, she said. The agency is sending a car for us. It's going to be here any minute. You have to hurry up and get ready.

I got out of bed and tried to shake away my sleepiness. A car? I asked Crystelle. What do you mean? A taxi?

In the kitchen a couple of the other models were drinking coffee. They glared at me as I poured a glass of water.

I've been here for two months, one said to the other as though I wasn't there. Never once did they send a car for me.

It's ridiculous, the other muttered.

I dressed quickly and splashed cold water on my face. I heard Crystelle call out to me from the living room. I parted the curtains and looked out to the street. There was a long black limousine parked in front of the building, its engine running.

This can't be right, I said. This has to be a mistake.

I called the agency. The receptionist laughed when I told her what was happening. Don't panic, she said. Take your time, get dressed. When you're ready, the driver will take you to your appointments.

I told Crystelle what the agency had said. She peered out the window at the car, shaking her head.

It must cost a lot of money to hire such a car, she said.

Don't think about it, I told her, brushing my hair. We'll probably never get a chance to ride in a limousine again. Let's just enjoy it.

In the living room my housemates were on the phone to the agency. They wanted to know why I deserved such special treatment.

She has no experience, one model said.

She doesn't even know New York, another said. Why is she being treated like she's something important?

I slipped out quietly, fearing they might ask me the same questions. I couldn't have answered them. I knew only that I wanted to get into that black limousine before it drove away and left me behind forever.

My schedule was completely booked for the few days that remained before the collections began. I went to nearly every design house and walked for casting directors. The agency told me that they were receiving calls asking for me to model in the shows. I was told that in a few days I would be very busy.

Everyone is interested in you, my agent said. They love the way you look, the way you speak. People are talking about you. We think we can turn you into something big.

I said nothing, fearing that the moment might burst and evaporate away. I remembered walking through Paris day after day, the discouraging looks and words I received at the design houses. Part of me didn't believe this good fortune was real. I had been in New York just a few days. I waited for the imaginary phone call that would tell me everything had been canceled.

Crystelle was also hired for many of the same shows at which I was scheduled to work. I imagined that we were talismans for one another, each infusing the other with an aura of luck that began when we met in the sky. She was also my ally when I came home at night. I began to understand that a new model being hired for so many fashion shows was very rare; while a few models at the apartment were nicer to me now, from the others I felt competitiveness and jealousy.

Two days before the collections my agency called. You have three more shows, my agent said. Can you believe it?

I think so, I said uncertainly. All of these designers want me to model at their shows? What if they're planned for the same time? I can't be in two places at once.

The agent laughed. Leave that to me, she said. I'll take care of your schedule. By the way, I have two appointments for you in the morning. One is with *Vogue,* the other is with *Harper's Bazaar.*

I looked at my open suitcase on the floor. It reminded me that I had planned to stay in New York only for a short time. Now less than a week had passed and I was being considered for work by two magazines that to me represented everything that fashion was about. Copies of these magazines had been passed from hand to hand in Russia until they fell apart and had to be taped together. For the first time I allowed exuberance to take hold in my heart.

Thank you, I said. I will be there.

I talked to another casting director about you, the agent added. Her voice sounded close and intimate on the phone.

Nothing bad? I asked.

Of course not, she replied. She just confirmed what I thought. You have a new look that people are willing to take a chance on. You're also a hard worker, that comes through right away. I think you have the makings of a very good start.

I think I understand, I said, repeating the words in my mind.

You will, she said. I don't know if it's sunk in yet, but your life has changed forever.

A week before I had been in Paris worrying about my week's rent. I had felt an unseen hand trying to pull me back to the hardships and chaos of Russia. My decision to come to America hadn't been thought out or planned. I had merely ridden the winds of the world in the direction that felt best.

Are you listening? the agent asked. Do you understand the magnitude of what's about to happen to you?

I think I do, I said, not really comprehending what she meant.

Part of me stepped back from the world and watched in silence. The sun rose, the stars appeared, the winds and rains caressed the earth. Fate had decided to bless me, for however long it wished. I watched my life unfold like a spectator at a great drama.

I wasn't sure what any of it meant—the cameras, the lights, the glamour. I knew I loved it, that it made me beam with delight. And that was enough. I didn't feel as though I had achieved much of anything, not in the scope of nature and the universe. But I was determined to enjoy this adventure as long as it lasted.

My agency spoke to me of great names that sounded like magic spells. Calvin Klein. Donna Karan. Ralph Lauren. Bill Blass. Isaac Mizrahi. I was scheduled to work in dozens of fashion shows and several print fashion spreads. I knew the weeks would pass in a quick blur. I tried to hold on to every moment, to remember each detail so that I could recount them to myself when times turned hard again.

It was time for the shows to begin. I repeated to myself like a mantra: work hard, enjoy it, let the beauty move you. My agency told me to go to Bryant Park, at Sixth Avenue and 42nd Street, for a show by a designer named Anna Sui. I had recently seen her creations in a magazine. They were colorful and fun, full of life and imagination. I stepped into the theater fantasizing about how I would wear her designs when I strode onto the catwalk.

Backstage seemed like a busy painting created by a hurried hand: models, makeup artists, hairstylists, Anna Sui's staff. I sat in an empty chair and waited for instructions. Someone called my name, and in seconds I was surrounded by men and women holding microphones and cameras.

You're Irina? a woman asked.

I said I was. How do you know my name? I asked.

Where are you from? a man said, thrusting a recorder close to my lips. Is it true you're an Eskimo?

I'm from Siberia, I told him. Yes, my people are Eskimos.

How did you get to America from Russia?

On a plane! I laughed.

But isn't it hard to leave Russia?

I was persistent, I said.

I remembered one of my first days in New York. My agency had asked me how I had come to America, where I was born, where I had traveled. I hadn't thought it was important, but I had told them everything. I understood now that my agency had told these reporters about me.

The questions continued. What city was I from? Was my country still a part of Russia? What languages did I speak? How long had I been in Paris? What were my plans for the future?

I don't know what my plans are, I said. I didn't even plan for any of this to happen.

Are you married? an older woman asked me. Do you have a boyfriend? Are you in love?

I paused. I had been working hard to stay alive for so long that the years had passed almost beyond my notice. Love had been a distant consideration. Images flashed in my mind of childhood crushes, flirting, the brief love I had known in Moscow. I hadn't felt alone until that moment.

I'm very busy, I said. Perhaps later there will be time.

The woman smiled at me. You're young, you don't have to worry about it, she said. Love takes care of itself.

Do you think so? I asked her.

A stylist arrived with a makeup brush in her hand. She wore a tight blouse and a short skirt and was smoking a skinny cigarette.

All right, people, leave Irina alone, she said. It's time for her to get ready.

I tried to recount how many questions I had answered. Thirty? Fifty? The reporters had been interested in everything I said. I realized how rarely I had ever spoken about myself, or explained my thoughts and feelings to anyone but my closest friends.

The makeup accented my cheekbones and eyes. I was dressed in a short skirt with matching blouse and handbag, very modern and chic. I watched the other models being dressed and saw faces I recognized from magazine covers: Naomi Campbell, Cindy Crawford, Linda Evangelista, Claudia Schiffer, Christie Turlington. They looked to me like pictures come to life, as though such perfectly beautiful women could not possibly exist in flesh.

I heard music from the hall outside. The lights dimmed. I walked onto the runway in an explosion of lights flashing. I saw cameras' eyes everywhere. I turned and took a deep breath. I looked up at the high ceiling then down at the audience. I felt different than I had in Russia, or even in France. I saw smiles and returned them. I felt a sense of joy that mirrored my own.

Minutes later I returned to the runway in another outfit. I felt my face radiate my joy and saw it reflected in the audience. I burst out with a moment of uncontrolled laughter.

After the show I was still dressed in the final outfit I had worn onstage. Reporters and audience members had stormed backstage before there had been time to change. Security guards watched over the models and the designer, their eyes alert for danger.

Anna Sui talked to a television reporter about the collection; she laughed and spoke in an easy tone, and I instantly liked her. Naomi Campbell spoke to three reporters at once.

I watched this commotion from the side, hoping that the answers I had offered earlier would be sufficient. I wanted to trap each moment in my memory. I wanted to stop time, or at least to slow it. I folded my arms and leaned back against the wall.

Irina, a man's voice said.

I looked around, expecting to see another reporter. I'm Irina, I said.

I stopped speaking when I saw his face.

Roland, I whispered.

He stood with his hands at his side, his face frozen in an uncertain expression. He had changed little since I had seen him last in Moscow.

I'm here to shoot the show, he said. I'm still working as a photographer.

The smile stuck on my face had been a smile for a stranger. Not for Roland. I felt my body stiffen with confusion. I wasn't sure I was seeing reality. Perhaps it had all been a fantasy. None of it was real.

He took a step closer to me. I'm so glad to see you, he said. I'm so happy.

The sound of his voice unlocked my spirit. I looked down, then back up at his face. It had been years. But somehow it felt as though I had never been apart from him.

I'm very happy to see you, too, I said.

I tried to phone, he said. I couldn't get a line from Moscow to Ulan Ude. It was impossible.

I wanted to think you were trying, I said.

In his eyes I saw that he told the truth. I saw his kindness, his strength and intelligence. I saw him burn with love for me.

Enough is enough, he said, touching my hand. I won't lose you again. Once is enough for ten lifetimes. That night Roland came to the apartment. He was carrying a huge bouquet of pink roses, which he set down gently on the coffee table.

As I basked in the warmth of his love, I tried to absorb everything that had occurred in the past two weeks. I wondered how all my good fortune had happened, and whether I deserved it.

A few nights later I went to Roland's uptown apartment. I stood at the window looking down as Roland pointed out the landmarks below: Lincoln Center, Central Park, Broadway, the Hudson River. Just about every American movie begins like this, I said. The camera flying through the sky, looking down at the lights of New York. And now here I am.

Roland came to the window from the kitchen, where he was cooking dinner. America is your second home now, he said.

I can stay, can't I? I asked. I'd love to stay!

Roland glanced out the window. Our perspective was that of angels or giants.

Would you marry me, Irina? he asked.

I looked at him. He took my hand.

I won't lose you again, he said.

As I accepted I looked from Roland's eyes to the city below. We were spirits who had crossed the world to be together. The lights outside stretched so far into the distance that they seemed to reach around the globe.

*　　*　　*

I worked every day during the collections, my schedule that of an established veteran rather than a newcomer. As soon as the shows were concluded I was booked to pose in pieces for *Vogue* and *Harper's Bazaar.* I felt as though I had stepped through a mirror and into another world.

During one of the final shows of the season I became friends with Zang Toi, a designer. I took him aside before his show and asked him if he could lend me a dress to wear next week.

Roland and I are going to city hall, I told him.

What? he asked. You're getting married? You just got here. You're living so fast.

Life is fast here, I told him. I'm just moving at the same speed as everything I see.

On the morning of my wedding I looked at my schedule. I had photo sessions in the morning, and Roland was working as well, but we found a sliver of time around midday and made an appointment at city hall. An administrator told us we would need a witness to be married, so I phoned Monica, an American model I had met in Japan.

What? she said. Married? I didn't even know you were in the country!

I'm happy; I'm in love, I said to her.

I'll come, Monica replied.

At a quarter after twelve I left the studio and stepped out into the warm May day. I looked at my watch. We had to go all the way downtown, and I had promised to be back in the studio in a couple of hours.

A long black limousine pulled up to the curb. I looked up and down the street, trying to find Roland's face in the crowd.

I'm over here, Roland said, getting out of the limousine.

We rode together to his apartment to change clothes. Roland had bought flowers, chocolates, champagne. I felt like a character in a movie.

My dress was short, covered with shiny flowers, and I wore red high heels. Roland wore an exquisite bright green jacket. When I looked at us in the mirror our colors seemed to sing of joy and hope.

At city hall we registered our names in a tiny office with wooden chairs and tables. The clerk said they would call us when our turn came. Roland and I sat together drinking champagne. Monica arrived to be our witness.

Other people were wearing jeans and informal shirts. Some had brought their small children. One couple stood together nervously in the corner; he wore a black tie and she wore a white dress. Roland and I, in our bright clothes, looked as though we had stepped out of a picture book. We started to laugh and couldn't stop.

When our turn came the woman who conducted the ceremony spoke in a fast monotonous voice. She sounded as though she had married a hundred people a day for the last twenty years.

Would you take Irina for your wife? she asked Roland.

Would you take Roland for your husband? she asked me.

We looked into each other's eyes and said yes. Now you can exchange rings, the woman said.

But we don't have any rings, Roland said.

She dropped her book on the table, stunned. No rings? she shouted.

No, no rings! Roland said. We don't have them, but we still want to be married.

She cleared her throat. All right, she said. I suppose we can go through with it.

I looked at Roland and widened my eyes. His lips curled into a smile. A moment later we covered our mouths with our hands to keep from laughing.

The ceremony was over. It seemed as though it had lasted thirty seconds.

That's it? I asked.

That's right, the woman said. She looked over my shoulder and shouted, Next!

We went outside and poured fresh glasses of champagne. Monica took pictures of Roland and me together. We held hands and laughed, feeling years of frustration and sadness turn into relief and happiness. With Roland my world opened anew. His knowledge and strength made me feel endless possibility. I felt that I now had an ally in my life who would always protect me and love me. I felt as though I had finally come home.

*   *   *

My good fortune continued. Photographers shouted my name when I walked the runways, and people recognized me on the streets of New York.

You *go,* girl, a young woman called out as she passed me on Rollerblades.

In a shop an Asian woman in her early twenties approached me shyly, with her eyes cast down at the ground.

Are you Irina? she asked me.

It seemed impossible that people knew me, knew my name and face. We were strangers. I felt as though they were talking about someone else, a woman like me but indescribably different.

I am, I told her.

She gathered her courage to look up into my eyes. I just wanted to tell you, she said, that you're doing something great for Asian women. You're breaking barriers in the magazines and fashion shows. You're showing the world that Asian women are beautiful.

I shook her hand and thanked her. I didn't have the words to explain that the only barriers I perceived of myself as breaking were the walls of my own spirit. I had fought and struggled because I was born into a world in which it was necessary. The fight is universal. The struggle belongs to everyone.

Roland brought me to the Whitney Museum in Manhattan for Richard Avedon's forty-year anniversary show. I had seen his photographs in Russia and knew the way in which he captured the spirits of his subjects. Avedon sat at a table before a long line, signing books commemorating his work.

We arrived late and had waited in line for a few minutes when a security guard approached us.

I'm sorry, but we have to cut off the line, he said. You came too late. You'll have to leave.

I clutched my book in my hand. There's no one behind me, I said. Why not allow me to reach the front?

We've been here all day, the guard said. It's over.

I walked away from the line, which had dwindled to just a few people. I waited a few minutes and, after the guard left, sprang to the table where Richard Avedon was putting away his things.

I just arrived in New York from Siberia, I said, handing him the book. Your exhibition is wonderful. I know your photographs from Russia. Your work is amazing.

The words came forth in a torrent. My body coursed with adrenaline in the great photographer's presence. I wanted to explain my life to him, make him know that to a Russian he was like a distant god. If not for the tricks of history I never would have stood on the same continent as him.

From Siberia? he asked, signing the book. But you're so tall. Aren't people in your part of the world much shorter than you?

They are, I said. Maybe it was the *Tungus* meteor that crashed in 1908.

He laughed and gave me the book. Maybe you're right, he said.

I would see him again a few years later and tell him how I had fought to stay in line to reach him. I wanted to tell him that it had not been the most difficult line I had faced in my life.

My parents saw my image flickering on their television screen when the station CNN interviewed me about my life and work. They told me later that our neighbors had gathered in my family's living room, watching me in amazement.

I was hired to work on a book for the remarkable Japanese designer Issey Miyake with photographer Irving Penn, one of the great living masters. Roland had showed me Penn's pictures and pointed out their technical elements and visual power.

We shot the pictures in a small studio on a hot early summer day. I looked into the eye of the camera, imagining myself as it saw me through its glass lens, trying to feel the power of Penn's genius coursing through me. He was in his seventies, and his every movement seemed infused with experience and purpose.

When the shoot was over I dressed in my own clothes. The studio was a cramped mess of cameras and designer clothes. Standing in my bare feet, I hunted around for my shoes. They were nowhere.

Has anyone seen my shoes? I said.

Penn's assistants laughed, and I joined them. It seemed impossible to lose anything in such a small space, but none of us could find my shoes.

I'll help you, Penn said. He hunted through a bag and pulled out a pair of his own sneakers. They're probably not the right size, but they'll be enough to get you home.

I put on the shoes and thanked him. I wanted to tell him that his photographs were so precious to me, that his old sneakers were like a golden artifact. Instead I waved good-bye and walked out to the sunny street. The shoes flapped against my heels as I walked. They were at least three sizes too big.

I went home with a smile that I couldn't erase. I was walking in Irving Penn's shoes. My life was a fairy tale that was written anew every day.

I worked on a photo spread for *Harper's Bazaar*. The photographer was Michael Thompson, the top model was Bridget Hall. Again I met people who before to me had been only names, or perhaps pictures in a book or magazine. The clothes were by Jean-Paul Gautier and were inspired by Mongolian dress.

The makeup room was set up like a hospital: brushes, lipsticks, powders, eyeliners, sponges, pens, pencils, all carefully organized on a huge table. I sat down and the stylist tugged at my hair, twisting it, inserting pins.

We're going to give you an incredible Mongolian look to go with these fashions, the makeup artist said.

I've been to Mongolia, I said. I grew up close to there. These fashions, you know, they really aren't much different from what Mongolians wear on the street every day.

There was a moment of silence. You're not kidding, are you? the hair stylist finally asked.

No, it's true, I said.

A chorus of voices filled my ears. What do Mongolians wear? How do they style their hair? What sort of makeup do the women wear?

I answered from memory, thinking again how tiny the world had become.

My life became hectic in a way that I never would have imagined during my long frustrating days in Paris.

The phone rang; it was my agency. We have a booking for you, they said, in San Francisco, with *Mirabella*.

But what about the European collections? I replied, feeling

sheepish. The daily bustle was still new to me. The challenge of scheduling my time seemed almost insurmountable.

Don't worry, the agency said. You'll fly straight to Milan from San Francisco. We'll get you there two days before the shows. The agency in Milan knows all about it.

When I stepped out of the Milan airport the Italian sky shone with a patchwork of stars; the sight made me think of quiet nights in Siberia.

A driver from the agency was waiting for me at the airport. He took calls from the agency on a portable phone as he drove.

Do you do this all year? I asked him from the backseat. You seem very young for a taxi driver.

He laughed. No way, I'm a college student. I do this for extra money and to meet the fashion crowd. His phone rang before I could ask him another question. In a couple of hours the sun would rise. My dream of a hot shower and some sleep would have to be abandoned. I was to be driven all day to a long list of "go-sees" with clients.

Some of the clients knew me from previous fashion shows, but everyone wanted to check my measurements to see if reality matched the description of my written profile. I worked into the evening trying on clothes, listening to the designers describe the focus of their shows for this season. It was late when I left the last fashion house and stepped into the cool night.

At seven in the morning I was woken by a call from my agency: there was a long list of things for me to do that day. A driver would pick me up in a half hour. I stretched my legs and poured a glass of juice. I cherished this moment of quiet and relaxation, wished I had just an hour more to myself.

On the first day of the Milan season I arrived at a museum for a show by a young, hip English designer. As I walked to the makeup room I stopped to examine some of the inventions of Leonardo da Vinci that were installed in a special space. I lingered over his careful drawings, centuries old, and experienced a strange sensation that all of history could be contained in a single moment.

The show itself was just around the corner from the exhibit. I saw a lot of young people drinking champagne backstage, talking in several languages, and smoking cigarettes. A young man named Adam, just arrived from London, styled my hair as I sat back and relaxed.

Another stylist went around to all the models, saying something I couldn't hear. By the time she reached me I was burning with curiosity.

All the shoes are size 42, she said to me. I hope that works for you.

I wear a 39, which meant that I would walk across the runway in shoes three sizes too big.

The show went perfectly in a blur of flashbulbs and music. A couple of the models teetered—including me—in the oversized shoes, but no one fell or broke a leg, even after drinking the cold champagne that waited backstage. I rushed from one fashion show to the next for the rest of the day, changing in and out of clothes, becoming a different character on each runway. I felt like a butterfly flying from one exotic flower to the next.

In the morning the agency called again. Great news, the voice on the line said. We have an important show for you.

The show was an anniversary collection for an important Italian designer; when I arrived at the hall the place was full of people drinking cocktails and talking like old friends. Television crews fought for floor space with the designer's staff wheeling carts of shoes and dresses backstage.

The collection was dedicated to the glamour of the Hollywood Golden Era. The clothes reminded me of images I had seen in films all my life, and as I wore them, I wondered if anyone recognized the glee that I felt in my heart. The fashion world, in many ways, still felt as though it belonged to other people and not to me. I still felt like a girl from Siberia who liked to play dress up. More and more, every day, I began to realize that I belonged here. This world was like any other; it belonged to everyone who took part.

The weather was warm and sunny all week until the final day of the Milan shows. In the afternoon the air turned cool and little flakes of snow fell from the sky. Backstage the models and stylists were complaining about the turn in the weather. I smiled to myself, thinking that nothing made me feel more at home than snowflakes.

Karl Lagerfeld had designed a Fendi collection that included warm coats and sheepskin. I saw him backstage and said, You must be very close to Mother Nature. She gave everyone a taste of the cold just in time for you to show your winter fashions.

Karl Lagerfeld laughed and returned to the task of dealing with the reporters that besieged him from all sides.

Camera flashes, microphones, tape recorders, reporters, beautiful faces, glamorous clothes. Before I knew it the Milan shows were almost finished. I sat in an auditorium, waiting for the car that would take me to the airport. A television crew arrived and set up to interview Claudia Schiffer. Her boyfriend, the dark-haired magician David Copperfield, made faces behind the cameraman to try to make Claudia laugh. People were rushing everywhere, trying to dismantle the fixtures and decorations from the shows. Everyone was as much in a hurry to leave as they had been to arrive. Again I tried to take a snapshot with my eyes, hoped that I could remember every moment of this beautiful chaos.

I boarded my plane to Paris. I watched Milan shrink and disappear from my seat next to the window, then fell asleep thinking of the hectic schedule that awaited me when I landed.

I rode a taxi to the small hotel next to the Bastille where I had a room; from there I could rush to my appointments using the Metro or taxis. As I raced through the streets to my first booking I looked out at the city from my cab. So much had changed since I left Paris; no longer did I have to walk the streets knocking on doors, facing rejection after rejection. But now there was no time for the cinema, for the theater, for the museums. I felt a pang of regret when I saw a tourist bus heading down the road in the direction of the Louvre.

When I arrived at my first fitting I noticed the way the young models looked at me; they recognized me, looked at me with naïveté and respect, and I was reminded that I was no longer a beginner in the fashion world. Still, I waited late into the night because I wanted to meet the designer, sitting on a stool in a side room and watching a dozen hair stylists making wigs. They sprayed and twisted the hair until it met their precise

requirements, their hands moving with confidence and exper-
tise, like sculptors or painters creating works of art.

The wigs were extraordinary, somehow both lush and severe,
and they were a major ingredient in the look of the show that
week. The shows took place in a circus, and backstage the
atmosphere was festive and pitched with excitement, just as it
had been in Milan. I saw many of the same reporters who
worked all the collections. The press was everywhere, recording everything that was said with an insatiable thirst, inter-
viewing models and taking photographs. The staff rushed from
one model to the next, explaining that there would be no runway for this particular show—instead there was a grandiose set,
like something from a Fellini movie.

At the end of the show James Brown came on stage and
sang; I listened to his propulsive and energetic music, my body
moving with its rhythm. This trip had been a series of snapshots, each more incredible than the one before. I felt the press
of people and rushing motion all around me like a river.

The next morning I got out of bed and poured a fresh cup
of *café au lait* with a croissant. The telephone rang. It was my
agent, his voice loud with excitement.

Yves Saint Laurent wants to see you, she said. In person. He
might want to use you for his show.

I hung up the phone, shaking my head with amazement. I
felt that I was living in a dream, that at any moment I would
awaken and find myself sitting in front of a sewing machine
in Ulan Ude. But when I stepped into the Paris sunshine the
dream did not dissolve. The streets teeming with traffic beckoned to me. Once Paris had seemed like it would be the end
of my adventure; now it was the beginning.

Yves Saint Laurent sat behind a large desk. At his feet sat a
big dog with alert eyes that scrutinized everything. The dog
seemed like a person, as important as anyone in the room—if
not more so.

Several members of the designer's staff were standing on
alert around us, ready to take notes and helping me with the
dresses.

The room was very quiet as I was buttoned into the first
dress, its fabric rich and black. I lifted my chin, gathered my

courage, and looked into the great designer's eyes. He seemed almost regal, very sure of himself.

I tried on another dress. There was stillness in the air, and the room was quiet. I became so nervous that I looked down at the dog, as though perhaps I could gain his approval and then his master's. But the dog stared at me with the same detached expression as his master, reserving his judgment.

Suddenly Yves Saint Laurent looked up at his staff. With a nod of approval his decision was made. Everybody started to clap for me as though I had just finished a successful performance. I looked down; the dog looked at me with approval also. The dog was very pleased with what I had done.

Modeling for Issey Miyake was thrilling; his shows always looked like conceptual-art events. He autographed a book containing his fashions, and I flipped to the page where I found the photographs of me that were taken by Irving Penn the day he loaned me his sneakers to walk home. The person in the picture looked young and energized by the situation in which she found herself. I remembered the awe I had felt in the great photographer's studio and tried to find it in the glint of my eye in the picture. In that single image I looked back through the corridor in time of the past year; I realized how much had changed, and yet how much I felt the same.

On the plane back to America I looked out at the low clouds over the Atlantic, imagined the great depths of water below. I fell asleep peering out at the stars, feeling as though the airplane might continue to ascend into the darkness of night until we reached another world entirely.

In New York I was able to sleep in my own bed, eat breakfast in my own kitchen with Roland. Images of Milan and Paris flickered in my mind like photographs that had just been developed, as the brisk reality of New York regained its hold on me.

I had received many requests to work shows. My agency told me that this was a very good sign, that in their eyes I had become a success. I wasn't sure what to think; to me, the fashion world seemed like a deep exotic forest through which I was traveling. I was simply doing my work and living each moment as it came. Still these words made my heart beat a little faster with excitement.

All of the fashion shows took place in an area around Seventh Avenue that was ten blocks long by three blocks wide. In the fashion district people rushed and mingled, oblivious to each other. There were businessmen in suits, bicycle messengers, punk rockers. Moving between them, as though negotiating a maze, were people pushing huge carts full of dresses, anxious to reach the next fashion show before it started. I moved from one appointment to the next, stopping in cafes for a quick cup of tea or pastry. I felt as if the entire world had temporarily been condensed into a few city blocks.

Sometimes I ventured from this realm into the wilds of Soho, where I visited Isaac's showroom for a fitting. Downtown, things were more brash and youthful, more colorful and vibrant. Isaac kept me laughing the entire time I was there with his refreshing sense of humor.

Outside I found a little pizzeria, where I ordered a slice and sat down. I was looking through my appointment book when I looked up and saw my friend Mark Jacobs, a designer, come through the door. When he saw me waving at him he came to my table.

He pointed at my address book and laughed. I can tell you where your next appointment is going to be, he said. It's with me. You're a few minutes late.

I swallowed my bite of pizza and began to apologize.

Don't worry, he said. This week is crazy. I can't keep my schedule straight either.

We walked together back to his showroom. Mark is very kind, with a shy manner that makes him very different from other designers, who are usually brash and outgoing. His studio was full of models when we arrived, and his designs were hanging from racks everywhere that I looked, like blossoms of color.

Afterward I took the "A" train uptown—just like in the song— and got off at Seventh Avenue, returning to the temporary center of my universe in the fashion district. I arrived at Oscar de la Renta's for a fitting, where I was given an orange silk dress that was slit in the side all the way to the waist. The dresser told me that, when I showed the outfit to the designer,

I should imagine that I was also wearing silk pants and high-heeled shoes.

I was escorted to the small office where Oscar de la Renta was working. He was dressed simply, his features reflecting dignity and experience.

I turned around in the dress and said, Please imagine with me that I am wearing silk pants and high-heeled shoes.

He thought for a moment then nodded. Okay, he said, I am pretending to see pants and shoes.

I was scheduled to be the second model onstage at his show, but at the last minute Oscar made a change: I was to be the first model to step out onto the runway.

It was the first time I had opened a show for a designer. I stepped out of the dark and projectors drowned me in a sea of light. A shiver ran up my spine. I stepped into the light as though I was being born into a new world. After I left the stage I was filled with an electric energy that would not disappear for the remainder of the shows there.

But by the end of the week my body felt drained with fatigue. I had worked so much that I no longer kept count of the shows. At one of the final shows I stepped into the runway lights to the sound of loud rock music; part of me flashed back to my communist youth, when we were told that rock 'n' roll would destroy our souls and bring down our country. Surely Lenin's head was scowling now in the Ulan Ude city square.

Now that it was over I lay down in my bed and looked up at the white ceiling. I could almost see the pictures there, projected from my recent memory. So many things had happened in such a short period of time. I had done the circuit—as they said in the fashion business—and experienced everything that came with it. I saw rushing photographers, nervous and excited designers, celebrities like Tony Curtis, who had been pleasantly surprised when I told him I had watched *Some Like It Hot* when I was a little girl in Siberia. Or The Artist Formerly Known As Prince, who told me about his allergy to being photographed. I hoped there was a cure for his disease.

Other images replaced these: the fashion contests in Moscow, the runways of Ulan Ude, the senseless accusations at school, the snow-covered walk leading up to my parents' theater. My grandfather saying that nothing ever truly begins or ends.

I modeled at the Academy Awards in Los Angeles. Before the show began I peered through the slightly parted curtains at the audience. I saw faces that I knew from movie screens now reduced to human dimensions. They were imaginary royalty made real. I felt again like the little girl in Buryatia who lost herself in her parents' theater.

Dreams and reality locked in an embrace. I picked up magazines at street corner newsstands and opened them to see my face staring back at me. The woman in the photos looked like she'd known all along that her life would take the course that it had.

Soon after I modeled at the Oscars a film producer approached my agent to ask if I would like to audition for a part in the sequel to a movie called *Mortal Kombat.* I read a few pages of the script and knew that I wanted the part for which I was being considered—a dangerous, mystical woman named Jade. The movie dealt with fantasy and adventure; I began to visualize fantastic sets and strange worlds in my mind.

I was drawn to the film because it portrayed incredible martial arts battles. Bruce Lee had been very popular in Russia, and I remembered the girls crying when we learned he died. I met with a trainer in Los Angeles and worked for a week in a hot studio, learning to kick, jump, to fight with my hands. It was exhausting work, and my face turned so red that my instructor called me the Lobster. But I felt my body respond to the new movements I was learning. Soon I was able to lose myself in the swirl of karate's dance.

I flew to London in October to rehearse and try on makeup and costumes. The director wanted to rehearse the love scene between my character and Liu Kang, played by the martial artist Robin Shou.

Let me give you strength for your battle, Jade said to Liu Kang, trying to seduce him. I pictured the snow that fell from the sky onto our characters in the scene. I freed my heart and let it beat with the love that Jade felt for Liu Kang.

Together we could melt the snow, Jade said. Together we could live our final days.

I worked long days learning to fight with long wooden sticks that were martial-arts weapons dating back to ancient times. Every morning I reminded myself that this would be my first American film. Another of my dreams was about to come true.

Shooting in London lasted two weeks; it was freezing cold, the days were long and exhausting. I focused on my character and on the choreography. We worked on a huge sound stage and shot the scenes in a different order than they were written into the script. In the evenings I tried to see as much of London as I could. I saw plays, sometimes waiting in line to buy seats for sold-out shows from audience members who might have an extra ticket.

Next the film crew flew to the Middle East, to Jordan; before we left the crew was given a set of specific instructions about how to behave. We weren't allowed to bare our legs or cross them, show our arms above the elbows, make any signs of the cross, or behave in an aggressive manner.

We arrived to shoot a series of scenes in the historic caves of Petra; the only way to reach the site was by horseback. We left for the location very early in the morning, before the sun had risen. I rode a horse for the first time since I had left Siberia; as the animal moved slowly up the rocky hillside I remembered my grandfather's horses running across the green plains of his village.

Petra was once part of an ancient kingdom called Nabataea, our guide said as we neared the place. When we reached it I gasped; it was walled in by high rocks, and I could see the temples and tombs carved out of the stone like tokens of the ancient past. We had to carry our film gear on our backs up steep steps cut out of stone to reach the filming location.

When the sun rose the sky turned bright blue; I heard the sound of running water. The stone glinted in the sun, formed deep shade where the gorges blocked the light.

I watched people emerging from the caves and asked my guide who they were. Do they live in those caves? I asked.

He told me they did, that they were Bedouins. I watched them with fascination as they grew closer. Their children were beautiful, their eyes dark and shining. They pulled horses and donkeys as they formed a great circle around the film crew setting up the day's cameras and sound recorders.

A ten-year-old, his dark hair tousled and his eyes a deep vivid blue, came up to me.

You must be Japanese, he said in good English, displaying an array of trinkets that glittered in the sun. You have lots of money—you have to buy something from me.

In the afternoon I watched the beautiful children playing in the sun; their cries of enjoyment in a language I couldn't understand seemed like voices of the ancient past. I closed my eyes and listened to them, drifting on the currents of history. In another life, in another time, I might have stood on the same spot, hearing the same sounds.

In January, I had a break from filming that I spent working the *haute couture* shows in Paris. I flew to Thailand in February; the shooting began again. Even though we arrived at night, it was so warm and sticky that my dress stuck to my back; in the morning it was even hotter.

The set was beautiful, like something out of a dream, but the warehouse where it had been built was so hot that my head began to pound as soon as I walked inside. Most of the crew had been there a month longer than me, and I heard that some of them had fallen ill from mosquito bites and the heat. Others had quit after Petra because the dust from the rocks had infected their lungs.

I began to work on fighting scenes, sweat flying from my forehead as I kicked and leapt. Between takes I watched quietly as the crew and actors spoke to each other in low voices. It seemed as though something had changed, that the air of happiness that had existed on the sets in London and Petra had turned into something more weary and less harmonious. We were told that our schedule was tight, our money was limited, and whatever scenes we couldn't film successfully on schedule would simply disappear.

The night before filming our most important scene I spoke with Robin at our hotel. We agreed that the next day we would work together and make the scene into something extraordinary.

The scene is greater than just the two of us, I said to him. It's for your fans, for the audience.

Early the next morning I walked onto the stage. The set was dark and frightening. Snow fell all around. Liu Kang and Jade were about to share a passionate kiss that would affect both their futures.

The snow was made of tiny pieces of shredded paper that blew about from winds created by huge fans. We were supposed to act as though it was cold, but it was so hot on the set that we had to constantly drink water to keep from becoming dehydrated. The set became even more tense because there would be no more filming after that day; if the scene wasn't successful it would be edited to a brief flash on the screen.

The first time we filmed the scene I was unable to kiss Robin.

The second time my hair fell into his mouth and he was unable to say his lines. Because he was lying on his back the paper snow fell into his mouth and choked him.

We waited while the cameras were set up for the close-up. We both felt that our time was running out, and Robin and I hadn't connected yet. I recalled the hillside in the Soviet Union, when Hadja Nasredin and I stood under the hot Asian sun and struggled to complete our scene. I knew I had to lose myself in my character and the moment.

I remembered the actors in Ulan Ude, the way they had taken a deep breath and, in the space of a single blink, transformed into someone else.

My blood boiled. My heart beat loud in my chest. The cameras whirred. Action, the director ordered.

You are too good to be true, said Liu Kang.

The same could be said for you, Jade replied.

I felt love for him course through me, so strong that I almost could not control it. I felt his hand push at me, as if to say that I was kissing him for too long a time.

I opened my eyes and said, Together we could melt the snow.

I kissed him again and added, Together we could live our final days.

At the end of the afternoon John, the director, said three magical words: Cut, print it.

My parents came to visit in the summertime; my father was very excited because he had an appointment with a New York theater director who was interested in using some of his music in a new production. When Roland and I met them at the airport my mother gave me a small envelope that looked yellowed with age.

This came for you in Ulan Ude, she said. It looks like it took a long time.

I waited until I was home to examine it. My name was written upon it in a small, meticulous hand. When I opened it I read several paragraphs before I fully understood what I held in my hand.

Roland, I called out. He rushed into the living room from the kitchen. It's unbelievable. This letter, it's from Lobsang. He sent this seven years ago.

We looked over the letter as though it was something that we had dug up from a time capsule. Lobsang was still a monk at the side of the Dalai Lama, living in a monastery in the Tibetan exile community at Dharmsala, India.

You have to write him, Roland said. Tell him where you are.

Lobsang's letter had taken so long to reach me because he hadn't known my full address; he had sent the letter through monks on a long journey from India to Tibet to Mongolia to Siberia. It was almost a miracle that I received it at all. I wrote him a long letter about myself, recalling his tender voice and loving smile, the evenings we spent together in Buryatia trying to find a common language in which to communicate.

He wrote me again, his letter finding me in New York. Lobsang had been studying for all the years since I had last seen him. He had grown more deeply spiritual, which was reflected in his new standing in a high position at the monastery. He said he was amazed and happy for all that had happened to me. When he said he had grown very fat, I could almost hear his joyful laughter in my ears.

I promised that I would go to see him one day. When I mailed another letter back to him I could feel the cycles of life moving within my life and through all others'.

In the midsummer heat of New York City I took a taxi to the Park Avenue offices of Woody Allen. He was making a film in which he depicted some aspects of the fashion world, I had been told, and I had been asked to audition for the part of a woman named Barbara. I whispered this name to myself as I rode the elevator up to the floor where I had been told to come. I stopped outside the door. This didn't seem like a famous filmmaker's working space; instead it looked like a doctor's office. I stepped through the door into a small waiting room. A couple of women were waiting in simple chairs, reading newspapers. A receptionist looked up from a stack of phone messages.

I'm sorry, I said. I think I have the wrong place. I'm looking for Woody Allen.

The woman behind the desk laughed. No, no, wait, she said. You have the right place. I'll tell him you're here.

I was ushered into a big room; my eyes were met with a splash of greenness. Green carpet on the walls, the floor. Standing was a gentle-seeming man with sparkling brown eyes behind his big glasses.

Hi, I'm Woody, he said to me.

Hi, my name is Barbara, I replied.

It took a second for him to register the joke I had made. We laughed together, but inside part of me was serious. I wanted to *become* the character who would be portrayed in the movie.

Woody Allen told me his assistant would read the scene with me. Allen's eyes bored into me like X rays as I read my lines, as though he was envisioning me in a frame of celluloid. As I performed the scene I couldn't banish from my mind a fantastic vision. I saw him as a doctor in my imagination, preparing to give me an actual X ray. He was dressed in a white lab coat, with a white hat bearing a red cross upon his head. This little room became his medical office. It was almost as though, for a moment, I had stepped through a door into another world. I concentrated hard to remember where I was, amazed that such a great artist worked in such nondescript surroundings.

We finished the short scene. There were no more lines. Woody Allen asked me to improvise with his assistant while staying in character. I had watched several of his movies in the past few days. I recalled their sense of reality and the way the actors spoke as though their lines had just come to them.

Do you want to go dancing tonight? the assistant asked Barbara.

Yes, I do, I replied, becoming one with my character. But

no, wait. I have to fly to Milan. I forgot all about it. It's always like that with me these days—a real disaster sometimes, not knowing where I have to be or what I'm doing the next day.

When we were done he thanked me and shook my hand. I stepped out into the afternoon heat shading my eyes from the glare of the sun. I had met a genius. Within the week I had been told that the part was mine.

I sat at a long table inside a bistro. To either side were actors and actresses, other models. The camera and sound crews worked quickly, calling out to each other as they made final adjustments for the scene. Lights cast shadows everywhere but illumined our table; cables crossed the room, forcing everyone to walk with cautious steps.

Food and drinks were served. There were no lines for me to read that day. Woody Allen had come through and told us to relax, enjoy ourselves. Drink and talk. Soon he would film us being as natural as possible.

From a small bag I took out a pipe that I bought the week before, when I had a moment of understanding about my character: I will be Barbara, and Barbara smokes a pipe.

I stuffed the pipe with aromatic tobacco and lit it. Smoke twirled around my face and formed filigrees in the light.

A pipe? the woman next to me asked.

I hope you don't mind, I said.

No, it's nice, she said. But it's unusual to see a woman smoke a pipe.

Not where I'm from, I said. My grandmother always said that smoking a pipe is healthier than cigarettes.

My grandmother's pipe smoked in my mind, its little ball of flame warm and bright. I saw her on the lake, the boat bobbing beneath us, her mouth turned up in a smile as she handed me one end of the fishing net to pull. The smell of tobacco made me feel as though I were in two places at once, that a part of me would always be under the Siberian sky.

Woody Allen saw the pipe; he came over to the table and looked at me for a long moment.

Hold that pipe closer to your face, he said.

He spoke with his cinematographer. They both agreed that they would start the scene with a close-up of my face and the pipe. I improvised a line of dialogue. In my heart, fresh winds were blowing across the plains.

I worked several days on the film, in scenes that took place in a New York disco and an art gallery. On the last day we shot through the night, ending at three in the morning. Just like modeling, it was more hard work than glamour. When we had finished I stepped out of the gallery into the early morning. Now Barbara lived inside me, just like the other characters I had become on other stages and runways. Dreaming and reality had become one again.

I walk up Fifth Avenue toward Rockefeller Plaza on a cool autumn New York afternoon, past the gothic spires of St. Patrick's Cathedral and the skylit atrium of the Olympic Tower. I see an ocean of faces rushing past me, shoppers laden with bags and businessmen speaking on cellular phones and toting heavy briefcases. I am moving through a canyon of shining shop windows and towering skyscrapers; I see my reflection in glass, the crystalline blue sky behind me.

I breathe the air of New York. I let my eyes feast on the splashes of color crowding the street, and each individual face which contains a story that I wish I could understand.

I feel neither old nor young. My life has taken me from the deepest reaches of snow-covered Siberia to the West, from a communist classroom to the fashion runways of Europe and America. I have felt history change around me like the ground shifting beneath my feet.

I stop at a crosswalk and let a cold breeze move through my hair. Winter is coming to New York. In the breeze I smell freshness, rebirth, like the spring that comes after the long freeze around Lake Baikal.

My life has been short; there is still much to come. I feel that there is nothing so special about me. Rather, it is this incredible world, full of possibility and promise, that is extraordinary.

I turn on 60th Street and walk into Central Park, where the leaves are falling from the trees. The squirrels hoard food for the long winter. People have begun to wrap scarves around their necks to fight off the chill.

I take a deep breath and walk faster.

I don't know what my life will be in the future, I don't know where I will be or what will fill my days. When I was a little girl in Siberia I could not have predicted that I would see the world, that I would be able to live out my dreams. How could I predict what will happen next?

Beneath a huge tree—now bare of its leaves—I stop. A lone squirrel pauses next to a thicket of twigs. I see a nut on the ground that he has missed and toss it toward him. He picks it up in his paws and springs up the tree.

Life and nature go on. The universe moves forward in time. I will be there with it, living my life as I always have, trying to embrace every adventure with all the power of my heart.

Wake up, little girl. The play is over.

I rub my eyes.

You were very brave, my mother says. You stayed awake almost through the entire play.

No! I say. It cannot be over.

I stand up and look around. The theater is the same as it has always been. My father is helping pack his orchestra's instruments. It breaks my heart that the actors have gone home.

Don't worry, my mother says, taking me by the hand. There will be another play tomorrow. All the actors will come back.

I am looking through an open door; the shapes outside are barely visible, which intrigues me even more than if I could clearly see. Determined, I take a step forward . . .

CAPTIONS

Page vii. Irina at age three. *Photo courtesy of author.*

Page 3. Irina in Ukranian costume in kindergarten at age five. *Photo courtesy of author.*

Page 47. Irina with her grandmother on her farm in Siberia. *Photo courtesy of author.*

Page 107. Irina in Uzbekistan on the set of her first movie. *Photo courtesy of author.*

Page 221. First modeling photos of Irina taken by Roland Levin in Moscow. *Photos courtesy of author.*

Page 275. Irina on the catwalk at Thierry Mugler's 25th anniversay show in 1995. *Photo courtesy of author.*

Page 310. Irina with her parents in traditional costume, posing with Harkonnen Chair designed by H.R. Giger © 1981. *Photo by Susumu Sato.*